# *Dzogchen*

## ESSENTIALS

RANGJUNG YESHE BOOKS · WWW.RANGJUNG.COM

PADMASAMBHAVA · *Treasures from Juniper Ridge* · *Advice from the Lotus-Born* · *Dakini Teachings* · *Following in Your Footsteps: The Lotus-Born Guru in Nepal* · *Following in Your Footsteps: The Lotus-Born Guru in India*

PADMASAMBHAVA AND JAMGÖN KONGTRÜL · *The Light of Wisdom, Vol. 1, Vol. 2, Vol. 3, Secret, Vol. 4 & Vol. 5*

PADMASAMBHAVA, CHOKGYUR LINGPA, JAMYANG KHYENTSE WANGPO, TULKU URGYEN RINPOCHE, ORGYEN TOBGYAL RINPOCHE, & OTHERS · *Dispeller of Obstacles* · *The Tara Compendium* · *Powerful Transformation* · *Dakini Activity*

YESHE TSOGYAL · *The Lotus-Born*

DAKPO TASHI NAMGYAL · *Clarifying the Natural State*

TSELE NATSOK RANGDRÖL · *Mirror of Mindfulness* · *Heart Lamp*

CHOKGYUR LINGPA · *Ocean of Amrita* · *The Great Gate* · *Skillful Grace* · *Great Accomplishment* · *Guru Heart Practices*

TRAKTUNG DUDJOM LINGPA · *A Clear Mirror*

JAMGÖN MIPHAM RINPOCHE · *Gateway to Knowledge, Vol. 1, Vol. 2, Vol. 3, & Vol. 4*

TULKU URGYEN RINPOCHE · *Blazing Splendor* · *Rainbow Painting* · *As It Is, Vol. 1 & Vol. 2* · *Vajra Speech* · *Repeating the Words of the Buddha* · *Dzogchen Deity Practice* · *Vajra Heart Revisited*

ADEU RINPOCHE · *Freedom in Bondage*

KHENCHEN THRANGU RINPOCHE · *King of Samadhi* · *Crystal Clear*

CHÖKYI NYIMA RINPOCHE · *Bardo Guidebook* · *Collected Works of Chökyi Nyima Rinpoche*

TULKU THONDUP · *Enlightened Living*

ORGYEN TOBGYAL RINPOCHE · *Life & Teachings of Chokgyur Lingpa* · *Straight Talk* · *The Sublime Lady of Immortality*

DZIGAR KONGTRÜL RINPOCHE · *Uncommon Happiness*

TSOKNYI RINPOCHE · *Fearless Simplicity* · *Carefree Dignity*

MARCIA BINDER SCHMIDT · *Dzogchen Primer* · *Dzogchen Essentials* · *Quintessential Dzogchen* · *Confessions of a Gypsy Yogini* · *Precious Songs of Awakening Compilation*

ERIK PEMA KUNSANG · *Wellsprings of the Great Perfection* · *A Tibetan Buddhist Companion* · *The Rangjung Yeshe Tibetan-English Dictionary of Buddhist Culture* · *Perfect Clarity*

# Dzogchen

## ESSENTIALS

*The Path that Clarifies Confusion*

*Compiled and edited by*
MARCIA BINDER SCHMIDT

*Translated by*
ERIK PEMA KUNSANG

*Introductory Teachings by*
TSOKNYI RINPOCHE

RANGJUNG YESHE PUBLICATIONS
*Boudhanath, Hong Kong & Esby*
2004

RANGJUNG YESHE PUBLICATIONS
55 Mitchell Blvd, Suite 20
San Rafael, CA 94903 USA

*www.rangjung.com*
*www.lotustreasure.com*

1 3 5 7 9 8 6 4 2

First edition 2004
Printed in the United States of America

Publication Data:
Schmidt, Marcia Binder.
*Dzogchen Essentials: The Path That Clarifies Confusion.* Translated by
Erik Pema Kunsang, Introductory Teachings by Tsoknyi Rinpoche.
Includes bibliographical references.
ISBN 978-962-7341-53-6 (pbk)
1. Eastern philosophy—Buddhism. 3. Vajrayana—Dzogchen (Nyingma).
I. Title.

COVER ART DETAIL: Padmasattva, Tsikey Gompa
DESIGN: Rafael Ortet

# CONTENTS

## PART THREE • THE MAIN PRACTICE

## PART FOUR • THE CONCLUDING ACTIVITIES

# PREFACE

*Dzogchen Essentials* offers an exciting and diverse selection of material, both new and traditional, for study and practice in the Dzogchen tradition. These teachings are principally about clarifying confusion, the third of the Four Dharmas that Gampopa and Longchenpa have made well known. The Four Dharmas are universal principles and describe, in the words of Tulku Urgyen Rinpoche, "what a spiritual practitioner needs to reach complete enlightenment in a single lifetime." Padmasambhava explained these Four Dharmas as follows:

> You must make sure your Dharma practice becomes the real Dharma. You must make sure your Dharma becomes the real path. You must make sure your path can clarify confusion. You must make sure your confusion dawns as wisdom.

> When you have understanding free from accepting and rejecting after knowing how to condense all the teachings into a single vehicle, then your Dharma practice becomes the real Dharma.

> When, in any practice you do, you possess refuge and bodhichitta, and have unified the stages of development and completion, and means and knowledge, then your Dharma becomes the real path.

> When you combine the path with the view, meditation, action, and fruition, then your path clarifies confusion.

> When you exert yourself in practice having fully resolved the view and
> meditation, then your confusion can dawn as wisdom.
>
> In any case, no matter what practice you do, failing to unify development
> and completion, view and conduct, and means and knowledge will be like
> trying to walk on just one leg.[1]

The third Dharma contains the teachings on letting the path clarify the mistaken ways we normally relate to perceptions of our environment, our body,
and our sense impressions. Rather than continue the habit of insisting on a
solid reality, we are offered a skillful alternative involving empowerment
and *yidam* practice: the development stage, visualization of deities, recitation of mantra, feast, and completion stage. *Dzogchen Essentials* contains
instructions on Vajrasattva practice, mandala offering, and especially guru
yoga. Underlying these practices is the essential intent of integrating them
with the view of the Great Perfection. This is the unique style of Dzogchen
as it was taught by Tulku Urgyen Rinpoche.

*Dzogchen Essentials* is for the serious, dedicated Vajrayana student. It carries on from *The Dzogchen Primer,* which can be used as support and background material. *The Primer* succinctly covers the Hinayana and Mahayana
vehicles, including the basis, the buddha nature, inherent to all beings;
refuge; the ten virtuous actions to adopt and the ten unvirtuous actions to
avoid; and the importance of extending oneself through the aspiration and
application of *bodhichitta*.

Dzogchen is the pinnacle of the Vajrayana, yet this pinnacle is poised
upon the foundation of the Hinayana and Mahayana, and it includes all
the precepts of those lower vehicles, even within a single practice. To quote
Chökyi Nyima Rinpoche:

> In Mahamudra and Dzogchen, the training is not to stray from the empty
> awareness that is the awakened state of the buddhas. This empty, aware
> state of all buddhas, the awakened state, is also compassionate.... By not
> straying from the empty and aware awakened state, one automatically
> never breaks the precepts of the lower vehicles.[2]

At the same time, Dzogchen is not for the ambivalent. The path itself is
like a very restrictive package tour; we cannot make our own itinerary,
even though we might be tempted to fall back into old habits of picking
and choosing. As Tsoknyi Rinpoche states, "It does not make sense to grab
at the highest teachings and reject the rest. It is pointless to invent some

personal idea of Dzogchen to train in. If you do, then Dzogchen becomes something fabricated, something you have made up. Calling your own theories Dzogchen is a foolish pretense that has nothing to do with the genuine, authentic teachings."[3]

How then do we enter the swift path of Vajrayana? It is by connecting with a qualified, living master who possesses an authentic lineage, and then requesting and receiving empowerment and pith instructions. Receiving empowerment means being authorized, matured, and sanctioned to engage in these profound practices. As Thinley Norbu Rinpoche says, "According to the Tantric system, the purpose of empowerment is to receive blessings and power. Many tantras reveal that if empowerment is not received, accomplishment will never be attained. The essence and root cause of buddhahood is within everyone. However, without the necessary condition of meeting a teacher who has the wisdom and the blessing of lineage, this essence of buddhahood will never blossom."[4] The first section of *Dzogchen Essentials* is dedicated to this important topic.

If we choose to train in the path of Dzogchen, we must be willing to surrender many of our preconceived ideas about the way things are. We must confront the possibility that our own mind cannot figure it all out and face the emotional challenge that we will have to rely on more than our own sense of reality in order to free ourselves from our predicament. All of these ideas are carefully explained in the material presented here. They are also laid bare for analysis as juicy topics for discussion in the facilitator guidelines. It is good at the beginning to establish a solid intellectual understanding about approaching the path of Vajrayana through study and careful analysis. We should verify our teacher's words with scriptural supports from the buddhas and other fully realized masters. By combining these two perfect measures, our teacher's words and scriptural supports, we embrace the third, the perfect measure of our individual intelligence. Next, we get experience through undergoing the process of practice. Finally, if we have done these things correctly, we can achieve realization.

At the start of the path, however, we face an odd dilemma: We need to trust that the methods will work even before we use them. Unfortunately, we are often more skeptical of the Dharma than we are of our own illusions. This creates an aversion toward Dharma practice that reinforces resistance, which is why we need to make a real effort to open ourselves up.

We could call that effort a leap of trust. Unless we make such a leap, we might continue with our critical attitude and remain unchanged. For me it is a little like flying in an airplane. As much as I have tried with my limited intellect, I have never been able to understand how that huge mass of metal gets off the ground. However, I do trust that it will, and I get on the plane and fly to wherever I am going. If I were to wait until I understood the workings of aerodynamics, I would never get anywhere.

It is the same with the *seemingly* conceptual practices. At one point, we take the leap and engage in them, and as we do so, we change. Having integrated practice into experience, we can see differences in how we behave and how we perceive the world and beings. We loosen up our conceptual constraints, and our mind-streams become more supple. But first we need to commit ourselves and practice.

Correspondingly, on a more mundane level, scientists and psychologists have conducted considerable research into the effects of meditation and prayer on healing and coping with illness. It is widely agreed that a positive mental outlook can have positive consequences, especially in these areas. This topic is beautifully explored in the work of Tulku Thondup in both *The Healing Power of Mind* and *Boundless Healing*. For the practitioner, then, consider how the profound methods of devotion and pure perception could be a much-needed alchemical component of transformation. When we are ready to broaden our "normal" mind-set, we are able to receive the blessings. As Tulku Urgyen Rinpoche says, "True blessings are the oral instructions on how to become enlightened in a single lifetime, which you can receive from a qualified master."[5] The next step is to have the merit and intelligence to employ them!

Here in the West, there is a lot of resistance to visualization practice altogether, including the preliminaries. Uninformed practitioners feel these are intellectual, cultural applications—completely conceptual. But actually, development stage practice mirrors the way things truly are. It is an effective method to bring us closer to the all-encompassing purity that is hidden from us by our confused perceptions.

As Tulku Urgyen Rinpoche says, "The development stage is like awakening from the dream state; it is manifesting what primordially exists. The purpose is to purify evil deeds, to prevent one's thinking from falling under the influence of the disturbing emotions. The purpose of *sadhana* is to enable blessings to enter our being and bless our mind-stream. The ritual is not to please the deities and fill their stomachs with offerings. It is for us to clear away our negative karma, purify our obscurations, and attain complete enlightenment. The correct seeing of mind-essence depends upon this purity."[6]

Employing these vajra yogas—deity, mantra, and samadhi—intrinsic to the development stage and completion stage, we can purify that which prevents us from recognizing and sustaining the natural state. These practices make our minds pliable and less coarse by peeling away the layers of hardened tendencies that we have accumulated over countless lifetimes. We are trying to affect the immaterial, which cannot be transformed solely by material means. We need to clear away what we unknowingly experience but cannot tangibly identify: the three ignorances, karma, obscurations, and habitual tendencies. Connecting with pure phenomena has a transformative power. We are working to link with the sublime. As Vajrayana practitioners, we are already initiated into a sacred mandala infused with the underlying principle of all-encompassing purity.

In addition to clearing away that which needs to be removed, these yogas expedite what needs to be gathered, namely, conducive circumstances and merit. Tulku Urgyen Rinpoche again addresses this: "Whether you can remain in the natural state or not depends on your merit. If you know how to recognize awareness, it is good to do so. If you do not know nor do any sadhana practice, you are doing nothing at all. You are merely eating through your mouth and shitting through your ass like a dog or a pig."[7]

There are various ways to apply these methods. First we can apply them as an imitation—feigning the way things are and our true nature, if we have not genuinely recognized mind nature. As we progress and purify and gather the accumulations, the imitation can transform into an experience of how things truly are. If we have recognized mind nature, then practicing according to the style taught by Tulku Urgyen Rinpoche and other masters, the accumulation of merit with reference point, and the accumulation of wisdom beyond reference point can be simultaneous. In this way, view and conduct are combined; the recognition of rigpa is the basis for every activity. There is no reason to think that one has to leave the view behind while engaging in the preliminaries and the development stage. On the contrary, progress in establishing the view is enhanced by these practices, and they in turn help to stabilize sustaining the view.

The structure of this book follows the order in which one approaches Vajrayana practice itself: Part 1, Ripening, explains the crucial step of empowerment; part 2, The Liberating Instructions, includes teachings on the preliminaries.; part 3, The Main Practice, explains deity meditation; and part 4, The Concluding Activities, covers feast and dedication. In *Dzogchen Essentials,* Padmasambhava and Jamgön Kongtrül's *Light of Wisdom,* volumes I and II, and Paltrül Rinpoche's *Words of My Perfect Teacher* are principal texts. Moreover, there is a wide range of pieces that support the style of the *kusulu,* or simple meditator, as well. These include selections by Tsele Natsok Rangdröl, Dilgo Khyentse Rinpoche, Dudjom Rinpoche, Tulku Urgyen Rinpoche, Chögyam Trungpa Rinpoche, as well as such living masters as Adeu Rinpoche, Sogyal Rinpoche, Dzongsar Khyentse Rinpoche, Mingyur Rinpoche, and Tulku Thondup. The facilitator's guidelines provide additional sources and information to enrich study groups and nurture the lone practitioner.

My heartfelt appreciation goes to all our lineage and living masters who are the source of the teachings I have assembled here. What an amazing legacy we have been given. It is such a wonderful opportunity to be able to share this wealth of wisdom from both ancient and modern sources. Sincere thanks go to all the teachers who have permitted me to quote their beautiful and inspiring slices of realization. The proper credits for all these are listed at the end of the book.

In particular, once again thanks to Tsoknyi Rinpoche, who continues to help with this project; to Tulku Thondup who verified the contents; to my husband and favorite translator, Erik Pema Kunsang, who acts as a sounding board and provider of material; to Michael Tweed, who edited many pieces and reviewed this manuscript, as did the exuberant Steven Goodman. Special mention to Cam Tran, who also offered transcriptions; to the meticullous type-setting maestro, Rafael Ortet, to Daniel Kaufer for proofreading, to the talented editor Tracy Davis, with whom it is a pleasure to work, and to the production sponsor, Richard Gere.

Again, I pray that this effort will encourage and assist all aspiring Dzogchen yogis to reach the collapse of delusion and attain complete and perfect enlightenment for the benefit of all beings.

*Marcia Binder Schmidt*
*Nagi Gompa Hermitage, 2004*

# *Dzogchen*

## ESSENTIALS

# INTRODUCTION

*Tsoknyi Rinpoche*

When embarking on the path, it is necessary to receive the ripening empowerment as the extraordinary entrance. Having received the ripening empowerment, one can then receive the liberating instructions.

What is the purpose of receiving the ripening empowerment? The very identity of empowerment is the fact that within the nature of your mind, the buddha nature, the three vajras are already primordially present. When we explain the natural state itself, the ground has the nature of enlightened body, speech, and mind. It does not require any empowerment in order to be that way, because the buddha nature is itself enlightened body, speech, and mind: essence is body, nature is speech, and capacity is mind. In this way, the three *kayas* are spontaneously present within the ground. Nevertheless, we have failed to recognize this. Due to the three types of ignorance—coemergent, conceptualizing, and single nature—essence as vajra body becomes confused into the ordinary body; nature as vajra speech becomes confused into ordinary voice; and capacity, the nature of the indivisible vajra mind, becomes confused into the normal state of mind. This is how our normal body, speech, and mind, which in fact have the nature of the three vajras, are confused due to the threefold ignorance—our failure to know our own basic nature.

In short, we have strayed into confusion. And as the confused way of experiencing gradually unfolds, we successively descend through the formless realms and the realms of form. While roaming through the experiences of the three realms, we totally lose track of the fact that our nature possesses the three vajras and the three kayas. As we cling to experiences, deluded perception solidifies until we experience our present body, voice, and mind.

Each time one is in a new body, due to the dualistic clinging to perceiver and perceived, the first thing formed is the channels. Based on the channels, energy currents begin to move, connecting with the newly formed sense faculties, and, based on all this, one has impressions of sights, sounds, and the other sense consciousnesses. Within all this, the experiences appear to have real substance, even though they are insubstantial. While our identity is that of the three kayas, due to confusion we perceive everything as the sceneries of the three realms.

That is our situation when we enter the Vajrayana path by connecting with a true and qualified master. Such a master's stream-of-being is liberated through realization and is capable of liberating others through his compassionate capacity. By connecting with such a person, we can be blessed with recognizing that within our ground, the seeds for enlightened body, speech, and mind are actually present as the three vajras and three kayas. The seeds in this context refer to the power or blessings for enabling our present body, speech, and mind to be "reinstated" in the ground.

In the presence of a qualified master, by receiving the empowerment for enlightened body, the disciple's ordinary body is empowered to be the vajra body. The seed for attaining this is planted in one's stream-of-being. By receiving the empowerment for enlightened speech, one is invested with the power to realize the unceasing quality of vajra speech. Please understand that seed, power, and blessings all have the same meaning. Receiving the empowerment for enlightened mind, transcending mental constructs, plants the seed for eventually arriving back in the state of vajra mind, the unconditioned basic space of original wakefulness. These are the reasons for the empowerments for enlightened body, speech, and mind.

The basis for empowerment consists in blessings, but the purpose is the above-mentioned *planting of the seeds of realization* within our present body, speech, and mind. Through this the yogi or yogini, the male or female practitioner, moves along the path following the various steps described in the guidance manuals.

Someone who practices Dzogchen trains in all the details connected to the Dzogchen view, meditation, and conduct. If one follows the Mahamudra path, the principle is the same. The path begins with receiving the blessings through empowerment, after which it is possible to embark on the journey. During this journey, it is through the development stage involving yidam practice that all our present experiences—the coarse, materialistic phenomena including environment, sense impressions, and the bodily form that appears as the five aggregates—are purified into being the deity and its pure realm and are realized as the identity of the vajra body.

Similarly, through the training in enlightened speech, including the seed syllable, mantra, and so forth, the various steps of receiving the blessings of the deity's voice, using a mantra with three, five, or any other number of syllables, the mantra is endowed with a certain power of blessings. By chanting the mantra, one's mind, one's voice, and the sound of the mantra gradually become indivisible, so that every movement of one's voice is purified into basic space and one realizes the identity of the vajra speech. The effort of recitation facilitates this, but the fact is that the seed is already planted in the voice. Please understand that "planting the seed" does not mean that some new seed is being introduced. Receiving blessings means *reconnecting* with the enlightened body, speech, and mind that are already present within the nature of the ground. *The purpose of empowerment is to invest us with the ability to be liberated into the already present ground.* In order to actualize this ability, it is necessary to make use of the skillful practices including development stage, completion stage, and the Great Perfection or Mahamudra or any other similar practice. All such practical steps serve to nurture and help these seeds to sprout and eventually blossom.

> Though of identical purpose, it is undeluded;[8]
> It has many means and minor hardships
> And is to be mastered by those of sharp faculties;
> Thus is the vehicle of Mantra especially eminent.

This famous quote about the superior quality of Vajrayana means essentially that the extraordinary function of Secret Mantra is dependent upon blessings. Blessings are obtained through empowerment, or, put another way, empowerment is conferred in the manner of blessings. This is the principle that makes Vajrayana superior to the Sutra system. That doesn't mean that one cannot become enlightened through the Sutra path; it has its own specific journey, and those who take it will sooner or later, by applying themselves to it with perseverance, definitely awaken to enlightenment. Whoever realizes his or her basic state by meditating will gradually uncover the naturally present vajra body, vajra speech, and vajra mind—this is definitely not an impossibility, and it is perfectly all right as well. The principle of blessings, on the other hand, is one of using instantaneous force to bring forth realization, setting its strength immediately ablaze, like flying with jet propulsion.

The skillful means of the path of blessings makes it possible for the real Vajrayana master to instill this ability in the disciple's stream-of-being. The authentic warmth of blessings conferred during empowerment nurtures and ripens the seeds in the practitioner's "ground," so that realization can take place instantaneously without the need to first go through a long period of meditation practice. This is why empowerment is considered so precious and important.

There are various types of empowerment. Secret Mantra, generally speaking, is composed of the traditional four major levels known as Kriya, Charya, Yoga, and Anuttara Yoga. Each of these has many sets of empowerments. For someone who primarily emphasizes the visualization aspects of development stage, it is sufficient to receive empowerment in the form called the permission blessing, which includes empowerment for enlightened body, speech, and mind. Permission blessing consists of a ceremony for being accepted by the deity and receiving permission for training in that particular yidam practice. Having received it, one is authorized to visualize the deity, chant its mantra, and compose one's mind in a particular style of samadhi. The Anuttara Yoga tantras, especially the nondual tantras, confer four empowerments—vase empowerment, secret empowerment, knowledge empowerment, and word empowerment. These can be very extensive, and it is excellent if one is able to receive all of them in full. But if this is not possible, it is perfectly sufficient for one's personal practice to receive the permission blessing in order to practice Vajrayana.

Once you have received these empowerments, it is possible to concern yourself with the stages of the path. As mentioned before, empowerment means blessings, sowing the seeds in one's stream-of-being. Next, these seeds—which are called path seeds, not ground seeds, since they are seeds for realizing the ground—must be realized, meaning that the qualities of enlightened body, speech, and mind must be fully brought forth. In other words, they need to be brought to maturation, which is often called ripening. The different stages of the path are necessary for this process of ripening.

The two main aspects of the path—the famous *ngöndro* and the main part—come into play after one has received empowerment. The ngöndro includes the general and specific preliminaries. The purpose of the general preliminaries is to thoroughly prepare one's mind-stream. Those teachings facilitate turning one's mind to the Dharma. These are followed by the specific or extraordinary preliminaries, beginning with taking refuge in combination with prostrations. Sometimes refuge comes together with forming the bodhisattva resolve. One takes refuge, bowing down and giving rise to bodhichitta over and over again. The repetition of such a practice causes a natural subsiding of all the blatant, selfish emotions that usually frequent our stream-of-being. The coarse channels and their twists and bends get straightened out. The "unrefined" states of mind, the rough emotions—hate, love, closed-mindedness, and all the rest—settle into the natural state. You repeatedly devote yourself to refuge practice with prostrations. Again and again you form the bodhisattva spirit. By bowing repeatedly, you offer your entire being, physically, verbally, and mentally. The atmosphere is one of abandon, completely surrendering body, speech, and mind. It is like presenting a mandala offering. When you surrender yourself in this repeated gesture of taking refuge, all your coarse, selfish emotions will be naturally depleted and begin to vanish.

At the same time, you experience your state of mind to be more free and easy, and you begin to be at peace with yourself. Eventually, this relaxed mental state of ease allows you to receive the Dzogchen pointing-out instruction. When someone receives the pointing-out instruction after the ngöndro, it is much easier to recognize the view of the Great Perfection. There is another tradition in which practitioners receive the Dzogchen empowerments and the pointing-out instruction before beginning the ngöndro—in other words, a sort of "baby realization" has taken place. They have had a glimpse of the view, but for some reason, and they do not know why, there is no progress at all. There are some people who are introduced to the nature of mind and then don't seem to get anywhere; no strength develops. The baby rigpa is feeble, like an undernourished plant. Even after a lot of "meditation," it is the same dried-up state of rigpa. They try all kinds of practice methods—*shamatha, vipashyana,* Dzogchen, Mahamudra—but there is not the slightest bit of progress in realization. It is as if the baby realization simply refuses to grow up. The solution for this hampered growth is to receive the blessings of a qualified master and to use one's body, speech, and mind to make one's blatant, selfish emotions subside. In this way, there are two traditions for receiving the pointing-out instruction, before and after doing the ngöndro.

The bottom line is that strong emotions obscure self-existing wakefulness and prevent progress in realization. Therefore, in order to conquer all these emotional states, we offer prostrations, which soften up the rigidity of our body, speech, and mind. Taking refuge again and again in all the buddhas and bodhisattvas, we are protected by their light rays and compassionate influence. We truly receive the blessings, and in this way we are definitely able to progress. These are the benefits and purpose of making prostrations.

Refuge and prostrations are followed by the meditation and recitation of Vajrasattva. We find Vajrasattva mentioned in various contexts sometimes as a bodhisattva, sometimes as a buddha. The Dzogchen tantras describe Shri Vajrasattva as the single embodiment of the compassionate activity of all buddhas. In the past, Vajrasattva took the pledge "May the emotional and cognitive obscurations present in the mind-stream of any sentient being who utters my name be naturally cleared away and vanish!" This was Vajrasattva's aspiration, his vow, and through this auspicious concurrence, such purification does happen.

Vajrasattva's identity is one of compassionate emptiness, and his nature is the capacity to dissolve all types of emotional and cognitive obscurations. This is why glorious Vajrasattva is regarded as so important in Vajrayana practice throughout all four schools in the Tibetan tradition of Buddhism.

It is best to receive the specific empowerment for Vajrasattva. In other words, you should request it, even in the form of a permission blessing. At this point, you don't need the incredibly elaborate version of the Vajrasattva empowerment, which is necessary only if you do a specific development stage retreat based on Vajrasattva. For the ngöndro, a permission blessing is sufficient.

Having received it, you commence the practice. Follow the text for your particular ngöndro as to how to visualize Vajrasattva. At some point, you should feel confident that the nature of your own mind, which is the unity of emptiness and cognizance, is in essence identical with Vajrasattva's mind of unconditioned wakefulness. Then settle naturally into the state in which your mind and his are indivisible. This is how to lay the foundation for the practices of the development stage. Every visualization practice shares this same basic principle.

As you continue with the visualization for the "downpour and purification of nectar," radiating and absorbing rays of light, you should feel confident that not only your own karmic misdeeds and obscurations but those of all sentient beings are totally purified.

There are two aspects to purification: One is to be purified in actuality—that is, the veils are being removed for real—while the other is psychological, in the sense of developing the feeling of being totally pure. We know the opposite of this feeling: "I'm useless! I'm a great sinner, and so are all other sentient beings. We have so many negative emotions; we are so selfish. There's no way I can be enlightened. I am incredibly bad!" People often develop such attitudes of denigrating their own worth.

Vajrasattva practice is radically different from training in low self-esteem. Instead one develops this attitude: "Through this practice and visualization of glorious Vajrasattva, all my negative traits from all my past lives are totally eliminated. I have no more negative karma. It's totally gone!" By repeating this attitude over and over, we make room for a sense of delight, of not being burdened by the thought of so many negative actions. The basic feeling of guilt that we all share begins to vanish. Then a clear and uplifted spirit—you could call it clear conscience—facilitates our ability to connect with the true instructions of Dzogchen. We have a very lucid and sincere feeling in our heart and feel ready to face even the most profound instruction. That is one of the important reasons for Vajrasattva practice.

Please do not regard Vajrasattva as merely a trick to alleviate psychological guilt. There *is* a real Buddha Vajrasattva presiding right now over his own buddhafield. He is not nonexistent. Someone who approaches him through the practice of Vajrasattva's body, speech, and mind does receive the blessings for removing karmic, emotional, and cognitive obscurations and for realizing the vajra body, the vajra speech, and the vajra mind. Even though it is possible to eliminate both the cause and the subtle obscurations during the ngöndro practice, the main emphasis in the teachings is on diminishing the effects—the coarse, selfish emotions.

The subsiding of negative emotions is an extremely meaningful discovery, otherwise one is stuck with a self-defeating attitude: "I cannot attain enlightenment! I'm totally wrapped up in negative karma and selfish emotions!" Such a habitual attitude makes our hearts shrink, and that timidity is a barrier that prevents liberation. It is my personal experience that the meditation and recitation of Vajrasattva is extremely beneficial in such a situation.

The next practice in the ngöndro sequence is mandala offering, which has the purpose of gathering the accumulations. Now, it could be difficult to understand the full meaning of the word *accumulations*, which refers to the accumulation of both merit and wisdom. The problem is that we have a strong habit of seeing causal relationships exclusively in terms of material substance. All the phenomena that we perceive due to notions of subject and object seem to possess a concrete substance with a physical nature. In other words, cause and effect seem to be based on matter. As long as we hold on to this perception, it is inherently difficult to see any causal relationship in something invisible, beyond matter.

Reality seems to be grounded in physical matter. This morning the sun rose in the sky, and that is why I feel warm right now. Everybody can understand this, naturally. This relationship of material cause and effect is obvious; it is perceptible through the five senses and so is readily accepted. This is why most people are inclined to regard reality as nothing more than that, and they find it difficult to fit the accumulations into their limited worldview. Spiritual practices seem confusing and do not make sense. At the same time, everyone experiences pleasure and pain, joy and sorrow, all of which have their own causal relationships. Since these causal relationships are not visible physical entities, one should wonder what they are made out of, but for some reason most people never do.

To embrace the spiritual path in an authentic way, we need to relate to certain invisible causal relationships. There are the consequences of our actions, the law of karma, the blessings of a master, and likewise the causality involved in gathering the accumulations, all of which play key roles. Understanding these topics is extremely important if you want to practice the genuine Dharma. You cannot grasp them as if they were objects perceptible through the five senses. As I get older and more experienced in the Dharma, I notice that certain topics are difficult for a lot of people to understand. But these topics are extremely important if one is to be an authentic practitioner and awaken to enlightenment.

Let's say that we create some of these accumulations today. We perform acts of giving, make mandala offerings, and we make these offerings out of respect. One may then wonder what their immediate effect is. It is difficult to see, since the real causal relationship involved here is invisible, immaterial, and yet those noble actions are extremely important. This is a crucial point. Unless we accept the fact of invisible causal relationship, our resistance could form a barrier against becoming an authentic spiritual practitioner. We sit nicely on our cushion doing our meditation sessions for a while, and then something happens in our lives that prevents us from really practicing. We want to progress on the path, but it doesn't happen or we don't go all the way. This and that, all kinds of stuff, block us.

I have noticed that a lot of people feel downcast, depressed, and uninspired for no obvious reason; they get no joy out of life. This happens even though their physical surroundings are pretty comfortable. In their hearts they feel a lack of courage and a sadness that seems hard to shake. Some psychologists call this low self-esteem, but it has many variations that spontaneously permeate people's spirit, such as the feeling that something is missing in one's life. This is exactly what is meant by a lack of merit, a shortage in the accumulation of merit, which is felt as an unexplainable sadness or depression.

Accumulations can be created based on physical matter or based on "insubstantial substance". The accumulation of merit itself is always made of insubstantial substance, and yet it is an actuality. When we gather a fair amount of merit, which happens through the power of interdependence, we spontaneously feel at ease. We are not burdened by anything; we feel free and easy, ready to rejoice. You could almost say a delighted atmosphere pervades our being. The bodhisattva spirit doesn't seem difficult at all; it comes naturally. The basis for this psychological atmosphere is the accumulation of merit.

In the context of Vajrayana practice, the accumulation of merit is most commonly created through the practice of mandala offerings. The basic principle in mandala offerings is an absence of clinging, casting away attachment. The stronger the attachment, the easier it is to become emotional in the dualistic sense and create negative karma. The more we are able to reduce clinging and attachment, the more we naturally shed our selfish emotions and negative karma. Continuing in this way, the accumulations of merit and wisdom increase as a matter of course.

While chanting the mandala offering with the various continents and the different directions, imagine that you give away each and every one of them—the four continents, the subcontinents, and your body, speech, and mind, the enjoyments of your five senses, your possessions, everything—to your guru and to all the buddhas and bodhisattvas. Then offer everything one more time, and again and again. By doing this repeatedly, you eventually gain the feeling that all of these things are experienced but insubstantial. You no longer hold the attitude that they are "my" things. In other words, you completely eliminate the clinging to "mine". Moreover, by making an offering of the five aggregates, you realize that the personal identity of "me" is devoid of true nature. By making an offering of all phenomena—whatever appears and exists in samsara and nirvana—you realize that the identity of any phenomenon is devoid of true nature. This happens due to the interdependence of cause and effect and the process of gathering the accumulations.

Up to this point we have dealt with the coarse, material aspects of our body, speech, and mind, by offering prostrations and by giving rise to the bodhisattva spirit. That was followed by purifying the more blatant aspects of negative karma and obscurations through the meditation and recitation of Vajrasattva. Next, since the stumbling blocks and hindrances for progress on the path to enlightenment come about due to a lack of accumulated merit, we make mandala offerings in order to ensure that the conducive circumstances for enlightenment are brought about fully and completely. Now we have come to the practice that brings forth the very heart of the Buddha's teachings within our personal experience.

It is taught that the basis of the entire Dharma depends upon the blessings of the guru. In other words, if the guru's realization is not transmitted into your mind-stream, your mind is not yet liberated. This is why we, in the Vajrayana tradition, consider the guru's blessings absolutely vital. You do not hear this statement much in the general Mahayana teachings or in the Theravada tradition. It is an extraordinary feature of the vajra vehicle of Secret Mantra to rely exclusively, as a single panacea, on devotion to the guru. In the Drukpa Kagyü tradition, you find this emphasized to the utmost—how many practitioners out of devotion took refuge, formed the bodhisattva resolve, practiced Vajrasattva, did mandala offerings, and finally realized the nature of all phenomena, all that appears and exists.

In this practice of focusing exclusively on guru devotion, please understand that the "guru principle" does not refer to just the physical body of flesh and blood. The practitioner realizes that the guru principle is the nature of the four kayas, and it is within that state of understanding that the practitioner supplicates the guru. First, true trust needs to take birth in one's mind-stream; then, as this trust is cultivated further and further, it becomes devotion. This devotion can become overwhelming—you could say blazing. It can feel as if your body and mind dissolve in this blaze. All concepts of me and mine melt away within the state of devotion. In that state, there is no room for a separate concept of personal identity or the identity of phenomena. The two types of self vanish within devotion.

The guru's blessings are always present, day and night. The buddhas and bodhisattvas, all the masters of the lineage, and your personal root guru are always full of blessings, continuously, throughout the three times. But how do these blessings saturate our own mind-stream to bring us to maturation? This happens when the concepts of me and mine have melted away in the state of devotion. It is this ego that prevents blessings from ripening our stream-of-being. The concept of self melts away in the atmosphere of devotion. This is when the warmth of blessings permeates you completely.

As far as my own personal experience, when I underwent the ngöndro training, I had already received some Dzogchen instructions. The awakened state of rigpa had been pointed out, and I had a lukewarm certainty about what it was. But the ngöndro helped me to progress. You could say a quick escalation happened. It was like making a fifteen-mile jump all at once without having to take all the steps in between. I feel that it was the ngöndro that was responsible for this progress. In my opinion, the ngöndro practice is the root of advancing the theory of rigpa to a truly liberated actuality.

The guru's blessings are necessary in order to make real progress. Otherwise, no matter how hard one tries by oneself, the struggle doesn't seem to have the power to give rise to true insight. No matter how fit one is, it's difficult to walk farther than twenty miles in one day. But when your guru suddenly sends you a helicopter, you jump inside and it takes off, and then those twenty miles are covered in a couple of minutes. It is taught that you can reach enlightenment by traversing the five paths and the ten *bhumis*, thinking that you are doing it all by yourself, but it takes a tremendously long time—three incalculable aeons. On the other hand, to make use of the skillful Vajrayana methods, especially the ngöndro training, and to receive the guru's blessings within your stream-of-being is like finding yourself inside a helicopter or even a jetliner. The power of the guru's blessings enables you to travel fifty miles in just a few moments. Traveling at this speed, your body, speech, and mind are swiftly brought to maturation and you awaken to complete enlightenment.

After the ngöndro, the next topic covered in *Dzogchen Essentials* is the Vajrayana practice involving a yidam deity. Westerners, first of all, do not know whether there really is such a thing as a deity or a buddhafield. Obviously, we Tibetans accept these things as a matter of course, but you are encountering such phenomena for the first time. You are in the habit of accepting only what you see, what belongs to your personal experience, and consequently wanting to exclude the possibility of anything else. Nobody told you about other types of phenomena. It's like life on other planets: It may exist, and it probably does, but we cannot see it, and therefore we believe it does not exist. Who can blame anyone for that?

This is why a proper explanation of deity practice has to be given: who the deity is, whether there is a connection between the deity and oneself, and whether the deity's identity is the same as, or different from, our own nature. We need to understand the principles of the deity's body, speech, and mind and their relationship to our own body, speech, and mind. In particular, we need to be thoroughly introduced to the fact of our own buddha nature. In other words, we need to have received the pointing-out instruction, for real. Next comes how to connect the deity residing in the buddhafield with oneself, and how that connection brings benefit. All these questions do arise, and they need to be answered.

The purpose of the link between a deity and oneself is to receive blessings. Our buddha nature—our ground composed of essence, nature, and capacity—is in fact the actuality of the three kayas. Specifically, the empty essence is *dharmakaya*, the cognizant nature is *sambhogakaya*, and the unconfined capacity is *nirmanakaya*. This indivisible unity of the three kayas is already present in a very real way as our basic nature. How does that relate to the deity living in some buddhafield? In the deity these three kayas have been fully ripened, totally matured, while in our case they are unripe. The difference between being fully ripened and being unripe consists in an obscuration—something that prevents full maturation. Therefore, in order to bring our own potential three kayas into the realm of actuality, to ripen them, we call out to the deity in the buddhafield, saying, "Please give me a hand, quickly! Please, I have some children and they need to grow up. I have three baby kayas here and they need to mature. Please help me! Also, clear away these obscurations that have prevented it from happening!" With this frame of mind we do the mantra recitation.

The basic principle in mantra recitation is to connect with the vajra body, vajra speech, and vajra mind. It creates—or you could say it revives—the link between our body, speech, and mind and the three vajras of the deity residing in the buddhafield and makes us receptive to the blessings. It is these blessings that, infusing our stream of being, help to mature and nurture the three vajras present as our ground, our buddha nature, so that they can fully manifest. In doing yidam practice intensively over a long period, gradually every barrier—clinging to duality, solidifying experience into perceiver and perceived, holding on to conceptual attributes—totally and utterly dissolves, is purified. The whole reason this is possible rests in the fact that we have only one mind. *When this one mind is occupied with nothing but pure phenomena, and the impure way of perceiving gradually dissolves, the three kayas present as our ground become an actuality.* The rays of light and the blessings and the power from the "three kayas deity" in the pure land—with which we connect through the yidam practice—allow the three kayas to be seen as indivisible from our own nature, so that finally we arrive at the state that is similar to, for instance, Buddha Vajrasattva in his own buddhafield.

In Vajrayana training there is a principle known as the "four stakes binding the life force."[9] You use the stakes to nail together the three kayas of the fully realized Buddha with your own potential three kayas so that they are indivisible. During this mingling, every type of delusion and negative emotion tries to escape, hide, and run away terrified until they vanish altogether.

The basic principles I have discussed here are nothing new. Whenever we need help, we go to someone who is capable and ask for support. The poor man goes to the bank to take out a loan. The bank manager agrees, and the poor man uses the loan to improve his situation. It is exactly the same with asking the buddhas and bodhisattvas for support and blessings to bring forth our full potential, the three kayas that are present in our basic nature. This is why we ask the yidam deity, "Please help, please give your support, please grant your blessings." This is why we practice the development stage.

# THE QUINTESSENCE OF
# WISDOM OPENNESS ⚯

*Padmasambhava*

*Emerging from samadhi, the Lotus-Born master taught this root yoga, the source of all mandalas:* ⚯

Having obtained the supreme freedoms and riches, and being weary of
    impermanence, ⚯
With intense renunciation, endeavor in accepting and rejecting what
    concerns cause and effect. ⚯
Those possessing faith and compassion ⚯
Who wish to attain the supreme and common siddhis in this very life ⚯
Should ripen their being through empowerment and, with totally pure
    samaya, ⚯
Take refuge, the root of the path, ⚯
As well as generate the twofold bodhichitta, the essence of the path. ⚯
All evil deeds and obscurations, the conditions opposing experiences and
    realizations ⚯
Of Vajrayana, the ultimate part of the path, ⚯
Should be purified through the profound practice of Vajrasattva. ⚯
In order to perfect the positive conditions, the accumulations of merit and
    wisdom, ⚯
Offer the mandalas of the oceanlike realms of the three kayas. ⚯
In particular, apply the key points of the essence of all the paths, ⚯
The guru yoga of devotion: ⚯

Amid an ocean of offering clouds in the sky before me, ⁸

Upon the lion throne and layered lotus, sun, and moon, ⁸

Is Orgyen Tötreng Tsal, the embodiment of all objects of refuge. ⁸

He has one face and two arms and is wrathfully smiling and glowing with resplendent light. ⁸

He wears the lotus crown, secret dress, gown, Dharma robes, and brocade cloak. ⁸

Holding a vajra in his right hand and a skull with a vase in his left, ⁸

He embraces the secret mudra in the hidden form of a khatvanga. ⁸

With his two feet in the reveling posture, he is within a sphere of five-colored rainbow light. ⁸

He sends out cloud banks of the all-encompassing Three Roots. ⁸

All that appears and exists is the essence of the glorious guru. ⁸


Perform the external practice in the manner of supplication, ⁸

And the inner practice in the manner of recitation. ⁸

Afterward, receive the four empowerments and dissolve Guru Rinpoche into yourself. ⁸

In the luminous state of your mind inseparable from the guru, ⁸

Experience one-pointedly the secret, ultimate guru. ⁸


Through the practice of the great emptiness, the space of suchness, ⁸

Where all the relative and ultimate dharmas ⁸

Are the great supreme dharmakaya of the inseparable two truths, ⁸

You will realize death as the natural state of luminosity. ⁸

Through the practice of the all-illuminating samadhi ⁸

In the illusory manner of nonconceptual compassion ⁸

Toward unrealized sentient beings pervading space, ⁸

The bardo will appear as the forms of the deities of the Magical Net. ⁸


Particularly, in order to purify the process of taking birth, ⁸

Practice the development stage that ends clinging to ordinary experience: ⁸


Visualize as perfected in instantaneous recollection in order to purify miraculous birth, ⁸

And visualize through the emanation and absorption of the seed syllable in order to purify birth by warmth. ⁸

Visualize the seed syllable, attributes, and bodily form in order to purify womb birth, ⁸

And visualize the cause and effect heruka in order to purify egg birth. ࿇
In all cases, visualize the mandala of the base and the based, ࿇
And the faces, arms, and attributes in total completeness. ࿇

For this, first, in order to become gradually trained, ࿇
Visualize yourself in the form of the single mudra ࿇
With vivid features, like a rainbow. ࿇
At best, regard it as the natural great absolute; ࿇
As the next best, envision the distinct general and specific features; ࿇
At least, plant the stake of unchanging concentration. ࿇
Place an image with all the characteristics before you ࿇
And focus your mind, eyes, and prana one-pointedly upon it. ࿇
When a vivid presence appears, abandon the defects of drowsiness and
    agitation, ࿇
Rest in the state where the form of the deity is the unity of appearance and
    emptiness, ࿇
And the experience will arise in which the turbulence of thoughts has
    subsided. ࿇

Sometimes rest, bringing consciousness to its natural state. ࿇
Sometimes transform the expression of your concentration into many
    different things. ࿇
In each session, bring the clear appearance of the deity to perfection. ࿇
In each session, plant the great stake of the essence mantra. ࿇
In each session, rest in the same taste of the deity and your mind. ࿇
In each session, accomplish the magical display of emanating and absorbing
    rays of light. ࿇
At all times, keep the pride of being inseparable from the deity. ࿇
Since the path illustrates the unity of ground and fruition, ࿇
Practice the total purity that stops the clinging to ordinary experience. ࿇
In between sessions, mend the samayas with feast gatherings and tormas. ࿇
Bring all that appears and exists onto the path ࿇
As the essence of the magical deity, mantra, and great wisdom. ࿇

If you practice one-pointedly in this way, ࿇
The experiences of movement, attainment, habituation, steadiness, and
    perfection will arise, ࿇
And you will actually meet with the form possessing the threefold
    vividness. ࿇

19

You will accomplish the truth of speech and a changeless mind. ৪

Next, fix your mind on the entire mandala circle, ৪
And when you have gradually attained its vivid presence, ৪
Emanate groups of buddha families filling the sky. ৪

Through the samadhi of the magical net ৪
Of the vidyadhara power-wielders, and appearance and existence as manifest
     ground, ৪
And by means of group practice in an assembly, ৪
The highest siddhi will be accomplished. ৪
With the perfect place, time, teacher, retinue, and articles, ৪
Correctly perform the "rite of the land" ৪
And practice the sadhanas of outer, inner, and secret retreat. ৪

Erect the sign mandala as the support for concentration, ৪
A vivid and complete image adorned with ornaments. ৪
Visualize yourself and the whole retinue, the self-existing mandala deities, ৪
As inseparable means and knowledge. ৪

By the light rays of approach and full approach, ৪
Purify the outer world into the Lotus Net realm. ৪
By the emanation and absorption of the light rays of accomplishment, ৪
Transform all the inner inhabitants into the forms of the Magical Net of
     the vidyadharas. ৪
Purify your being by the great accomplishment. ৪
Then, through the vivid presence of the deity forms and the rays of the
     mantra, ৪
And through the samadhi of bliss and emptiness and the practices of
     uniting and freeing, ৪
When completing six, twelve, or eighteen months, ৪
As the outer signs you will actually have a vision of the deity, ৪
The mandala will emit light and the nectar in the vase will boil, ৪
The skull cup will tremble and the butter lamp will ignite by itself. ৪
As the inner signs, your body, speech, and mind will be blissful, your prana
     and awareness will be clear, ৪
And you will perceive all the dharmas of fixation and grasping as illusory. ৪
As the secret signs, your mind will be changeless in one-pointed samadhi, ৪
And the assembly of deities will be perfected within you. ৪

Since at this time you will have realized the supreme siddhi, §
You can display various miracles of the one taste of appearances and mind. §
Even without changing body, your mind will initially accomplish §
The Vidyadhara of Full Maturation in the form of a deity. §
You will attain the Mastery of Life, the Vajra Body, §
And by means of the supreme family of the Great Mudra of the five
    aspects, §
You will perfect the ten bhumis and realize the great regency, §
The Vidyadhara of Spontaneous Accomplishment. §

The intent of recitation, the auxiliary of the development stage, §
Has four visualizations of approach and accomplishment. §
First, upon the moon in your heart center, §
Within the center of the five-pronged golden vajra, §
Is the letter HRIH upon a moon, glowing like a flame. §
The mantra garland surrounding it §
Is self-resounding and revolves continuously. §
To fix your mind on this, like the moon with a garland of stars, §
Is called the intent of approach invoking the mind of the deity, §

The mantra garland emanating from there emerges through your mouth §
And enters through the mouth of the wisdom being before you. §
Passing through the bodily form and the navel lotus, §
It enters your navel and revolves as before. §
Light rays and essences gather in your heart bindu. §
Imagine that the wisdom of great bliss is stabilized §
And that all the siddhis are mastered. §
This concentration like the wheel of a firebrand §
Is the intent of the full approach to the deity. §

This can also be exchanged with the form of the consort, your own
    radiance, §
Or with any of the different emanation visualizations §
In order to invoke the surrounding assembly of deities. §

By the light rays emanating from the mantra, §
Offering clouds make offerings to the noble ones and gather the blessings
    back into you. §

The obscurations are purified, the accumulations perfected, and you have
    obtained the empowerments and siddhis. ፄ
As they emanate again, the karmas and disturbing emotions of the beings
    of the three realms are purified. ፄ
Emanating and absorbing like the emissaries of the king ፄ
Is the intent of mastering the accomplishment of siddhis. ፄ
At this time the outer world is the vajra realm of Akanishtha. ፄ
Appearances are deities, and all the animate and inanimate sounds are
    mantras. ፄ
Thoughts are the display of nondual wisdom. ፄ
During this, to recite in the great state of appearance and existence as
    manifest ground, ፄ
Is the practice like a beehive broken open, ፄ
The intent of the great accomplishment of siddhis. ፄ

You should apply these four intents of vajra recitation ፄ
Chiefly to the practices of the single form, the elaborate form, ፄ
The group, and the gathering. ፄ
The next practice should be entered when the vivid presence of the former
    is perfected. ፄ

However, through the intent of these instructions of mine, Self-born Lotus, ፄ
The way of practicing the recitation intents of approach and
    accomplishment ፄ
Combined into one in a single sitting session ፄ
Has been taught in order to swiftly produce blessings and signs. ፄ

Through the internal way of profound HUNG recitation, ፄ
Clinging to the appearances of the development stage is stopped and the
    power of awareness increases. ፄ
Through the secret and most profound method of the prana recitation of
    great bliss, ፄ
Samadhi is stabilized and pliancy is attained. ፄ

As to the ultimate practice of dissolution into luminosity, ፄ
By HUNG HUNG HUNG the world and its inhabitants along with your body ፄ
Gradually dissolve into the seed syllable, the letter HRIH. ፄ
This again dissolves into the innate state of nonconceptual luminosity. ፄ

Where the past has ceased and the future has not yet arisen, ᢀ
In the unimpeded state of present wakefulness, ᢀ
Rest in the manner of mind looking into mind. ᢀ
No matter what thoughts may arise at this time, ᢀ
They are all the display of the single mind essence. ᢀ
As the nature of space is unchanging, ᢀ
You will realize the all-pervasive mind essence to be changeless. ᢀ
This is the Great Perfection, the ultimate of all vehicles, ᢀ
The unexcelled meaning of the self-existing Mind Section. ᢀ

Whoever practices this ultimate yoga ᢀ
Will have limitless secret signs and virtues. ᢀ
The great power of experience and realization will gradually be perfected, ᢀ
And they will attain the wisdom of the Ever Excellent Padma. ᢀ
By then uttering PHAT PHAT PHAT, ᢀ
Perceive yourself and the world with its inhabitants as the mandala circle. ᢀ
Within the state of the unity of the development and completion, ᢀ
Further increase the two accumulations of merit and wisdom. ᢀ

This essence of the ocean of tantras and oral instructions ᢀ
Is complete and concise and has immense blessings. ᢀ
It is easy to practice and is the path to enlightenment in one lifetime. ᢀ
It contains the key points in the intent of the Magical Net of the
    Vidyadharas ᢀ
And of the Direct Vision of the Ever-Excellent Mind Essence, ᢀ
Which I have gathered as the vital blood in my heart. ᢀ

I, the great Self-born Padma, have taught it ᢀ
For the benefit of the present king, his sons, and my disciples ᢀ
And for the benefit of qualified beings in the future. ᢀ

Future generations, do not let this nectar dissipate, but collect this essence ᢀ
And accomplish the supreme and common siddhis! ᢀ
My children, practice continuously! ᢀ
Practitioners of knowledge mantras, never be apart from development and
    recitation! ᢀ
Yogis, bring your realization to encompass dharmadhatu! ᢀ
Samaya, seal, seal, seal.

Having expounded this most affectionate instruction, pouring out from the treasury of his realization, he entered the all-magnetizing samadhi. ❈

*This was the fourth chapter from the Wish-fulfilling Essence Manual of Oral Instructions, on the Quintessence of Wisdom Openness, the root samadhi which is the source of all mandalas.* ❈

PART ONE

# RIPENING

# 1

# THE RIPENING
# EMPOWERMENTS

*Tsele Natsok Rongdröl*

Regarding your questions about the meaning and definition of obtaining empowerment, my reply will be accompanied by quotations from the tantras and arranged under two headings: general and specific.

Entering the door to the teachings of Secret Mantra Vajrayana depends upon two things: ripening and liberation. Unless you first obtain the ripening empowerments, you are not authorized to hear even a single verse of the tantras, statements, and instructions. (Unauthorized) people who engage in expounding on and listening to the tantras will not only fail to receive blessings; they will create immense demerit from divulging the secrecy of these teachings. A person who has not obtained empowerment may pretend to practice the liberating instructions, but, instead of bringing accomplishment, the practice will create obstacles and countless other defects. This is mentioned in the *Buddha Skull Tantra*:

> As a lute cannot be played without strings,
> Though all other parts may be present,
> The person who lacks empowerment
> Will not be successful in the practice of mantra and meditation.

---

From Tsele Natsok Rangdröl, *Empowerment* (Boudhanath: Rangjung Yeshe Publications, 1993), "The Ripening Empowerments."

The *Tantra of the Heart Mirror of Vajrasattva* further states:

> Just as a boatman without oars
> Cannot cross to the opposite bank of a river,
> There will be no accomplishment without the support of empowerment.

The shortcomings of failing to obtain empowerment have been mentioned in countless such ways. Regarding the advantages of receiving empowerment, the *Tantra of the Heart Mirror of Vajrasattva* says:

> Having fully obtained all the empowerments,
> The entire Secret Mantra is accomplished without hardship.

The *Tantra of the Brilliant Expanse* further says:

> The noble child who has obtained empowerment
> Accomplishes all wishes in this life
> And attains true enlightenment in the next.

Innumerable other similar quotations exist.

The basic materials or seeds for the empowerments in question are already spontaneously present within one's own nature. The master's blessings and the symbolic indications (of the words, gestures, and implements used during the ritual) provide the circumstances for their growth. As an analogy, consider the enthronement ceremony of a universal monarch. The person enthroned must unmistakenly be of royal birth, and yet until he is established on the throne he is only called prince, never king. Once he has been enthroned and has been conferred with rulership of the kingdom, he becomes king in actuality.

Similarly, while the seeds of the four empowerments are primordially present in the disciple's nature, the original wisdom will not be actualized until these seeds have been ripened through empowerment. Once the disciple embarks upon the path of ripening and liberation, the wisdom of his own nature will be actualized. This is described in the *Subsequent Tantra of the Bathing Elephant*:

> The mind-essence of sentient beings is the luminous nature of self-awareness,
> The unfabricated awakened state, a continuity that is spontaneously present.
> Once you embark on the path of ripening and liberating this luminous
>    nature,
> You clearly perceive the fruition within your own being.

I shall now explain empowerment in terms of its essential identity, etymological definition, categories, and purpose.

The *Tantra That Embodies the Four Rivers of Empowerment* describes the essential identity of empowerment:

It purifies, ripens, and refines your being,
Infuses you with innate wakefulness,
And implants in your mind-stream (the seed of) the fruition
Of attaining the indestructible thirteenth bhumi.

Thus, empowerment is the king of all methods that cause the original wisdom inherent in yourself to naturally manifest.

The etymological definition of empowerment is like this: Formerly your body, speech, and mind followed deluded habitual tendencies and possessed no independent power. The method that now provides you with natural authority over the indivisible state of the four kayas is called empowerment.

The Sanskrit word for empowerment, *abhishencha*, literally means "to cleanse defilements," in the sense that the power of the four empowerments removes the obscurations of body, speech, mind, and cognition. The Sanskrit word *abhisheka* is also used, meaning "to instill with an entitlement." What kind of entitlement is one instilled with? The vase empowerment entitles or authorizes you to visualize your body as a deity, the secret empowerment to practice the channels and energies, the wisdom-knowledge empowerment to practice coemergent bliss and emptiness, and the precious word empowerment to practice the unity beyond concepts.

The Sanskrit word *abhisiddhi* is also used, meaning "to be accomplished" or "to be ripened." How is one ripened? The vase empowerment ripens the physical aggregates, elements, and sense factors into a deity; the secret empowerment ripens the voice and the inhalation, exhalation, and abiding of the breath into the nature of mantra; the wisdom-knowledge empowerment ripens the *bindu* essences into great bliss and all sensation into coemergent wisdom; and the word empowerment ripens all that appears and exists into all-encompassing purity, the all-pervasive continuity of dharmakaya.

The categories of empowerment differ according to the various sections of tantras. To quote the *Wisdom Bindu*:

Empowerment with water and empowerment with crown
Are described in the Kriya tantras.
The vajra, bell, and name (empowerments)

Are clearly explained in the Charya tantras.
The empowerment of no return
Is elucidated in the Yoga tantras.

According to the Kriya tantras, the disciple is rendered a suitable vessel by the water empowerment, the crown empowerment, and also by means of the knowledge entrustment, and so on. In the Charya tantras, the additional empowerments of vajra, bell, and name, which together (with the two above) are called the five knowledge empowerments, are conferred on the disciple. The Yoga tantras include an additional empowerment called the irreversible master empowerment, or the empowerment for accomplishing vajra conduct. A general method for bestowing these empowerments is used by the Sarma and Nyingma schools of Secret Mantra.

Inner Secret Mantra's special Anuttara tantra tradition for conferring the complete four empowerments also does not fundamentally differ from the teachings of the Sarma and Nyingma schools (regarding the outer tantras), although there are numerous minor variations within the four. According to the Sarma schools, the empowerments of Chakrasamvara, Hevajra, and Guhyasamaja are for the most part alike.

The Kalachakra system teaches that the water of the initial vase empowerment is for purifying the defilements of the five elements, accomplishing the *siddhis* of the five consorts, and attaining the first bhumi. The crown empowerment is for purifying the defilement of the five aggregates, accomplishing the siddhis of the five buddhas, and attaining the second bhumi. These two empowerments purify the obscurations of the body and implant the seed for attaining the vajra body.

Similarly, the tiara-streamer empowerment is for purifying the defilements of the ten winds, accomplishing the siddhis of the ten consorts, and attaining the third bhumi. The vajra and bell empowerments are for purifying the defilements of the right and left channels, accomplishing the siddhi of the male and female chief figures, and attaining the fourth bhumi. These two empowerments purify the obscurations of speech and implant the seed of vajra speech in your being.

The empowerment of yogic discipline is for purifying the defilements of the eight consciousnesses, the sense faculties, and the sense objects; accomplishing the siddhis of the male and female bodhisattvas; and attaining the fifth bhumi. The name empowerment is for purifying the defilements of doer and deed (subject and object), accomplishing the siddhis of the male and female wrathful ones, and attaining the sixth bhumi. These two empowerments purify the obscurations of mind and implant the capacity to attain the state of the vajra mind.

The permission blessing and supportive ritual are for purifying the defilements that obscure the nature of original wakefulness, accomplishing the siddhi of Vajrasattva and consort, the lord of the family, attaining the seventh bhumi, and connecting with the fruitional state of vajra wisdom. These seven empowerments[10] are called the seven empowerments to initiate immature beings, and it is taught that the person who has obtained them becomes a lay practitioner (*upasika*) of Secret Mantra.

Following that, the vase empowerment implants the capacity to attain the eighth bhumi and validates one as a novice (*shramanera*) of Secret Mantra. Through the secret empowerment one attains the ninth bhumi and becomes a fully ordained practitioner (*bhikshu*) of Secret Mantra. By means of the wisdom-knowledge empowerment, one attains the tenth and eleventh bhumis. Through the fourth empowerment, one attains the twelfth bhumi and becomes a great lord of beings. Thus, as the Kalachakra system teaches, the empowerments guide you through progressive stages.

All the other tantras divide the vase empowerment into the five knowledge empowerments followed by the empowerment of the conduct of a vajra master. Then follow, one after the other, the secret empowerment, the wisdom-knowledge empowerment, and the word empowerment. There are numerous systems of classifying empowerments.

According to the Nyingma school of Secret Mantra, there are two ways of dividing empowerments: either into the "four rivers of empowerment," corresponding to their origin, or into the "four steps of empowerment," corresponding to their method of bestowal. The four rivers of empowerment are:

▸ the empowerment of the scripture of teachings
▸ the empowerment of the yidam deity
▸ the empowerment of the learned pandita
▸ the empowerment of the expression of awareness.

The four steps of empowerment are the vase, secret, wisdom-knowledge, and word empowerments.

The subdivisions of each of these are described in the scriptural system of the *Magical Display of the Peaceful and Wrathful Ones*:

Perform the empowerments of the crown and tiara,
The rosary, armor, and the banner,
The mudra, the parasol, and the vase,
The food and drink, and the five essential components.

These are the ten outer benefiting empowerments. They are followed by
the empowerments for the abilities of expounding, learning, sadhana practice, engaging in various activities, and acting as a vajra master. These are
called the five inner enabling empowerments. All fifteen are subdivisions of
the vase empowerment.

Following these, the secret empowerment, the wisdom-knowledge
empowerment, and the empowerment of the indivisible great bliss are
bestowed. These three are known as the three profound empowerments.
Thus, there are a total of eighteen different empowerments.

The scripture called the *Eight Sadhana Teachings of the Assemblage of
Sugatas*[11] divides empowerments into two categories: the special wisdom
empowerment and the general compassion empowerment.

The special wisdom empowerment includes twenty-six empowerments:

▸ the eight empowerments based on the outer indicating mandala of material substance, which upwardly embodies Kriya and Charya[12]
▸ the nine empowerments, based on the inner 725 deities, which bestow
  the complete blessings of Mahayoga and Anu Yoga
▸ the three empowerments of complete bodhichitta, based on the secret
  union of the father and mother aspects, for quickly traversing the paths
  and bhumis
▸ the six empowerments of the entire Ati of royal anointment, based on the
  innermost thatness mandala of self-aware wisdom.

The thirteen general compassion empowerments include the eight enabling empowerments of the all-encompassing teachings, and the five benefiting empowerments.

All these add up to 39 empowerments, while the detailed subdivisions
amount to 237 different empowerments.

According to the root text of the teaching cycle of *Lama Gongpa Düpa*,[13]
the great ripening empowerment scripture entitled the *Heart Mirror*, the
empowerment categories include:

▸ the outer vase empowerment in 10 parts: the 5 knowledge empowerments and the 5 supportive empowerments
▸ the inner empowerment of the all-encompassing teachings of the vajra king, in 117 parts
▸ the secret empowerment of the vajra master, in 34 parts
▸ the quality empowerment of the offering articles of precious accomplishment, in 25 parts
▸ the activity empowerment of the attendants acting to tame beings, in 21 parts; and
▸ the seven empowerments of permission blessing for the complete entrustment of the teachings.

Thus, there is a total of 213 parts.

According to the system of the grand empowerment of the *Scripture of the Great Assemblage (Düpado)*, the chief of all the empowerments of the Nyingma school and the general empowerment of the nine gradual vehicles,[14] there are:

▸ the preliminary 16 major supreme empowerments by means of the chief deity Vajrapani, indivisible from Vajrasattva, with twelve other retinue deities in the mandala. These purify misdeeds and obscurations and lead one away from the abodes of the lower realms.
▸ The vehicle of gods and humans of the higher realms discloses eleven mandalas and 123 empowerments.
▸ The vehicle of the *shravakas* has five mandalas and 39 empowerments.
▸ The vehicle of the *pratyekabuddhas* has four mandalas and 45 empowerments.
▸ The bodhisattva vehicle of aspiration and application has ten mandalas and 53 empowerments.
▸ The vehicle of Kriya has six mandalas and 62 empowerments.
▸ The vehicle of Ubhaya[15] has one mandala and 28 empowerments.
▸ The vehicle of Yoga has the twofold mandala of Vajradhatu and 99 empowerments.
▸ The vehicle of Mahayoga, of the unexcelled Secret Mantra, has the two aspects of peaceful and wrathful: the peaceful has six mandalas and 362 empowerments, while the wrathful has six mandalas and 640 empowerments.
▸ The vehicle of scripture Anu Yoga has eleven mandalas and 855 empowerments.

▸ The vehicle of Ati Yoga of the Great Perfection has one mandala and 18 empowerments of the expression of awareness.

Serving as the support for all of the above is the longevity empowerment of accomplishment, with one mandala and 58 empowerments. In short, without counting the different entrances to the mandala of the *Great Assemblage* (*Düpado*) tradition establishes that there are, in all, 54 mandalas of colored powder and 55 mandalas of three components, in which dwell 1,980 deities. The total number of empowerments amounts to 2,440.

The different categories of empowerment belonging to either the old or new schools of Secret Mantra are merely subdivisions of the four empowerments. They are not individual components of a complete structure consisting of the preliminary steps of preparation, the accomplishing and offerings of the main part, and the concluding ritual actions. The precise number of these categories differs greatly among the various empowerment texts of the Sarma and Nyingma schools. How can one possibly establish a fixed number of categories when each system of teachings has an inconceivable number of major and minor empowerment texts? Briefly, all the methods of ripening in the unexcelled Secret Mantra are without a single exception included within the four categories of vase, secret, wisdom-knowledge, and word empowerments.

In addition, many scholars of the Sarma schools have raised numerous objections against certain empowerments found among the different vehicles, such as the empowerments of the shravakas and pratyekabuddhas found in the empowerment manuals of the Early Translation school of Secret Mantra.[16] Generally speaking, aside from the Secret Mantra, empowerments are not found in the sutras or in the Vinaya. Nevertheless, the context (of the *Great Assemblage*) demonstrates that all teachings are complete and included within the path of Mantrayana.[17] Practice of the short path of Mantrayana suffices for the sharpest type of person possessing the capacity for instantaneous realization, but people with gradual capacity are to be guided by means of the gradually ascending vehicles. The *Two Segments* describes this principle:

At first, give the mending-purification,
And then teach the Vaibhashika.
Likewise, with the Sautrantika.

This describes the shravaka teachings. Next:

> After that, teach the Yogacharya.

This describes the Middle Way and so forth of the Mahayana vehicle.

> And next, teach the Hevajra.

This refers to the actual part of Vajrayana and corresponds to the prescribed gradual way of teaching.

Furthermore, regarding the context of taking precepts, most of the empowerment manuals state:

> The trainings of discipline—
> The precepts of individual liberation, of bodhichitta,
> And the vidyadhara precepts of Mantrayana—
> I will always abide by and observe.

Even though empowerment manuals appear in various lengths, all agree on one single point: Although those who receive these precepts are indeed not eligible for the proper Vinaya title of shramanera or bhikshu, they still possess the three complete sets of vows of Mantrayana. This can be understood simply by examining the previously mentioned steps of the Kalachakra empowerment. Again, one may think that the mandalas and empowerments of the different tantric vehicles should only be performed in accordance with their individual systems, and that it would be unreasonable to perform them exclusively in accordance with the Anuttara system. In fact, the lower vehicles and tantras are always included within the higher ones, but it is impossible for a higher vehicle or level of tantra to be included within the levels below. For example, the king is never controlled by the ministers—the ministers are always under the power of the king. Similarly, it is the nature of things that all the lower vehicles are completely contained within the Unexcelled Higher Vehicle. Nevertheless, the Sarma school empowerment text, *Vajra Garland*, teaches that the key point involving the different systems of bestowing empowerment is "knowing one that frees all" and does not divide them into different sections of tantra. It also explains the method used to divide the various sections of tantra, and how empowerment is conferred in accordance with each individual system.

The empowerments for the nine vehicles of the Nyingma school include two traditions:

▸ the method of conferring empowerment for all other mandalas in their totality within the Single Great Mandala of the Unexcelled

▸ the method of disclosing the mandalas of the individual sections of tantra, and then bestowing empowerment in accordance with each of their different systems.

In either case, these empowerments are without exception part of the flawless tradition of Padmakara and the other sublime *vidyadharas*, *panditas*, and *siddhas*, and they are exactly in accordance with the intent of the numerous tantras of the three yogas.[18] They are not fake teachings fabricated by dirty old family men of the Nyingma school dressed up as tantrikas. I merely mention this as an additional point.

Regarding why the empowerments are always divided into four types, you might ask, "What are the purposes and functions of these four?" I will reply in terms of their basis of purification, the objects to be purified, the means of purifying, and the results of the purification.

All the aggregates and elements of beings—the vessel and its contents—are the basis of purification of the vase empowerment. The speech and *pranas* present (within oneself) as syllables are the basis of purification of the secret empowerment. The essential elements and bindus present (within oneself) as great bliss are the basis of purification of the wisdom-knowledge empowerment. The mind-essence that primordially is dharmakaya is the basis of purification of the word empowerment. Why is this? Because the basic materials are spontaneously present within oneself as these four aspects.

Then you may wonder, "Well, if they have been spontaneously present in myself since the beginning, what is the need for conferring the four empowerments?" The empowerments are necessary because of the existence of the following four deluded habitual tendencies that obscure the ground, seeds, or basic materials:

▸ the delusion of fixating on the world and beings as ordinary and solid
▸ the delusion of fixating on the speech as ordinary
▸ the delusion of fixating on the mind as ordinary
▸ the habitual tendencies of fixating on the three doors as being separate

The means of purifying these four (fixations) is the four empowerments. Moreover, the purposes of the four empowerments are:

- to abandon the four types of desire that should be discarded: watching, laughing, touching, and embracing
- to realize the four mudras that should be accomplished: the samaya mudra, the dharma mudra, the karma mudra, and the mahamudra
- to savor the experiences of the four joys: the wisdom of joy, the wisdom of supreme joy, the wisdom of transcendent joy, and the wisdom of co-emergent joy
- to receive the four mandalas: the mandala of colored powder, the body mandala of the father and mother aspects, the mandala of the secret lotus, and the mandala of self-cognizant wakefulness
- to authorize and make one suitable to perform the four practices: the development stage of the deity, the *nadi*-prana and the recitation, the swift path of the bindus, and the path of liberation of Mahamudra and the Great Perfection
- to comprehend the four views that should be realized: the view of Mind Only, the Middle Way, Secret Mantra, and Mahamudra and the Great Perfection
- to accomplish the fruition of the four kayas: nirmanakaya, sambhogakaya, dharmakaya, and svabhavikakaya;
- to gain mastery over the four activities for the welfare of others: pacifying, increasing, magnetizing, and subjugating.

The purposes of and necessity for the four empowerments are included within these points. Their benefits are beyond the grasp of thought, as the *Secret Treasury of the Dakinis* mentions:

> When the unripened person has fully received the ripening
> empowerments and abides by the samayas,
> He will provisionally attain all siddhis and ultimately achieve the fruition
> of the three kayas.

This is mentioned innumerable times in the various sections of the tantras.

# 2

## SOWING THE SEEDS

*Padmasambhava & Jamgön Kongtrül*

This has two points: a brief statement mentioning the topic and the detailed explanation of the meaning.

### A Brief Statement Mentioning the Topic

The *Lamrim Yeshe Nyingpo* root text says:

> Now, for the steps of planting the seeds: ☙

Having already trained your being through the general paths, enter the stages of the special paths. The first of these is the steps for planting the seeds of buddhahood within yourself.

### The Detailed Explanation of the Meaning

This has two parts: the actual planting of the seeds and explaining their life force, the samayas.

---

From Padmasambhava and Jamgön Kongtrül, *The Light of Wisdom*, Volume II (Boudhanath: Rangjung Yeshe Publications, 1998), "Empowerment."

## The Actual Planting of the Seeds[19]

This has three points: the person to whom empowerment is to be given, the empowerments to be conferred, and the way of conferring empowerment.

### The Person Being Given the Empowerment

The *Lamrim Yeshe Nyingpo* root text says:

> Having motivated his being through renunciation, the person of
>     Mahayana nature ❀
> Should train his mind thoroughly in the twofold bodhichitta. ❀
> Within this person of good fortune who wishes swiftly to attain
>     buddhahood ... ❀

The person to whom empowerment is to be given is described in the *Ornament*:

> Who through knowledge doesn't dwell in existence
> And through compassion doesn't dwell in peace.

In this way, such a person should possess the Mahayana potential, and his being should be motivated by true renunciation, through knowledge and compassion, of the two extremes of samsaric existence and nirvanic peace. The signs of that are mentioned in the *Ornament of the Sutras*:

> To precede an action with compassion,
> To have aspiration and patience,
> And to correctly engage in virtue—
> These are taught as the signs of the (Mahayana) potential.

Such a person should have awakened this nature by means of learning and so forth. Through having trained his mind fully in the twofold precious bodhichitta, conventional and ultimate, he should desire to quickly realize and achieve the state of buddhahood for the benefit of sentient beings, in as short a time as one life, without requiring the long duration or hardship of three incalculable aeons.[19] Such a person of excellent fortune is a suitable vessel for planting the ripening seeds.

# 3

## AWARENESS-DISPLAY
## EMPOWERMENT

*Padmasambhava*

*The explanation of the empowerment for awareness-display according to the Unimpeded Realization of Samantabhadra.*

> To Samantabhadra and Vajrasattva,
> To Garab Dorje and Manjushrimitra,
> To Shri Singha and all the other masters,
> To the lineage masters of the three kayas, I pay homage.

The great master, bearing the name Lotus-Born, whose body is untainted by the flaws of a womb, whose radiant manifestation was born from a self-appeared lotus flower, is the victorious king of wrathful beings, conqueror of the four maras, whose bodily form is like the vajra, unchanging and indestructible.

This king of might, attainer of the marvelous supreme accomplishment, was invoked by the compassion of the dharmakaya buddhas, empowered by all the sambhogakaya buddhas; and when all the nirmanakaya buddhas conferred together, he appeared as the regent of Buddha Shakyamuni, on the Jambu continent that lies on the southern side of Mount Sumeru. He subjugated disciples in the eight great charnel grounds, served as the regent

---

Awareness-Display Empowerment" is from *ḳun bzang dgongs pa zang thal gyi rig pa rtsal gyi dbang gi 'grel ba* by Padmasambhava.

on the Vajra Throne of India, and by the power of former vows, he arrived in the snowy land of Tibet, causing the teachings of the Buddha to spread and flourish.

Later on, in the Cave of Samye Chimphu, he conferred the four empowerments in completeness upon King Trisong Deutsen and Lady Tsogyal, the Princess of Kharchen. It was at this time that the king and lady saw wonderful signs and gained the warmth of practice, so that out of faith and devotion they made this request:

Please listen, great master. What is the meaning when, at the beginning, one is conferred empowerment with attributes and articles including the vase, within the mandala of colored powder?

The master replied: Listen here, King and Lady of Kharchen. All the teachings of the truly and completely awakened one are taught in three ways: as expedient meaning, covert intent, and definitive meaning. Among these, the expedient meaning has the purpose of skillfully guiding sentient beings with incorrect perception to the higher realms. The covert intent is for when a bodhisattva uses his ingenuity as a method for liberating beings from samsara's sufferings.

The definitive meaning has three progressive stages. As the fruition of all the teachings of the lower vehicles, the view of the Middle Way free of focus is to settle into a state free of limits. What the sutra followers call absence of conceptualizing is to settle into the state that is free of perceiver and perceived. Up to this point there is no actual conferring of empowerment other than a mere sign or indication.

According to all the tantras of Secret Mantra, one is conferred the vase empowerment. To take the view of emptiness as fruition purifies the obscuration of karma, and to be given the vase empowerment opens up the doorway for the inner part of Secret Mantra, the five wisdoms that are indicated through words. Thus it is the symbolic empowerment.

This vase empowerment is the very first empowerment. It enables you to purify the obscuration of disturbing emotions, opens the door for the profound teachings, and is the occasion for being empowered to cultivate the yidam deity and practice the sadhana. Its result is to become capable of mastering everything belonging to the vessel and its contents.

Thus he spoke. Again they asked: Please listen, great master. At the time of the secret empowerment, why does one need to train in the nadis and pranas?

The Master spoke: Listen here, King and Tsogyal. Within the *dharma-dhatu* of Akanishtha, the dharmakaya and sambhogakaya and that which we call the mandala of wisdom experience do not consist of the material body, so they have no nadis based on the self-existing body of wisdom but rather a bindu sphere of the five lights of natural radiance. They have no karmic prana but are endowed with the four wisdom winds. Their bodily form is unchanging, their speech is unceasing, and their minds remain in the unmoving state of equality. For them there is no need for the secret empowerment, since means and knowledge are nondual.

In the nirmanakaya, even though it has a physical form that is like a magical illusion, the wisdom nadi has great strength, and the wisdom wind has great force. So the nirmanakaya has no defilement of disturbing emotions. Thus it turns into a wisdom body by simply being shown the symbolic secret empowerment.

In sentient beings, who have a form produced through ignorance, the nadis of disturbing emotions have great strength, the karmic wind has great force, and the wisdom channels and winds require skill to be found; therefore, it is most important to train in the channels and winds. When one has trained, ignorance subsides into a latent state and the nadis of disturbing emotions become refined; and when the karmic pranas are purified, the entire body becomes the wisdom mandala. Therefore, this training in the nadis and pranas is very important. Training in the channels and winds while in the human body transforms it into the wisdom body.

In the three lower realms, the wisdom nadi and wisdom wind lie latent so that there's no path of liberation. The bodies of most animals face downward, and therefore they have the channels and winds for being dull and mute. The bodies of most hungry ghosts are horizontal, and therefore they have the channels and winds for craving. The bodies of most hell-beings are head-down, so they have the channels and winds for agony. This being so, beings in the three lower realms are not suitable vessels for the pith instructions.

In the human body, a quarter of the channels and winds belong to the wisdom type, so bring forth perseverance and train in the nadis and pranas!

Thus he spoke. Again they asked: Please listen, great master. At the time of being conferred the wisdom-knowledge empowerment, what is the meaning of promoting the pure essence elements?

The Master spoke: Listen here, King and Tsogyal. The meaning of *wisdom-knowledge* is that the karmic winds of disturbing emotions are purified through training in the nadis and pranas, so that the winds move evenly within the empty channels, which gives rise to the experience of emptiness. That is called knowledge. At that time, there are various methods for promoting the essence elements, such as relying on nutritious food, wearing warm and soft garments, using the enjoyment of beautiful ornaments, making use of auspicious gemstones, and keeping a gorgeous companion. By means of these, one should, just like a spring flowing forth in any dry valley, exert oneself in the methods that promote the pure essence elements. Without letting it dissipate like water in a bad place, one should instead, like letting the water flow together to fill a nice pool from which one can irrigate the four directions, guide the pure essence element upward. This will block the channels of disturbing emotions, suppress the karmic winds, and advance all the channels and winds of wisdom.

The indestructible bindu of the life force in the heart center supports the wisdom mandala. When leading the pure essences, it will promote all good qualities so that your body is full of color and radiance, your voice speaks in a way that produces joy, and your mind becomes serenely free of thought. At that time, if you connect this with profound pith instructions, the stage of no return requires no effort. Even if you leave it to itself, when passing from this life you will take rebirth in the god realm of the Thirty-three Devas.

In this way, you become capable of the actions and activities that bring forth wisdom by means of the bindus. If the yogi who practices this path of the wisdom-knowledge empowerment does not possess empowerment and practice, he will not perfect the qualities of the path and bhumis.

Thus he spoke. Again they asked: Please listen, great master. Please explain in detail the meaning of pointing out that the nature of one's mind is dharmakaya, when conferring all four empowerments in completeness.

The Master spoke: Listen here, King and Tsogyal. In general, all the experiences belonging to samsara and nirvana are the unity of appearance and emptiness, while the empty quality is predominant. This entire world—above and below, and in the cardinal and intermediate directions—is within the empty expanse of space. In between, the earth, mountains, and rocks all perish and become empty in the end. The phases of the moon and the changing of the four seasons are also signs of being empty.

All sentient beings and life forms are born and die as well. Compared to the beings who obtain a physical body, a great many more don't have one. Moreover, attaining nirvana means being liberated within the dharmadhatu space of emptiness. In this way, everything becomes empty and so all that

43

appears and exists is the state of emptiness. Therefore, do not be attached and do not cling to duality. Without being attached to anything whatsoever, remain in the continuity of the great all-pervasive state of realizing emptiness that belongs to no category whatsoever. Let be in the state that is free from mental constructs.

Be certain that emptiness is the essence of most teachings. From the very beginning, that is the special quality of the view that is intended with this purpose. If you fail to understand the meaning of emptiness, you will involve yourself in clinging to the perceived objects of the six collections and continue to roam in samsara. If you gain certainty concerning the nature of emptiness, you interrupt the stream of samsara, and delusion is completely purified. On the other hand, if rather than true emptiness you stray into the idea of emptiness or fail to understand the state of equality and instead dissipate into a state of indolence, there is no straying more severe than this "emptiness". Rely therefore on a master for the key point of profound instructions and persevere in the practice.

Thus he spoke. Again they asked: Please listen, great master. Please explain to us in detail the meaning of conferring the most supreme among all empowerments, the empowerment of awareness-display, the key points of practice, and the meaning of gaining mastery over awareness.

The Master spoke: Listen here, King and Tsogyal. One engages in the four empowerments mentioned above progressively. One journeys through the levels and paths in succession and is not able to awaken instantaneously. They are teachings taught by the nirmanakayas for the sake of sentient beings.

The empowerment for awareness-display is taught by the buddhas who are by nature spontaneously perfected and, sending out compassionate emanations from the dharmadhatu of Akanishtha, they teach it for the sake of instantaneously awakening those who are of the highest fortune. It is therefore not possible to attain buddhahood without having received the empowerment for awareness-display.

All the buddhas of the past awakened after receiving the empowerment for awareness-display.

Everyone who presently attains enlightenment also awakens after receiving the empowerment for awareness-display. And every buddha who attains enlightenment in the future will also awaken after having received the empowerment for awareness-display. It is impossible to attain enlightenment unless you have obtained it.

*Samaya. Seal, seal, seal.*

# 4

## TRANSMISSION

### *Chögyam Trungpa Rinpoche*

Our next topic is the transmission of vajrayana teachings from teacher to student. Before we can discuss transmission, however, it seems necessary to go back a step and examine our level of sanity and discipline. We need to examine what we have accomplished in our relationship with the world. If we have not been able to make a relationship with our suffering, frustrations, and neuroses, the feasibility of transmission is remote, extremely remote, for we have not even made a proper relationship with the most basic level of our experience.

I could say to you, "Forget all that. Forget your pain and suffering; it is going to be okay." I could give you all kinds of antidotes: tranquilizers, mantras, and tricks. I could say, "Soon you'll feel good. Soon you'll forget your pain, and then you'll be in a beautiful place." But that would be an enormous falsity, and in the long run, such an approach is ungenerous and extremely destructive to the spiritual path. It is like giving our children tranquilizers whenever they begin to misbehave so that they will fall asleep. It saves us the trouble of getting a babysitter and changing diapers, but the child becomes a complete zombie. That is not the human thing to do, we must admit, and giving someone a spiritual tranquilizer is just as primitive

From Chögyam Trungpa, *Journey without Goal: The Tantric Wisdom of the Buddha* (Boston: Shambhala Publications, 1981), "Transmission."

as that. We suffer tremendously if we treat spirituality in that way, and we have to pay for it later on. Enormous problems arise—both resentment and discontent.

One approach that is used in presenting spirituality is to say that if we have any questions, we should just forget them. We should regard them as outside the circle of the spiritually initiated. We should forget all our negativity: "Don't ask any questions; just drop them. It is important that you have hope, that you go beyond your questions. Only if you accept the whole thing will you be saved." That strategy is used to take advantage of the sanity of human beings—which is unlawful.

Someone may tell us that, if we commit ourselves to a particular practice or path, within four weeks we are going to be okay; we are going to be "high" forever. So we try it, and it works—but not forever. After six weeks, at most, or perhaps after only ten days, we begin to come down, and then we begin to panic and wonder what is going on. Usually, the most faithful students blame themselves, feeling they have mismanaged the practice: "I must have some problem that I haven't cleared up yet." But that is not the case at all. The problem is the way they were indoctrinated into their spiritual practice.

We accept what is presented to us with an open mind, which is beautiful, but then its truth does not hold up. Because of the basic deception involved in our initiation, all sorts of holes begin to develop. Unfortunately, we become the victims of those lies, deceptions, or charlatanisms, and we feel the effects constantly, over and over again.

So we have a problem with spiritual transmission, a problem of how to get real transmission from a competent master into our system. At this point, we are talking purely about the beginner's level and the preparations that might be needed in order for spiritual transmission to occur in the very early stages. It is necessary for us to sharpen our cynicism, to sharpen our whole critical attitude toward what we are doing. That cynicism provides a basis for our study and work. For instance, if we are building a bridge, we begin by constructing the framework. It could be made of timber or iron rods, but the skeleton must be built before we pour the concrete. That is an example of the cynical approach. It is absolutely necessary to have that kind of cynical attitude if we are going to build a bridge, and it is necessary to be cynical in our approach to spirituality as well.

We need to encourage an attitude of constant questioning, rather than ignoring our intelligence, which is a genuine part of our potential as students. If students were required to drop their questions, that would create armies and armies of zombies—rows of jellyfish sitting next to each other. But, to use a local expression, that is not so neat. In fact, it is messy. Preparing a beautifully defined and critical background for what we are doing to ourselves and what the teaching is doing to us is absolutely important, *absolutely* important. Without that critical background, we cannot develop even the slightest notion or flavor of enlightenment.

Enlightenment is based on both *prajña*, or discriminating awareness, and compassion. But without cynicism, we do not have either. We do not have any compassion for ourselves because we are looking for something outside of ourselves, and we want to find the best way to get it. We also do not have any prajña, or clarity. We become completely gullible, and we are liable to be sucked in without any understanding, none whatsoever.

Transmission is like receiving a spiritual inheritance. In order to inherit our spiritual discipline, in order to have a good inheritance, we should become worthy vessels. In order to become worthy vessels, we have to drop the attitude that we are going to be saved, that there is going to be a magically painless operation, and that all we have to do is pay the doctor's fees. We have the notion that if we pay the doctor, everything will be taken care of. We can just relax and let him do what he wants. That attitude is simpleminded. It is absolutely necessary to think twice. The questioning mind is absolutely necessary; it is the basis of receiving transmission.

I am not stressing the importance of critical intelligence because Buddhism is just now being introduced to America and the West. It is not that I think students here might be more gullible. Buddhism is a strong tradition that has existed for 2,500 years, and throughout the ages students have been given these same instructions. Throughout the ages they have contributed their neuroses and their mistakes to help shape the methods and means of the Buddhist lineage. A learning process has been taking place for 2,500 years, in fact, even longer. And we have inherited all of that experience. So this approach is ages old rather than a sudden panic. It is an old way, very old and very traditional.

One of the responsibilities of the lineage holder is not to give an inch, but to keep up the tradition. At this point, tradition does not mean dressing up in robes and playing exotic music or having dakinis dancing around us, or anything like that. Tradition is being faithful to what we have been taught and to our own integrity. From this point of view, tradition is being awake and open, welcoming but at the same time stubborn.

According to tradition, the teacher should treat his students in this stubborn way: He should require that his students practice properly, in accordance with the tradition of the lineage. There are problems when a teacher is too kind to students who do not belong to the teacher's race and upbringing. Some teachers from the East seem to be excited by foreignness: "Wow! Finally, we are going to teach the aliens, the overseas people." Because of this fascination and out of a naive generosity, they make unnecessary concessions. Although such teachers may be liberal enough to include Occidental students, to take them to heart and be very kind to them, their extraordinary kindness may be destructive.

Such teachers regard Westerners as an extraordinary species, as if they came from the planet Mars: "Well, why don't we teach them, since we have a captive audience of living Martians here?" That misunderstanding is an expression of limited vision, of failing to see that the world is one world made up of human beings. A person who lives on this earth needs food, shelter, clothing, a love affair, and so on. We are all alike in that regard. Westerners do not need any special treatment because they invented the airplane or electronics. All human beings have the same psychology: They think in the same way, and they have the same requirements as students. The question is simply how one can teach students no matter where they come from.

In that respect we can follow the example of the Buddha, who presented the teachings to the Indians of his time in a universal fashion. It is much more enlightened to view the world as one global situation. Everybody is united: We are all samsaric people, and we all have the potential to become enlightened as well. We do not have to be particularly kind toward one part of the world or another, or for that matter, aggressive toward one part of the world or another. We are one world; we share one earth, one water, one fire, and one sun.

Wherever a student comes from, his or her attitude is very important. To receive transmission, a student should be humble and open but not wretched. Being humble in this case is being like a teacup. If we are pouring a cup of tea, the cup could be said to be humble. The cup has a sense of being in its own place. When we pour tea into a cup, the cup is at a lower level and the pot is at a higher level. This has nothing to do with the spiritual trips, higher consciousness, lower consciousness, or anything like that. We are talking pragmatically. If we are going to pour tea into a cup, the cup obviously should be lower than the pot. Otherwise we would be unable to pour anything into it.

Water obviously has to flow down. It is very simple. Like a humble cup, the student should feel fertile and at the same time open. Because tea is going to be poured into this particular cup, the cup has a sense of open expectation. Why not? We are no longer wretched people who are not up to the level of receiving teaching. We are simply students who want to know, who want to learn and receive instructions. Also, one cup is not necessarily better or more valuable than another. It could be made out of many things—ordinary clay, porcelain, gold, or silver—but it is still a cup as long as it can hold water or tea.

To be a proper cup, we should be free from spiritual materialism, thoroughly ripened, and brought to spiritual maturity so that transmission can take place. Then, in our basic being, we feel the quality of "cupness"; we feel our whole existence thirsting to receive teaching. We are open to the teachings. That is the first step in transmission: like the cup, we are on a certain level of experience that is not absolutely wretched or full of holes. We don't feel that we are deprived.

In fact, being a cup is an absolutely powerful thing: there is a sense of pride. Because our cup has such a strong quality of cupness, the teapot cannot help but fill it with knowledge or teachings. The teacher cannot wait to pour into us. We are seducing the teapot with our cupness: our pride, our self-existence, and our sanity. Two magnetic processes are taking place: the cup is magnetized by the teapot, and the teapot is equally magnetized by the cup. A love affair takes place; a fascination takes place.

Transmission means the extension of spiritual wakefulness from one person to someone else. Wakefulness is extended rather than transferred. The teacher, or the transmitter, extends his own inspiration rather than giving his experience away to somebody else and becoming an empty balloon. The teacher is generating wakefulness and inspiration constantly, without ever being depleted. So for the student, transmission is like being charged with electricity.

Transmission also requires the dynamic expression of the student's own emotions. As students, our aggression, our lust, and our stupidity are all included. According to vajrayana, everything we can think of, including the emotions, is workable. In fact, transmission cannot take place without emotions, because they are part of the food of transmutation. And since they are so energetic and powerful, we do not want to exclude any of them.

As long as we separate our philosophy and our concepts of morality from our emotions, there is no problem. This does not mean that we should be completely loose, seemingly free from philosophy, morality, and ethics, but that self-existing ethics take place constantly. To receive transmission it is absolutely necessary to be an ordinary human being: confused, stupid, lustful, and angry. Without those emotional qualities, we cannot receive transmission. They are absolutely necessary. I do not think this is a particularly difficult requirement to fulfill. Everybody seems to have a pretty juicy helping of them.

Our emotions are regarded as the wiring or electrical circuit that receives transmission. We could say that we have three wires—one for passion, one for aggression, and one for naiveté, ignorance, or slothfulness. These three form a very busy electrical device that would like to receive transmission. We are hungry for it; we are dying for it. And on the other side, there is the electrical generator which is somewhat smug, knowing that it is ready to transmit at any time.

So we have a good machine and we are beautifully wired; now we are just waiting for the generator to convey its charge—which in Sanskrit is called *abhisheka*. Abhisheka literally means "sprinkling," or "bathing," or "anointment." It is a formal ceremony of empowerment, a formal transmission from teacher to student. Abhisheka cannot take place unless the necessary wiring has already been set up, and to change our analogy slightly, abhisheka cannot take place without a good electrician, the teacher, or guru, who will know when to switch on the current.

In an abhisheka there is a sense of destruction, a sense of flow, and a sense of fulfillment. Those three principles of abhisheka are analogous to electricity in many ways: when we turn on a switch, the first thing that happens is that the resistance to the current is destroyed. Then, the current can flow through the circuit; and finally, the electricity can fulfill its purpose. If we turn on a lamp, first the electrical resistance is destroyed by turning on the switch, then the electricity flows, and finally the lamp is lit. In the same way, in receiving abhisheka destruction comes first, right at the beginning. Anything that is disorganized or confused and any misconceptions about receiving abhisheka get destroyed on the spot—immediately.

According to the tantric tradition, it is better not to get into tantra, but if we must get into it, we had better surrender. Having surrendered, we must give up the idea of survival. Survival means that we can still play our games, play our little tricks on the world. We have our usual routines, the little gadgets that we play with, the little colors that we pull out of our personality to make sure that we exist. But in tantra, it is not possible to play any games. So at the beginning it is necessary to give in completely. We have to surrender to groundlessness: there is no ground for us to develop security. As well we surrender to the fact that we cannot hold on to our ego, which by innuendo means that we surrender to the enlightened state of being. Then, actually, we do not have to do anything. Once we open, we just open.

All that is part of the first principle of abhisheka: destruction. When that first level of abhisheka takes place, it kills any unnecessary germs in our system. At that point, we have no hopes of manipulating anything at all. Then the flow of energy can take place. And after that, there is fulfillment: we finally begin to see the reality of what is possible in tantric experience. It is necessary for anyone involved with the discipline of vajrayana to understand the three principles of destruction, flow, and fulfillment. I am glad we could discuss these principles publicly, so that you will have a chance either to prepare yourselves or to run away. That creates a very open situation.

The student always has a chance to run away. We seem to have the concept that tantric discipline imposes itself on us, but what we are discussing is entirely self-imposed. The student might freak out at any time; he might feel weighted down, over-clean, and over-filled. But in order to receive transmission, he has to stay in his own place, which is not particularly pleasurable.

To conclude, the role of the guru in transmission is to electrify the student's vessel, so that it becomes clean and clear, free of all kinds of materialistic germs, and then to pour essence into it. And if he is to be electrified at all, to be cleaned out and filled up, the student must be waiting and ready. He has to be willing to be made into a good vessel. As a good vessel, the student feels that he is opening and taking part constantly. And as a good vessel, he could hold all sorts of heavy-handed liquids. In a good vessel, we could drink alcoholic beverages; that is, we could drink up dualistic thoughts. We could drink the blood of ego, which is killed on the spot.

# 5

## EMPOWERMENT AND SAMAYA

*Chökyi Nyima Rinpoche*

In general, we need to understand that the entirety of samsara is futile and pointless to pursue. In particular, we need to understand that karma and selfish emotions are like poison. Selfish emotions make us create an enormous amount of negative karma and negative actions that only create suffering. In this way, selfish emotions are the basis for deluded experience. If you are weary of samsara and want to renounce everything, you should abandon karma and disturbing emotions.

The objects of our compassion, from the core of our hearts, should be all sentient beings, who repeatedly undergo self-created suffering. The Mahayana scriptures frequently mention that each and every sentient being has been our own father and mother, our own brother and sister, our child, our intimate, in various lifetimes. We are connected to everyone, without a single exception. By practicing the true view and pure compassion, we can truly help others and bring them to a permanent state of liberation and enlightenment. Do so with this kind of motivation: "By training in the true view and pure compassion, I will bring all sentient beings to enlightenment!" At all times, keep this very precious bodhichitta attitude. Do not

From Chökyi Nyima Rinpoche, *Present Fresh Wakefulness: A Meditation Manual on Nonconceptual Wisdom* (Boudhanath: Rangjung Yeshe Publications, 2001), "The Heart of the Practice."

let it be mere lip service, but endeavor to make it deep-felt, from the core of your heart. Keep disenchantment with and renunciation of samsara as the very foundation of your practice, as well as loving-kindness and compassion. In addition, train in the true view, the pure view of recognizing mind-essence.

At all levels of Buddhist practice we combine two aspects, means and knowledge. In the general level of Buddhism, the means is the pure ethics, the discipline, as well as meditative concentration. The result of that is the knowledge, the insight of realizing there is no ego, there is no self. In this way, we can attain freedom. In the Mahayana teachings, the means are the first five of the six *paramitas*, while the knowledge is the sixth, *prajña-paramita,* or transcendent knowledge. Through these two aspects, we realize the true view of compassionate emptiness: profound emptiness that is indivisible from great compassion. In this way, we can progress through the paths and bhumis, all the way through the tenth bhumi to the eleventh bhumi of true and complete enlightenment.

When it comes to the vajra vehicle of Secret Mantra, the special quality of Vajrayana is pure perception. Because everything to begin with is already pure, whatever appears and exists is all-encompassing purity. To train in seeing everything as pure is a very profound method that is part of the means. The knowledge aspect in Vajrayana is nondual original wakefulness, the recognition of the very nature of our minds. It is only due to temporary confusion, moment-to-moment mistakenness, that we apprehend the existence of an "I" where no such personal identity exists, and of a "that" and a "you," where no such entities truly exist. Through such temporary mistakenness, all samsara's manifold experiences come about. Both the shared and individual types of experience are due to this moment-to-moment confusion.

To clear away this mistakenness, this impure way of perceiving, we not only train in pure perception but also in recognizing the true view of thought-free wakefulness. There are a variety of means to facilitate this in Vajrayana. They include the reflections called the four mind-changings, the ngöndro of the four or five times 100,000, as well as the development stage, recitation, and completion stage. Vajrayana methods are very easy, there are plenty of them, and they do not require much hardship. However, they are tremendously effective for purifying momentary confusion.

Let us take the example of the connection between firewood and fire. A lot of firewood makes a huge fire that can burn for a long time. You could

53

say that the fire's size and its ability to burn for a long period is thanks to the firewood. Nevertheless, when the firewood is used up, the fire is finished. Fire does not burn without wood. In the same way, the accumulation of merit is necessary and beneficial. When, in addition, this merit is combined with the accumulation of wisdom—with the view of profound emptiness—then that merit fuels the wisdom that enables us to transcend samsara. Therefore, means and knowledge, merit and wisdom, are extremely important. Knowledge can make us free of samsara. Perfect knowledge comes through the accumulation of merit. As is said, *the knowledge is the outcome of the means.*

The training in goodness with a conceptual focus means to avoid what harms others as well as what causes us to harm others. It follows that as we avoid inflicting harm, we are also able to do what is helpful for others. We are then able to create the circumstances that are beneficial for understanding; we are able to connect with teachings, to arrive in places where there are spiritual teachers. It becomes increasingly easy, naturally.

You may at present be unable to practice meditation; you may for a while lack the opportunity to embrace the practices of development stage and completion stage; but you can still sincerely take refuge in the Three Jewels, the Three Precious Ones, the Buddha, Dharma, and Sangha. Accept these three objects as your help and support. By forming this virtuous frame of mind, at some future point you will be able to reconnect with the teachings. You will be able to come into circumstances where you can learn, understand, and practice. Being able to practice the Dharma comes about through the combined power of the blessings of the Three Jewels and our own trust and devotion. It is said that although the blessings of the Three Jewels are like a hook that is always present, unless the ring of our openness of trust is also present, the hook cannot take hold of the ring.

The bodhisattva vow is the sincere wish to help others. We think, "As much as I am able to do so, I will help other beings directly and indirectly; I will do whatever it takes." The bodhisattva precepts are based on the resolve to bring all sentient beings to enlightenment. This is not just during the ceremony of taking the bodhisattva vow, but also on a daily basis—whenever we do any practice, it is part of the chant. Whenever we sit down to do a meditation session, we take the bodhisattva vow: It is like a prelude to meditation practice. It may seem that it doesn't help that much, that it is just a nice way of thinking. This is not true. From the initial vow comes the force to truly help others, which enables a bodhisattva to be courageous and brave, to embrace the vast activities that accomplish the benefit of all other beings in actuality. This actual ability springs directly out of intention. A bodhisattva first forms a strong resolve, the very deep-felt and strong wish to be of help to others. The vow we take is the seed of the bodhisattva activity. From this seed, the ability will come in the future to actually put it to use for the benefit of others. Taking the bodhisattva vow has tremendous benefit.

The Vajrayana precepts are called samayas. They are obtained through receiving empowerment. Through receiving the four empowerments of Vajrayana practice, we are introduced to the basic nature of things—how things really are.

Through the vase empowerment, the first of the four, we are introduced to the fact that whatever we see, all sights, are visible emptiness—not just the celestial palaces, buddhafields, and deities that we visualize, but everything we see. The second empowerment introduces us to the fact that all sounds, not only of mantra, are audible emptiness. To recognize this is to realize the voice of the victorious ones. Through the third empowerment, we are brought to the understanding that all sense impressions, especially but not only the blissful ones, are indivisible from emptiness. That is very important for us as humans, because the samsaric level we are in is called the Desire Realms. For beings in this type of realm, attachment to pleasant sensations and the feeling of desire are very strong; they run very deep. Through the third empowerment, we are introduced to the state of wakefulness in which bliss and emptiness are indivisible, in order to be free of that habitual attachment to pleasure. The fourth, the precious word empowerment, points out our innate nature of mind, intrinsic wakefulness, as being indivisible emptiness and awareness.

The best situation, of course, is to receive the four empowerments and simultaneously realize what is intended and pointed out, within our own experience. In that particular way, being empowered and being realized go hand in hand. If this does not occur, the empowerments at the very least still bestow blessings. This makes one receptive to realizing the intended meaning of the empowerment at some point in the future.

Honestly, the mind transmission of the buddhas is empowerment. The symbolic transmission of the knowledge holders, the vidyadharas, is also empowerment. And the oral transmission of masters, the teachings we receive, is a way of being empowered as well. I often teach about the nature of mind, about the value of recognizing it, and how to train in that. These teachings are also connected to the meaning of empowerment. Actually, there is no empowerment without teaching, and there is no teaching without empowerment. Still, there is a difference between the two.

The path of Vajrayana is means and knowledge: means as the development stage and knowledge as the completion stage. Without an understanding of the purpose, the development stage could resemble a child playing in a sandbox. Development stage has both temporary and ultimate benefit. These benefits are logical and profound and can be proven through the instructions and our own experience. The practice of development stage gradually reduces our attachment and clinging to the solid reality of our body and dwelling place. As a matter of fact, everything is already the unity of experience and emptiness, or *visible emptiness*, so visualizing things as being in such a way is in harmony with how things actually are; there is no conflict. All sounds are already *audible emptiness*; the voice of all buddhas is audible emptiness. All sensations, if we really look closely into how they feel, are nothing other than *blissful emptiness*. This is especially true when we apply the key points of the vajra body with the three channels and five chakras to ignite the *tummo* fire and to experience the blissful heat. Through experiencing the example wisdom, we are enabled to realize the true wisdom, the real wisdom, which is the naked state of *aware emptiness*.

There is a reason for these practices. In general, all phenomena originate dependently, based on causes and conditions. Mind is very powerful. When the mind directs itself toward what is good, we can do tremendous good. When it is directed in a negative way, we can do immense evil.

Isn't it true that someone who forms the deep-felt wish "May I benefit innumerable beings! May I attain that ability to truly help others in vast, vast numbers!" can do great good things out of that attitude? The converse is true for one who forms the strong wish "May I gain power over a great number of people and destroy my enemies." Out of such a malicious wish, one can do tremendous evil. Motivation itself has no physical form. A person who forms such a wish looks like an ordinary person, and yet the forming of that type of wish could be extraordinary. The power of noble aspiration is great, but so is the power of a negative wish.

Some people say, "Buddhism may be good, but its followers do not really do anything for others. Buddhists merely sit and make good wishes for other beings; they do not really do anything about it. People belonging to other religions reach out—they establish hospitals, they build schools, they actually do something for others." In terms of immediate benefit, it is accurate to say that. If we are concerned with what is of lasting benefit, there is a lot more to say. Certainly it is one type of benefit to help others while they are still alive, by curing them, educating them, giving them food, clothes, shelter, and so forth. This is called mundane benefit. You help to establish them in a nice, comfortable state in this world. But if you can influence their attitude toward developing greater compassion and understanding, that is an even greater benefit that could be inexhaustible, because they can take those qualities along. The giving of material things is good, but giving protection against fear is an even greater gift. Greater than that still is the gift of the teachings, which helps people's minds reduce disturbing emotions and increase compassion and knowledge. Giving the understanding of the nature of things is not a gift of temporary benefit: It is of lasting value.

Everything comes about through a connection between causes and conditions. Therefore, if we train in a way in which means and knowledge are in unity; if we train in a correct, pure way, we will realize a result that is equally pure and perfect. A perfect coincidence of causes and conditions may seem very simple, but it is not. Many factors need to synchronize for anything to happen. For example, we need many items to make a delicious cup of tea. We need water, a cup, and a clean pot. We need fire of some sort. Also, we need tea leaves, not to mention milk, sugar or honey, and maybe spices. Even for something as simple as a cup of tea, if one factor is missing, it will not be perfect.

In the same way, without the means we do not have their outcome, which is knowledge. Of course, it would be much better to understand without using any methods. If food would simply be prepared spontaneously, without our doing anything, that would be wonderful. If we could arrive somewhere without traveling, it would be the best. But these things don't happen. Therefore, please don't frown upon the importance of taking refuge and the bodhisattva vow, purifying obscurations, perfecting the accumulations, the four mind-changings, ngöndro, development stage, completion stage, and so forth. Do not underestimate the value of these practices. A small method can yield a great result. Do not belittle the means. When we do not underestimate even a small method, that small method can help develop the eventual profound outcome of all these methods, which is the knowledge in which egolessness is an actuality.

In all three vehicles in Buddhism, we practice in a way in which means and knowledge are combined in a unity. This is true whether we train in the knowledge that realizes egolessness, or in the profound view of compassionate emptiness, or in the basic state of nondual thought-free wakefulness. Whatever method helps you to progress in that, please use it. When something makes it more difficult, please avoid it. There are two guaranteed helpful circumstances: devotion and compassion. These two methods are the best ways to purify obscurations and perfect the accumulations. Moreover, when it comes to overcoming obstacles, sidetracks, and pitfalls in our practice, there are two practices that are very safe, simple and always efficient: devotion and compassion. *Sincere devotion and sincere compassion overcome any and all hindrances.*

I have also explained to you the purpose and benefits of precepts and vows. The heart of Vajrayana practice, the real purpose, is pointed out during empowerment. That is the wisdom, which is the nature of the empowerment. To be truly empowered, to realize original wakefulness, traditionally requires a lot of preparation. This is why purifying the obscurations and perfecting the accumulations are necessary. But just purifying and accumulating is not enough. It is important that we do not separate means and knowledge. As I mentioned before:

> This coemergent wisdom, beyond description,
> Is recognized only through the practices of gathering accumulations and
>     purifying one's veils
> And through the blessings of a realized master.
> Know it to be delusion if you depend on other means.

STUDENT: Could you explain a little more about samaya?
RINPOCHE: The Sanskrit word *samaya* in Tibetan is *damtsig*, and there are several ways of explaining its literal meaning. To make this very simple, *dam* means sublime, and *tsig* is a statement. Thus, samaya is a statement that is true, genuine, pure, real. To apply oneself in a way that is in harmony with how the truth is, is called keeping the samaya. Whatever we see is visible emptiness. This is how it actually is. This is also what we need to realize. The realization that all sights are visible emptiness is the vajra body of all buddhas. This is how it is proclaimed. That statement is real, true, and sublime. Keeping that is called keeping the samaya of vajra body. The same applies to all sounds being audible emptiness, and mind being aware emptiness. That is an unfailing truth.

When the samayas are described in detail, there are hundreds of thousands that can be listed. But all of them can be condensed in this way. The foremost samaya is when you compose yourself in a state in which you in actuality *experience the fact that all sights, sounds, and awareness are visible emptiness, audible emptiness, and aware emptiness*. That is the best. Next best is to have the conviction that this is so: "Whatever is seen is visible emptiness. Whatever I hear is audible emptiness, the voice of all victorious ones. And mind is aware emptiness, self-existing rigpa, intrinsic wakefulness; it is really so." To have that certainty is called keeping all the hundreds of thousands of samayas.

The opposite of this is to regard whatever I see or hear as a solid reality that is permanent, has concrete attributes, is formed, and really exists. With regard to the thoughts and emotions that move in our minds, failing to recognize the very identity of that which thinks or feels as self-existing wakefulness is known as damaging the samayas of mind. Being opposed to trusting that our nature could be dharmakaya or rigpa, having an opinion against that, is known as turning against the sublime samaya statements, against *the unfailing truth of what is*. As long as one keeps that orientation, one is removed from realizing what is true and real.

# PART TWO

# THE LIBERATING INSTRUCTIONS

*6*

# NURTURING THE SEEDS

## *Padmasambhava & Jamgön Kongtrül*

The third topic is Nurturing, which has two parts: a brief statement in the manner of connecting with the words above and a detailed explanation of the meaning.

## A Brief Statement in the Manner of Connecting with the Words Above

The *Lamrim Yeshe Nyingpo* root text says:

> Now come the stages of the path to nurture the seeds 𑁍
> By the pure person whose being has thus been ripened: 𑁍

Now come the stages of the path of the profound methods to nurture the planted seeds on the path of enlightenment. This pertains to those whose being has thus been ripened through the four empowerments, who have kept their body, speech, and mind completely pure by not transgressing the samayas, and who wish to quickly attain the siddhis through the path of Mantra.

From Padmasambhava and Jamgön Kongtrül, *The Light of Wisdom*, Volume II (Boudhanath: Rangjung Yeshe Publications, 1998), "Nurturing."

The actual path of Vajrayana is the two stages of development and completion. When the general meaning of these two is described further, there are five points: the identity, definition, divisions, sequence, and purpose of each of the two stages.

## THE IDENTITY

First, the identity of the development stage is the "yoga of the imagined deity." The characteristic of this is the visible and empty form of the deity, which is produced from fabrication and labeling and is concurrent with melting bliss.

The basis for the special qualities is the form of the deity, which is conceptualized by thought. The four special qualities are as follows:

1. The special quality of the ritual is to have the complete stages of the ritual of development, as taught by the Victorious One in the tantras of Mantra.

2. The special quality of its own result is ability and the development of magical powers.

3. The special quality of the essence is the aspect of extraordinary melting bliss sealed by emptiness.

4. The special quality of function is to have the three aspects of purification, ripening, and perfection complete.

The identity of the completion stage is the "yoga of the deity of actuality." The characteristic of this is the apparent and empty form of the deity, which is unfabricated and concurrent with the melting bliss. Being unstable in this is the causal completion stage, while stability is the resultant completion stage.

The basis for the special qualities is the nonconceptual wisdom, while the three special qualities are:

1. The special quality of the cause, which is to concentrate on the key points of the vajra body.

2. The special quality of the function, which is to purify the nadis, and to purify the pranas and bindus in the central channel.

3. The special quality of manifestation, which is great bliss simultaneous with empty form.

## THE DEFINITION

Second, the (Sanskrit) equivalent for development stage is *utpattikrama*. *Utpatti* means "fabricated" or "labeled," and therefore it means to develop by means of fabricating or labeling something new through conceptual thinking. At the same time, the basis for that which is fabricated or labeled is the completion stage. The (Sanskrit) equivalent for completion stage is *nishpannakrama*. *Nishpanna* means "unfabricated," "completed," or "perfected," and therefore it means that which is spontaneously present without being fabricated. *Krama,* in both cases, means "stage" in the sense of method or successive steps on the path.

## THE DIVISIONS

Third, when divided in terms of their identities, there are two parts: The development stage is the path and associated aspects of the yoga of the imagined deity, which is fabricated and labeled; the completion stage is the path and associated aspects of the yoga of the deity of actuality, which is free from fabrication.[20]

Concerning the object and means of purification, there are also two divisions: the development stage—which is the yoga of the conventional truth connected to the relative mundane aspect of arising—and the completion stage, which is the yoga of the ultimate truth connected to the absolute mundane aspect of ceasing.

In terms of application, the development stage has four ways of practice corresponding to purifying the habitual tendencies for the four types of rebirth. This is mentioned in the *Magical Net*:

> In order to purify the four types of rebirth
> There are also four types of development:
> The quite elaborate, the elaborate, and the unelaborate,
> As well as the very unelaborate.

The completion stage has the following ways of practice:

> The stage of relative self-consecration, which is the practice of nadis,
>     pranas, and bindus.
> The mandala circle supported by another's body.

The general stage of the inexpressible coemergence, the great ultimate
luminosity, which is sealing both of the above.
The special Great Perfection: the sections of Mind, Space, and
Instruction.

## The Sequence

Fourth, in order to purify your being prior to entering the path of the
natural state, you should apply yourself to the development stage as the preliminaries for the path. In order to train in the actual natural state after having purified your being, the completion stage is the main part of the path.

Phrased differently, the accumulation of merit lays the basis for the accumulation of wisdom and is also the cause for dispelling hindrances for
the arising of the special accumulation of wisdom, the original wakefulness
that is utterly perfected. Thus, the practice of the development stage must
precede (the completion stage). This is why the *Commentary on the Vajra
Essence* states:

> To those bound by thoughts and habitual tendencies,
> First teach the conceptual rituals.
> When the nature of thought is understood,
> Then let them engage in nonthought.

The *Five Stages* further mentions:

> To those who fully abide in the development stage
> And wish for the completion stage,
> These methods are taught by the perfectly Awakened One,
> Like the progressive steps of a staircase.

In short, there is a sequential dependency of the objects to be purified that
are the deluded imputing and their seed aspects, the means that purify that
are the support and the supported, and the accomplished results that are the
common and the supreme.

## The Purpose

Fifth, the purpose of the development stage is to abandon the fixation on
an ordinary world with ordinary beings, to form the auspicious link for the

seven impure bhumis of the path and the *rupakaya* of the fruition, and in particular, to accomplish the mundane siddhis that are the actual results.

The purpose of the completion stage is to abandon the defilement of the habitual tendencies of transition, to form the auspicious link for the three pure bhumis of the path and the coemergent body, *sahajakaya*, of the fruition, and in particular, to accomplish the supreme siddhi of Mahamudra, the actual result.[21] The *Subsequent Essence Tantra* describes this:

> The mundane siddhis are achieved
> Through the practices of the development stage.
> The siddhi that transcends the world
> Is gained through the practice of the completion stage.

## A Detailed Explanation of the Meaning

This has four parts:

1. The practice of the development stage, the union of appearance and emptiness, which is connected to the vase empowerment.

2. The practice of the profound path, the union of clarity and emptiness, which is connected to the secret empowerment.[22]

3. The practice of the *phonya* path, the union of bliss and emptiness, which is connected to the third empowerment.

4. The practice of the Great Perfection, the union of awareness and emptiness, which is connected to the fourth empowerment.

# 7

## THE DEVELOPMENT STAGE

### *Padmasambhava & Jamgön Kongtrül*

THE PRACTICE OF THE DEVELOPMENT STAGE, THE UNION OF
APPEARANCE AND EMPTINESS, WHICH IS CONNECTED TO THE
VASE EMPOWERMENT

This has three parts: stating the purpose of the development stage, the actual development stage, and concluding the topic.

STATING THE PURPOSE OF THE DEVELOPMENT STAGE

The *Lamrim Yeshe Nyingpo* root text says:

> First, connected with the vase empowerment, 8
> Train in the general and special development stages, 8
> In order to purify the clinging to the ordinary perceptions of the world
>     and inhabitants. 8

As for these progressive stages of the path, there are four paths connected with the respective four empowerments. The first of these is the path connected with the vase empowerment. For that, you must train in the general

From Padmasambhava and Jamgön Kongtrül, *The Light of Wisdom*, Volume II
(Boudhanath: Rangjung Yeshe Publications, 1998), "The Development Stage."

development stages that correspond to Mahayoga and the special development stages that correspond to the two higher yogas. This is in order to purify the conceptual thinking that clings to the perceptions of the inanimate world and its animate inhabitants as being of ordinary concreteness.

## THE ACTUAL DEVELOPMENT STAGE

This has two parts: a brief statement as a summary, and a detailed explanation of the meaning.

### A Brief Statement as a Summary

The *Lamrim Yeshe Nyingpo* root text says:

> For that there are the deities to be accomplished and the means to
> accomplish them, 𝄇
> The path of how to accomplish, and also the fruition. 𝄇

For example, when pursuing a business venture, the object to be accomplished is wealth of great value; the means that accomplishes it is a profitable business; the way to accomplish it is to be skilled in trading; and the accomplished result is to easily attain the desired wealth. Similarly, for the development stage there are the three types of deities to be accomplished, renowned as: the utterly pure deity of dharmadhatu, the deity that is of the identity of wisdom, and the blessed deity with attributes.[23] The means that accomplish them are all those comprised of preliminaries, main part, and conclusion. The ways to accomplish them are the sadhanas of the single mudra-form, elaborate form, and group assembly. The accomplished fruition is the four vidyadhara levels.[24] I will gradually explain how they manifest in dependent connection.

### A Detailed Explanation of the Meaning

This has four parts: the deity to be accomplished, the means by which to accomplish (the deity), the path of how to accomplish (the deity), and the result of having accomplished in such a way.

The deities, the objects to be accomplished, are in general the three types mentioned above. Among them, the first type is luminous awakened mind, the natural state of unconfined empty cognizance. This is endowed with the threefold wisdom of essence, nature, and capacity that is primordially present without distinction in all beings. This is the samaya being, *samaya-sattva*.[25]

The second type is the wisdom being, *jñana-sattva*, the dharmakaya of all buddhas, which pervades the entirety of samsara and nirvana. These two are primordially indivisible, and this nature of nondual samaya being and wisdom being is the basis for purifying defilements, just like (the metaphor of) the wish-fulfilling jewel.

This is what the causal vehicles describe by such names as potential (*rigs*), basic constituent (*khams*), *sugata*-essence *(bde gshegs snying po)*, and so forth. Within Mantra, the Kriya scriptures call it thatness of self; the Ubhaya scriptures call it awakened mind, bodhichitta; and the Yoga scriptures call it awakened mind without beginning and end, or ever-excellent awakened mind.

The Mahayoga scriptures call it self-knowing awakened mind of the superior indivisible truths transcending objects of experience, or the greater dharmakaya of the superior indivisible truths. The Anu scriptures call it great bliss child of nondual space and wisdom, the root mandala of awakened mind.

The scriptures of the Instruction Section teach that within the heart of all embodied beings dwells mind-essence, the luminous dharmakaya of awakened mind, supported by the (sphere) comprised of the five pure essences. Other sources teach that the experiential basis for all these phenomena consisting of the impure aggregates, elements, and sense sources is known as the innate aggregates, or the alternate aggregates, elements, and sense sources, which are utterly pure as the original mandala of the deities of the three seats of completeness. This is in agreement with the statement that the extremely subtle three doors remain, from the very beginning, as the identity of the deities of the indestructible three vajras.

Although this is true, one is deluded by apprehending these as something other because of not recognizing one's natural face. This lack of understanding is the defilement to be purified, like (the metaphor of) the mud. For example, just as a jewel cannot fulfill its function as long as it is not free from the defilement of mud, similarly, unless you realize your nondual nature, just having it is of no avail; you must purify the defilement.

Now, as for the means to purify, the development stage purifies the imputed aspect of the temporary delusion, while the completion stage purifies the seed aspect. How does this happen? The stream-of-being that manifests in the form of deluded phenomena, karma, disturbing emotions, and suffering is itself transformed into great bliss. The way this transformation takes place is by means of this vital point: that the nature of whatever is perceived dawns as pure experience by letting it be in its very nature, without removing or adding anything. It is for this very reason that here, in the vehicle of Secret Mantra, the nature of the truth of origin is experienced as the truth of the path, and the nature of the truth of suffering is experienced as the truth of cessation. Since this is also the principle of taking the fruition as the path, it is far superior to the philosophical vehicles of the paths of abandoning, covering, and purifying the basics (disturbing emotions). Having in this way identified the indivisible samaya being and wisdom being as the basis for accomplishment, the actual objects to be accomplished in this context are the "deities of attributes" that manifest from their blessings or expression.[26] Their identity is the Three Roots: the vidyadhara gurus of the three lineages, the yidams of the nine gradual vehicles, and the dakinis of the three abodes. Their forms, as the various manifestations of peaceful and wrathful, detached and passionate, lord of the mandala and retinue, are found in inconceivable numbers. However, "you should meditate on me, Padma Tötreng, the single embodiment of the three mysteries, qualities and activities of all the Three Roots, if you wish to quickly attain blessings and the two siddhis that are far superior to all others." ...

## Declaring the Means to Accomplish

This has two parts: a brief statement and a detailed explanation

## A Brief Statement

The *Lamrim Yeshe Nyingpo* root text says:

> Whichever is the case, for the stages of the means to accomplish them, ꙮ
> Engage in the preliminaries, the main part, and the concluding actions. ꙮ

Regardless of which of these outer, inner, secret, or most secret gurus (yidam deities) is to be accomplished, for the progressive stages of the means to accomplish them, engage in the training through these three points: first in the preliminaries, the steps of gathering, purifying, abandoning adversity, and creating what is conducive; next in the main part, the yogas of the development stage along with the subsidiary practices; and finally in the concluding actions, the fulfillment of the activities.[27]

# 8

## CONCEPTUAL MEDITATION

### *Tsele Natsok Rangdröl*

In general, a correct realization of the nature of emptiness is the source of all Dharma teachings. It is therefore called mother of the victorious ones, space of phenomena (dharmadhatu), and discriminating knowledge. It is also called the womb of the queen consort, space, source of dharmas, ewam, and so forth. All these and other such types of symbol, meaning, and sign belonging to Secret Mantra are taught using symbolic terminology in order to illustrate this nature of emptiness.

(This correct realization of the nature of emptiness) is the source of the categories of eighteen types of emptiness taught in the sutras of the definitive meaning, as well as of all different aspects of development and completion of Mantrayana. For example, just as external space is the basis for or source of all worlds and beings, all the phenomena of samsara and nirvana at first manifest from the expanse of emptiness and ultimately dissolve back into the space of emptiness. The *Tantra of Immaculate Fruition* mentions:

> The ground that produces all of samsara and nirvana, without
> exception,
> Is the utterly unformed dharmadhatu.

From Tsele Natsok Rangdröl, *Empowerment* (Boudhanath: Rangjung Yeshe Publications, 1993), "Conceptual Meditation."

Pervading everywhere, a vast expanse
Of spacelike wakefulness,
Arising from the state of nonarising
Myriad magical displays appear in all possible ways.
All that appears and exists, samsara and nirvana, take form from the
  unformed
And manifest in actuality.
Everything is one in the nature of the basic state,
The dharmata that transcends mental constructs.

Not realizing this nature as it is creates the basis for confusion to arise. Ignorant of the inherent quality of the unity of emptiness and cognizance, such people uphold wrong beliefs such as nihilistic voidness or limited emptiness. These wrong views will only lead to the lower realms. On the other hand, within the correct realization of emptiness, there does not exist someone to go to the lower realms, the act of going, or a place to go.

In particular, in the context of Mahamudra, Ground Mahamudra is the original basic state or sugata-essence that is primordially and spontaneously present as your innate nature (*dharmata*) free from change and alteration, increase and decrease—an empty cognizance endowed with a core of awareness. Path Mahamudra is the purification of the defilement of temporary delusion by means of the numerous profound and swift procedures, such as shamatha and vipashyana, development and completion, means and knowledge, the two accumulations, and so forth. Fruition Mahamudra is the attainment of mastery over the Dharma kingdom, the identity of the three kayas of buddhahood, that need not be sought elsewhere but is self-existing within yourself as a great spontaneous presence. These are the qualities of realizing emptiness as it is.

Whether or not the conceptual practice of emptiness creates the circumstances for rebirth in the lower realms depends upon the individual person. Moreover, there are different types of conceptual practices. In the general vehicles, there are Dharma teachings using conceptual love and compassion, bodhichitta, and the six paramitas. The special Secret Mantra has conceptually based teachings, such as the extensive and condensed development stages or the meditation practices of the channels, winds, and essences. But when you embrace these practices with the sublime key point, then conceptual and nonconceptual are simply indivisible. So what is this sublime key point? It is simply threefold purity. Taking the example of bodhichitta, this is to realize that the object for generating the resolve, the one who generates it, and the mental state of the resolve itself are all of one taste within the space of natural emptiness. The same goes for the paramitas and so forth. Once you understand this, then all the practices that are conceptual or with a reference point become causes for unexcelled complete enlightenment. The *Sutra Foretelling Goodness* says:

> All phenomena are devoid of a self-nature
> And are free of the attributes of sentient beings or buddhas.
> The belief that the attributeless has attributes
> Takes you far away from buddhahood.
> Thus dharmic people are tainted by concepts.
>
> When fully understanding that things have no substance—
> That any deed is beyond a doer—
> It is fully revealed that clinging to names is empty.
>
> The one who understands that causes and conditions have no self-nature
> Is free from attachment and therefore also knows the Dharma.
> The one who understands that Dharma of nonattachment
> Will see buddhahood with the eyes of purity.

Similarly, it is essential to understand correctly that all the conceptual visualizations such as the development stages of Mantrayana are also to be practiced in this very same way. That is to say, in whatever development stage you practice, exactly in accordance with what has been pointed out by your master during the vase empowerment, everything that appears—the world and its contents of beings, the aggregates, elements, and sense bases—is to be visualized with the certainty of being what they are: the nature of the deity since the beginning. This way of visualization does not mean to mentally construct something to be what it is not. Such an imputation would be an incorrect relative truth, like the example of a piece of charcoal, which never becomes a conch however much you imagine it to be so.

Similarly, the practices and visualizations of the nadis, pranas, and elements are profound key points, methods that form the coincidences for realizing the primordially present nature, the basic state of things. They are not imagining something to be what it is not.

Anything you visualize turns into "conceptual straying" if visualized as a permanent reality with fixation on it as being solid. You should resolve that the visualization is a display of the Mahamudra of your mind—visible while being devoid of self-nature, just like a magical illusion or the moon in water. In its ultimate nature it is beyond constructed concepts. In this way, there is definitely no basis whatsoever for any obstacle, flaw, or straying. The *Essence Tantra* describes this fact:

> In the coemergent mind-essence
> There is neither a meditation nor a meditator.
> There is no deity and also no mantra.
> In the nature free from constructs,
> Both deity and mantra are perfectly present.
>
> As the method for realizing this,
> Just like refining and crafting gold and silver,
> Since you cannot shape and craft silver ore
> Before it has been melted,
> You must establish the fruition
> By means of the ripening empowerment and the development stage.

The scripture continues:

> The five aggregates are the five families of buddhas,
> And these five families are the five wisdoms.
> The five elements are the five consorts.
> All the outer and inner vajra sense bases
> Are the supreme mandala of male and female bodhisattvas.
>
> From the continuity of the single dharmakaya,
> In order to benefit all sentient beings,
> The emanated buddhafields fill space
> And infinite bodily forms are displayed.
>
> Ultimately there is no development stage
> Since the wakefulness of your own perception is complete as the deity.
> The deity is your mind and your mind the deity,
> Just like a crystal and colored light are indivisible.
> This nonduality of deity and mind
> Is the nondual realization of the victorious ones.

Moreover:

> Just as milk from a milking cow
> Permeates its entire body but does not appear when you pull its horns,
> While milk appears when you tug the udders,
> Likewise, with the dharmakaya of self-awareness,
> If you know the key points of the methods and oral instructions
> Concerning the innate state of the three vajras,
> All the attributes of body, speech, mind, qualities, and activities
> Will appear as direct perception and not as inference,
> And you attain complete buddhahood in a single lifetime.

In accordance with this statement, when you apply the key points upon the ground in which the body, speech, and mind since the beginning are the three vajras, through the profound methods of the path of ripening and liberation, you realize the fruition, the qualities of the body, speech, and mind of the victorious ones. This is the special feature of the vajra vehicle of Secret Mantra, the profound key point of taking the fruition as path. If you receive the master's oral instructions and blessings for the stages of development and completion with and without concepts, this is not difficult.

# 9

## THE PERFECT DEVELOPMENT STAGE

### Tsele Natsok Rangdröl

Next, one begins the development stage with purifying into emptiness by means of the SVABHAVA mantra. This mantra is meant to remind the practitioner of the essence of emptiness, the original natural state of all phenomena, the nature that primordially pervades all of samsara and nirvana. Yet nowadays many people believe that the purpose of this mantra is the temporary emptiness of rendering inconcrete the appearances of the world and its beings.

What is the real reason for remembering the great emptiness of the primordial natural state at the beginning of the development stage? The reason is to acknowledge Prajñaparamita, the mother of all phenomena, out of whose space all the phenomena of (samsara and) nirvana must necessarily originate. It is precisely the natural expression of this emptiness, the magical display of its unceasing cognizant quality, that emanates and manifests in the form of a celestial palace and various types of deities. No matter how this magical display appears, recognize that it is not made of material substance but is the unity of appearance and emptiness. This great unity has never separated from the space of the immense emptiness of your mind-essence. This is what is given the name development stage.

From Tsele Natsok Rangdröl, *Empowerment* (Boudhanath: Rangjung Yeshe Publications, 1993), "Development Stage."

As for the particular group of deities you visualize, through vivid presence, you avoid falling into the extreme of nihilism; through recollection of the pure symbolism, you avoid falling into the extreme of eternalism; and through stable pride, you avoid sporadic or fragmented visualization. The purpose of these methods is to prevent your three doors from departing from the three vajras, and they are found in most of the tantras and sadhanas of both the new and old schools. However, only a very few people practice in this way.

Some people explain that visualizing the development stage in the beginning and dissolving into the completion stage at the end is intended to bring birth and death onto the path and is the system of Nagarjuna and his followers and others. Others hold that practicing development and completion as a unity is the system of Naropa and his chief disciples. Although there are many different types of systems, there is undoubtedly no real difference between the basic intent of these sublime masters. The different systems are suited to different occasions and to the diverse inclinations and capacities of those to be tamed.

Some masters have said that these variations stem from the different systems found in the many sections of tantra, while the ultimate meaning is that development and completion are nothing other than a unity. Why is that? It is because initially the ground is the unity of the two truths, while the fruition that is ultimately realized is the unity of the two kayas. Therefore everything at first manifests out of the expanse of emptiness, and at the end again dissolves into the primordial continuity of the natural state. Thus it is taught that both manifesting and dissolving are in fact no other than a unity, the cognizance and emptiness of your mind-essence. Yet nowadays people practice development and completion separately, alternating one with the other.

Furthermore, any practice of development and completion should be performed exclusively as the cause for the unexcelled enlightenment of oneself and all beings pervading space. However, it seems that present-day practitioners of development stage and sadhana recitation struggle blindly with deities and mantras for the temporary, selfish gains of increasing their life span and wealth, or in order to alleviate a particular disease or evil influence, or with the intention to attain minor accomplishment in yogic activities to bring benefit or avoid harm. Such people will hardly arrive at the perfect development stage. Clinging to deity and mantra as ordinary reality without correctly understanding the threefold symbol, meaning, and sign embodies great danger, as illustrated by the story of how one can be reborn as a hungry ghost with the form of Yamantaka. Therefore, no matter what type of teaching you practice, understand the importance of taking to heart the authoritative scripture and the perfect oral instructions of your master.

*10*

# THE THIRD DHARMA
# OF GAMPOPA

*Tulku Urgyen Rinpoche*

*Grant your blessings that the path may clarify confusion.*

Now we have reached the third Dharma of Gampopa: how to let the path clarify confusion. Confusion here is understood as that which obscures our innate nature and prevents enlightenment. Everyone has buddha nature, all sentient beings without a single exception. Unfortunately, we don't know what we possess. We have fallen into confusion and we are wandering in samsara.

To let the path clarify confusion, path should be understood within the context of ground, path, and fruition, a structure that encompasses all the teachings of Sutra and Tantra. The ground is the buddha nature, *sugatagarbha*, the dharmakaya of all the buddhas that is present in all sentient beings. It is compared to pure, undefiled gold endowed with supreme qualities and free from any defects. How is the buddha nature present in everyone? The example given is that of oil in a mustard seed. When pressed, a mustard seed always yields oil. In the same way, in all sentient beings there is the essence of buddhahood, the buddha nature. No one lacks it. All the buddhas

From Tulku Urgyen Rinpoche, *Repeating the Words of the Buddha* (Boudhanath: Rangjung Yeshe Publications, 1999), "The Four Dharmas of Gampopa," and *As It Is*, Volume I (Boudhanath: Rangjung Yeshe Publications, 1999), "The Four Dharmas of Gampopa."

and bodhisattvas have buddha nature, as well as all sentient beings down to the tiniest insect, without any difference whatsoever in size or quality.

The buddha nature, the sugatagarbha, encompasses all of samsara and nirvana. Space is beyond center and edge. Wherever space pervades, there are sentient beings. Wherever there are sentient beings, buddha nature is present. That is what is meant by the statement that buddha nature encompasses all of samsara and nirvana, all worlds, all beings.

Although buddha nature is present in everyone, we fail to recognize it. This ignorance is the main cause for wandering in samsara. Due to the ignorance of not knowing their own nature, sentient beings have strayed into confusion, like pure gold that has fallen into the mud and is temporarily defiled. Buddhas did not stray into confusion but retained their "natural seat." The difference between buddhas and sentient beings is the difference between knowing and not knowing our innate nature.

Although gold is gold, when it falls in the mud it gets covered by dirt and becomes unrecognizable. Gold temporarily covered by mud is the example for sentient beings who fail to recognize their own nature. All sentient beings are buddhas, but due to temporary obscurations they do not realize it. The ground is likened to pure gold, while the path is like gold that has fallen in the dirt and is covered by defilements. In this context, the path means the state of confusion.

Buddhahood, the realized state of all awakened beings, means not straying onto the path of confusion but recognizing the state of the ground as being pure gold. Due to the power of confusion, we have now strayed onto the state of the path—the pure gold is temporarily covered by mud. We are temporarily under the power of confusion. Because of the sleep of ignorance, we go through the dreams of the three realms, taking rebirth among the six classes of sentient beings again and again, endlessly.

Intrinsic to our buddha nature are qualities called the three kayas, or the innate body, speech, and mind, also known as the three vajras. The vajra body is the unchanging quality of the buddha nature; the vajra speech is its inexpressible, unceasing quality; and the vajra mind is its unmistaken quality. In this way the vajra body, vajra speech, and vajra mind are inherently present as our buddha nature.

At this time the unchanging vajra body is obscured by our transient, perishable physical body. The unceasing, continuous vajra speech, the voice of the nature of equality, is temporarily obscured by the repeated utterances of our normal talk. Likewise, the unmistaken vajra mind is obscured by our deluded thinking. Although the body, speech, and mind of all the victorious ones are present in our buddha nature, they are obscured by our ordinary body, speech, and mind.

Since we are under the power of confusion, we are at the stage of the path, and we need to clean away this dirt or confusion that covers our basic state. The way to do this is through Vajrayana practices and teachings that let the path clarify confusion, thus purifying the obscurations of our body, speech, and mind. The most eminent and profound method is through the three principles of Vajrayana practice: deity, mantra, and samadhi. By training in the development stage consisting of deity, mantra, and samadhi, we actualize what we already are.

Development stage is usually understood as visualizing the support, which is the buddhafield and the celestial palace and what is supported therein, the form of the deity. The palace and deity are considered to be the pure world and pure being. We may think that this is a product of our imagination, but in fact it is an exact replica of the original state of all things. It is how things already are in actuality. It is also called the great mandala of the manifest ground. Thus, *visualization is ultimately not a matter of imagining something to be what it isn't, but rather seeing it as it actually is. It is acknowledging things as they already are. This is the essential principle of Vajrayana. Within this principle are contained both development stage and completion stage.*

Development stage is not like imagining a piece of wood to be gold. No matter how long you imagine that wood is gold, it never truly becomes gold. Rather, it's like regarding gold as gold: acknowledging or seeing things as they actually are. That is what is meant by training in deity, mantra, and samadhi. The body, speech, and mind of the deity are contained within the three aspects of Vajrayana practice: development, recitation, and completion.

All appearances are the mandala of the deities, all sounds are the mandala of mantra, and all thoughts are the mandala of enlightened mind. The nature of all apparent and existing things—of this entire world and all its beings—is the great mandala of the manifest ground, our basic state. These three mandalas are present as our ground. The practice of a sadhana is based on manifesting from this ground. Sadhana practice is also based on some very essential principles: that the tantras are contained within the statements, the statements within the oral instructions, and the oral instructions within the application of the sadhana itself.

Let me rephrase this vital point. *In Vajrayana, a sadhana is the act of manifesting what is originally present in the form of the threefold mandalas of deity, mantra, and samadhi.* When practicing a sadhana, we are not superimposing something artificial atop the natural state of things. Rather, it is a way of acknowledging our original state, in which the nature of all forms is deity, the nature of all sounds is mantra, and the nature of mind is samadhi. This is the basic principle of development stage. And the differences in profundity between the teachings of Sutra and Tantra lie in how close the teachings are to the original nature. The closest, the most direct, are the Vajrayana teachings.

What are the reasons for development and completion stages? The profound development stage enables us to attain enlightenment in one lifetime and in one body through deity, mantra, and samadhi. And completion stage means that the deity is none other than our originally enlightened buddha nature. Its essence is present as body, its nature radiates as speech, and its capacity is pervasive as mind.

As previously mentioned, our originally enlightened essence contains within itself the awakened state of all buddhas as the three aspects of vajra body, vajra speech, and vajra mind. Training in these three vajras is intrinsically contained within the profound state of samadhi, which is none other than one's own nature.

To properly practice development stage, we need to let go of any ordinary, materialistic worldview. Don't chant the lines for the deity while thinking, "I am in this world, in my ordinary house, in my ordinary body." We need to first dissolve everything into profound emptiness, then visualize the celestial palace, the throne of the deity, and all the other details. Through this profound training in deity, mantra, and samadhi, we are able to let the path clarify confusion.

Remember, in practicing the development stage, we are not imagining that we are something that we are not. Everyone possesses the enlightened essence that is endowed with the three vajras, the three aspects of enlightenment. The way to acknowledge that fully is through deity, mantra, and samadhi.

To reiterate, development practice is simply knowing the nature of things *as it is*. Training in this is like knowing the jewel to be the wish-fulfilling jewel that it actually is. It's not like we're imagining an ordinary stone to be a jewel. A stone will never possess the value or qualities of a jewel, no matter how hard we visualize. There is incredible profundity in the development stage practice.

Development stage or visualization does not mean to imagine something that is not already present. The vajra body of all the victorious ones is within ourselves, intrinsic to our buddha nature. By practicing the development stage, we remove the obscuration that covers this nature and prevents us from realizing it. The unceasing vajra speech of all the buddhas, the king of all melodious expressions, is also present in ourselves. Recitation of the three types of mantra—*vidya, dharani,* and *guhya*—enables us to remove the obscuration of our ordinary voice. The mind of all the buddhas, non-conceptual wakefulness, is also inherent to our nature, but it is covered by our momentary conceptual thinking. Simply resting in the evenness of the state of samadhi reveals our innate vajra mind.

Do not consider development stage to involve imagining. Development stage means to mentally create or imagine the form of the buddhas. Even though visualization is at this point an artificial construct, a mentally fabricated act, still it is an imitation that resembles what is already present in us. Until we are able to practice the ultimate development stage, we need to visualize or mentally create pure images in order to approach that absolute state.

The ultimate development stage involves simply resting in the essence of mind of all the buddhas, out of which the two form kayas—the sambhoga-kaya of rainbow light and the nirmanakaya of a physical body—spontaneously manifest. In fact, the buddha nature is the starting point for development stage, and this innate nature is actualized through practicing the samadhi of suchness. Development stage is created out of the samadhi of suchness, which is the dharmakaya of all the buddhas. Out of dharmakaya unfolds sambhogakaya, which is the samadhi of illumination, and from sambhogakaya the nirmanakaya appears by means of the samadhi of the seed syllable. That is how the development stage should take place.

The samadhi of suchness is the recognition of the buddha nature itself, the flawless and primordially pure state of dharmakaya. If we have not recognized this nature in our personal experience, we can approximate or fabricate it by imagining that all phenomena, all worlds and beings, dissolve into emptiness, by chanting, for instance, the mantra OM MAHA SHUNYATA JÑANA VAJRA SVABHAVA ATMA KOH HANG. Out of the great emptiness, the clarity of cognizance unfolds like the sun rising in the sky and spreading light. That is called the samadhi of illumination, which is in essence the sambhoga-kaya. Out of space there is sunlight, and from the sunlight a rainbow appears. This is the analogy for nirmanakaya, the samadhi of the seed syllable from which the form of the deity manifests. Nirmanakaya is visible but not tangible; we cannot take hold of it with our hands, and yet it appears. We should imagine the form of the deity as apparent but without self-nature. Just as a rainbow in the sky is not substantial or material in any way whatsoever, the deity is not composed of flesh and blood.

The development stage takes place within the framework of the three kayas. Dharmakaya is all-pervasive like space. Within this "space," the sambhogakaya is vividly present like the light of the sun. Nirmanakaya appears like a rainbow to accomplish the welfare of beings. Just as the sun cannot rise and shine without the openness of space, the unceasing sambhogakaya cannot manifest without the nonarising nature of dharmakaya. Without space the sun cannot shine; without sunshine a rainbow cannot appear. In this way, the three kayas are indivisible.

Thus, the practice of the three samadhis provides the framework for visualizing the deity. Next, we invoke the ultimate deity from the realm of Akanishtha and dissolve it inseparably into ourselves. Then we make praises and offerings and so forth. All these seemingly conventional activities in the development stage resemble the activities of ordinary human beings, just like when we invite important people to visit, praise them, and give them good food and presents. The purpose of the development stage is to purify our habitual tendencies as human beings. It is not to appease some external gods by giving them offerings. Deities are not subject to pleasure when being worshipped or displeasure when not; it is we who benefit by purifying our obscurations and gathering the accumulations.

As I said earlier, when practicing development stage, do it with a sense of vastness, immensity, and openness. Don't visualize the deity in your own little house, in this little world. Everything is first dissolved totally into great emptiness, into vast space. Within the vastness of space, the mandala of the five elements is created. On top of it we imagine the immense Mount Sumeru. At the summit of Mount Sumeru is the celestial palace, and inside it is the throne with a seat of a sun and moon disk. It is on top of this throne that we appear in the form of the yidam deity, whichever it may be. This is how we should practice the development stage, not imagining we are sitting in our own little room.

The main purpose of development stage is to destroy our clinging to a solid reality. It is our fixation on concreteness that makes us continue in samsaric existence. The development stage dismantles that. How do we approach that? By imagining that the world is a buddhafield, our dwelling place is the celestial palace, and the beings in it are the divine forms of deities, visible yet intangible like a rainbow in the sky.

Similarly, the recitation of mantra destroys our fixation on our normal discontinuous speech, which stops and starts. Mantra is called the king of verbal expression. It is the unceasing vajra speech. Finally, the unmistaken vajra mind destroys our normal conceptual thinking.

At the end of the period of recitation comes the completion stage, which in this context is the dissolution of the palace and the deity into emptiness and the reemerging from the state of emptiness in the form of the deity. The purpose of dissolving is to eliminate our habitual fixation on appearances as being real and permanent, as well as the tendency toward the view of eternalism. By reemerging in the visible yet insubstantial form of the deity, we also destroy the basis for nihilism, the view that nothing whatsoever exists. Thus, by training in eliminating the tendencies for both wrong views, this practice truly is the path that clarifies confusion.

In short, this was about how to let the path clarify confusion. At present we are under the power of confusion. Through these practices we will be able to eradicate this confusion and realize the vajra body, speech, and mind of all the buddhas. A good metaphor for this confusion is the hallucinations caused by the psychedelic drug datura. Normally we see ourselves and other people as having one face, two arms, and two legs. But when intoxicated by datura, all of a sudden we see people not as they are but with ten heads, twenty arms, fifty legs, or the like. Currently we are under the influence of the drug of ignorance and continue deluded within the six realms of samsara. When the effect of datura wears off, we again perceive people as they are in their natural state. But right now the effect of the drug of ignorance has not yet worn off; we are still under the power of confusion. In order to clarify confusion on the path, we need to practice the stages of development, recitation, and completion.

# 11

# THE PRELIMINARIES

*Dilgo Khyentse Rinpoche*

### THE GENERAL PRELIMINARY PRACTICES

The *Ultimate Wish-Fulfilling Jewel Empowerment* says:

> First, the guru Samantabhadra, the great lord of sky-yogis, should accept disciples who, with exceedingly deep devotion and unwavering trust, yearn to quickly attain complete enlightenment.

As so stated, here and elsewhere, a qualified sublime master, a glorious protector, should, when accepting worthy disciples who yearn for liberation, first ripen them through empowerment as a preparation for the path, so that they can practice the most profound meaning of Dzogchen, which is the ultimate quick path among all means to attain the state of the lasting happiness of complete liberation, the essence of the 84,000 divisions of the Dharma, the summit of the nine gradual vehicles, and the heart of the oral instructions of the vajra vehicle of Secret Mantra.

As the *Ultimate Instruction Manual* says:

> Then, having fully ripened your being through empowerments, ...

From Dilgo Khyentse Rinpoche, *The Mind Ornament of Samantabhadra* (Boudhanath: Rangjung Yeshe Publications, 1995), "The Preliminary Practices."

In this way, prior to beginning the preliminary practices, the following empowerments should be performed in accordance with the tradition. As to the general, within the mandala of the peaceful and wrathful ones, there are the benefiting empowerments to accept the devoted ones and the enabling empowerments for the diligent ones. As to the extraordinary, the ground empowerments of primordial purity and spontaneous presence, the path empowerments of entering Trekchö, and the fruition empowerments of Tögal, should be given following the *Ultimate Wish-Fulfilling Jewel Empowerment,* and are respectively divided into four: elaborate, unelaborate, very unelaborate, and extremely unelaborate empowerments.

After the ripening (empowerments), the preliminaries for the liberating instructions follow. The precepts of Secret Mantra are obtained through empowerment, the mere receiving of which empowers you to hear, read, and practice the profound meaning. However, it is the samayas that sustain the life force of the empowerment in your stream-of-being. As the root text says:

> Keep your mind-stream pure by keeping the precepts,

In this way, it is crucial to protect the (vows) of individual liberation, bodhichitta, and Secret Mantra in general and, in particular, the roots and branches of the general, special, and supreme samayas, like protecting your eyes and to keep your stream-of-being pure. Immediately upon your receiving the vase empowerment, all three vows are born in your stream-of-being. So, in order to develop them further, protect them through being mindful, alert, and careful; then the qualities of the paths and bhumis will quickly arise without difficulty.

Next, concerning the general preliminaries for the path, there are generating an attitude of renunciation, taking refuge, arousing bodhichitta, Vajrasattva, the mandala offerings, and the seven branches that are part of the guru yoga.

> And endeavor in the steps which purify obscurations and gather the
>     accumulations.
> Retreat to snow mountains, caves, or forests,
> And, in solitude, sit on a comfortable seat,
> Supplicate your master one-pointedly,
> And motivate yourself with compassion and the thought of
>     impermanence.

As was just stated, contemplate as follows: "I will train and familiarize myself with the fact that nothing lasts forever, neither the world nor the beings within it. I have no doubt that samsara is futile and am resolved to the fact that all samsaric activities have nothing but evil deeds as their cause and misery as their effect.

"Therefore, I recognize that this body with its freedoms and riches is the perfect condition facilitating Dharma practice, a support superior to that of a god. I recognize that it is difficult to find, so, without squandering it on the pointless activities of this present life, I will concentrate on the essential Dharma. With renunciation as the basis for Dharma practice and with trust in the consequence of karma as its main pillar, I will exert myself to the utmost, applying all thoughts, words, and deeds to virtuous actions. Since death comes without warning and its circumstances are not certain, I won't plan far into the future.

"That which is meaningful is the excellent path of increasing happiness, the precious state of liberation. Therefore, I will apply myself exclusively to that which attains it, namely, virtuous thoughts, words, and deeds. Following a qualified master for the means and instructions on how to accomplish this, and for all the essential points on what to adopt and what to abandon, I will enter the path of liberation without error or mistake, doing exactly as he says."

Thinking this, in the space before you, as the single wisdom display of the glorious protector root guru Samantabhadra, the assembly of the peaceful and wrathful deities, along with a retinue of the Three Roots and guardians, are manifest, filling the sky. In their presence, you and all other beings act in unison with body, speech, and mind. To take refuge from now until enlightenment, completely surrendering with single-minded trust and devotion, is the relative, causal refuge. To maintain the continuity of the nondual view by recognizing that all of them are primordially indivisible from self-existing awareness, the wisdom comprised of essence, nature, and capacity, is the ultimate, resultant refuge. With these two as a unity, say:

NAMO

In the empty essence, dharmakaya,
In the luminous nature, sambhogakaya,
And in the manifold capacity, nirmanakaya,
I take refuge until enlightenment.

Accumulate the set number.

To open the gate to all paths, contemplate as follows: "Although we are all primordially enlightened within the single state of nondual dharmata, through a compassionate attitude I will bring those sentient beings who do not realize the natural state as it is, and who are tormented by delusion and karmic consequences, to the unmistaken ultimate state," while chanting:

HOH ৪

In order to establish all beings equal to the sky ৪
In the state of buddhahood, ৪
I will realize the dharmakaya of self-existing awareness ৪
Through the teachings of the Great Perfection. ৪

Thus, as the life force of the path, firmly keep the resolve toward enlightenment, which is emptiness suffused with compassion.

If the momentary conceptual obscurations are not purified, you will not behold the natural face of self-existing wakefulness. Therefore, while possessing all the vital points of the four powers, visualize above your head Vajrasattva inseparable from the guru, with one-pointed concentration on the downpour and purification of the nectar.

Recite the hundred syllables and the six syllables as many times as you can. At the end, to practice the ultimate repentance of the great primordial purity of dharmakaya that is beyond confessor and confessed is the royal purifier of all obscurations and is singlehandedly sufficient to remove obstacles on the path.

With the attitude of offering the spontaneously perfect universe of a billionfold Mount Sumeru realms—an ocean of undefiled riches, the natural forms of the luminous dharmadhatu wisdom—to the field of accumulation, the all-encompassing buddha mandalas of peaceful and wrathful ones of the three kayas, accumulate the set number of mandala offerings. That is the mandala practice, a simple and effective enhancement to the path.

In particular, the authentic experience of true original wakefulness within your stream-of-being depends on nothing other than your guru's blessings. So, in the sky before you, visualize your guru as Samantabhadra with consort, a brilliant deep blue, unadorned, naked, and sitting resplendently with crossed legs upon a lotus and moon within a sphere of rays of rainbow light. Full of trust and devotion, make supplication, totally surrendering your entire being.

Although the accumulation of merit is primordially perfected within the innate nature, accumulating and purifying are important methods that fully actualize it. So, in the presence of the visualized supports for the accumulations together with the one-pointed attitudes for the seven branches, repeat this suitable chant:

> To the skylike sugatas
> I prostrate as great luminosity;
> In the state of awareness, I present offerings;
> In the unceasing expanse, I apologize, and
> As it is permanent and never obscured, I rejoice.
> Turn the Dharma wheel beyond being and nonbeing,
> Remain as something to be experienced.
> May the supreme certainty be attained.

It is exceedingly good if you can complete 100,000 prostrations combined with the seven branches, the essence of accumulating and purification. At the end, with the great bliss wisdom of the guru's three vajras indivisible from your own three innate doors, in this primordially pure state receive the four empowerments, mingle your mind with his, and rest in evenness. This is the meditation practice of guru yoga, the essence of the path, taking effect. So, to exert yourself until the resultant signs manifest is to bring the training to perfection as a prelude to the path. Then the experiences and realization of the main part will occur without any hardship. Therefore, resolve the oral instructions and apply them correctly. In order to do that, abide in secluded places, such as retreats in snow mountains, caves, or forests, which are free from distractions and bustle and where the conditions for meditation training are complete. Thus, establish an abode of one-pointed practice.

## THE SPECIAL PRELIMINARIES

Since there are many average disciples who proceed gradually along the path these days, it is essential to first accomplish the concentration of mind by means of the development stage based on the *General Practice Manual of the Peaceful and Wrathful Ones,* completing the full number of recitations.

In an elaborate way, you can use a mandala or heaps, *amrita, rakta,* and *torma*s, or in an unelaborate way, imagination alone is sufficient. Either way, the basis for accomplishment is the totally pure Ultimate Being Samantabhadra, unconstructed primordial purity, appearing in the form of the peaceful wisdom (mandala) of *vajradhatu.* The spontaneously present display of luminosity appears in the forms of the sporting wrathful *herukas* who destroy the origin (of samsara), namely, confused grasping thoughts. With this as the basis for accomplishment, the method for accomplishment is the unity of development and completion, perfected in an instant's recollection, in which samaya being and wisdom being are nondual, and all that appears and exists is the display of the ground. Through this, you will ultimately realize the state of dharmakaya, primordially pure space, and of rupakaya, the unity of luminous awareness. Thus, while understanding that this (method, the unity of development and completion) is vital for realizing the level of the never-ending adornment wheels of body, speech, mind, qualities, and activities of the three kayas of enlightenment, correctly follow the practice manual (sadhana) of the peaceful and wrathful ones and cultivate the clear forms, stable pride, and pure recollection of the visualizations of the development stage.

As enhancement, do as many recitations of the peaceful and wrathful ones as you can, such as 400,000 for each (syllable). Perform the feast offering occasionally, such as on the tenth day of the waxing and waning moon, and at the beginning and end of a recitation retreat. Without missing a day, chant the petition-offering to the guardians of this teaching, composed by Tersey Rinpoche. All these details should be known from the general system of approach and accomplishment practice. If you have sadhana articles physically present, you should receive the siddhis when completing the practice. Furthermore, after you have gone through this (practice of) the development stage, to combine it with the exclusive practice of the view, meditation, and conduct of Trekchö will then be a self-sufficient path of development and completion. Therefore, for those who do not immediately engage in the path of effortless Tögal, it is fine to practice in such a manner. Understand that this is the unmistaken tradition of the forefather gurus.

# 12

## GREAT VASTNESS

*Dzongsar Khyentse Rinpoche*

For a follower of the Hinayana or Mahayana paths, there are the sutras and the shastras. The sutras contain the direct teachings of Buddha Shakyamuni, whereas the shastras are commentaries composed later by a disciple of the Buddha, such as Nagarjuna. Moreover, there are instructions on how to practice. For instance, many chapters of Shantideva's *Way of the Bodhisattva* contain very clear instructions.

Studying the Dharma can be compared to learning how to drive. There is a driving manual that explains what things are, how they work, the rules of the road, and so on. Similarly, the sutras and shastras contain the basic knowledge you need in order to practice the Dharma. When you actually learn how to drive, depending on your individual skills, your driving teacher's style, and the various practical situations you encounter, you receive personalized instructions. These are not necessarily presented in the same order as the information in the manual. Instructions can come in most unexpected ways.

In Vajrayana, there are the tantras as well as the pith instructions. For centuries, Dharma practitioners have studied the tantras while practicing according to the pith instructions. Some students place great emphasis on the tantras, the actual texts containing the theory of the view. Those who

Printed with permission of the author. © 2004 by Dzongsar Khyentse Rinpoche.

are more intellectually or academically oriented can get quite caught up in explanations and theories. Other students who are more emotionally oriented; they tend to get caught up in the instructions. This was a common fault in the past and continues to be so today.

Let's suppose you have devotion, trust, and the merit of having met a qualified master; for you, even without elaborate explanations on the theoretical aspects of the tantras, a mere instruction from your master can *potentially* lead you somewhere. Your practice could be as ridiculous as being told to have a cup of tea every hour, but it could still untie your knot of delusion and take you to a state where you would be released from all kinds of grasping and fixation. This, however, is quite risky, as our devotion is often temporary and fickle. In fact, as our devotion is most often *not* based on even a minimal understanding of the view, it is little more than a manifestation of our insecurity. If such is the case, our devotion can become rather unhealthy. Moreover, the merit to encounter a true qualified master is extremely rare. Of course, this is not to discourage you by any means. You can always aspire to one day meet a qualified master and develop the virtues of devotion and trust. If you have such good fortune, you don't have to read the driving manual; all you have to do is listen to your teacher and do as he or she says. But that's quite difficult.

Pith instructions appear in many different forms. Although we often talk about them as supplementary, the ngöndro teachings are actually pith instructions. They come directly from unbroken lineages of gurus, out of lineage masters' experiences and visions. If you want to know why Vajrasattva, guru yoga, and mandala offering work, then it's good to study a text like the *Guhyagarbha Tantra,* which elucidates the ideas of equality and purity and explains why everything is pure and equal from the beginning. When applied, the tantric texts and the pith instructions complement one another.

The ngöndro contains advice to help us stop our chain of thoughts. Personally, I have found it wise to follow Jamgön Kongtrül's suggestion and spend at least half of the session just sitting and developing a sense of renunciation by contemplating impermanence and such. Doing so actually sets the atmosphere and tunes your mind, so that at least some inspiration arises to actually practice. Otherwise, as samsaric beings, we have so much to do, and everything is *so* significant, from petty shopping lists to important meetings. If you let such mundane matters bother you, they will. Instead, if you reflect on impermanence and the like, if only for a few minutes, your mundane, incessant thoughts will at least temporarily pause. That's quite important.

Then after that, if you want to elaborate, it's good to clear the stale air. As I said, pith instructions, like this one, can sometimes seem illogical. For instance, if you are oriented more toward the Hinayana or Mahayana approaches, you might wonder what the stale air is and why it is so important in the ngöndro practice. Of course, it has its own enormous theory in the *Guhyagarbha Tantra,* but you might question why we have to subdue the gross and subtle winds and why this results in our whole perception changing. In spite of the numerous explanations, there's the simple fact that clearing the stale air helps us break the chain of thoughts that we are experiencing. Moreover, clearing the stale air tunes us in to renunciation mind and purifies our perceptions. Normally, when we practice, we don't spend much time on these things, and so our practice tends to be rather weak.

Having evoked renunciation and cleared the air through the nostrils, next be confident that the place where you're practicing is not ordinary. You will not find such a suggestion in the other vehicles; it is exclusive to Vajrayana. The whole purpose of Dharma practice, whether ngöndro or the main practice, is to understand the great purity and equality. This is the great vastness, *longchen,* the vast space where everything fits, everything! The different schools of Buddhism variously call it nonduality, the realization of emptiness, the union of samsara and nirvana, and so on. The fact that everything is nondual is not a recent invention nor a Buddhist one; it is the actual nature of phenomena from the beginning. As the Buddha said, "Whether the buddhas appear on this earth or not, the essence of phenomena never changes." The nonduality aspect, the great vastness, is unchanging. It has never been fabricated, nor is it something that we create.

What does this mean in practical terms? Devotion is integral to being a Vajrayana practitioner. Wanting to be free of delusion implies accepting that we are deluded. Within our deluded state, we have to learn and believe that we need to create a pure reality. Here comes a pith instruction: This is why we have to think that the place where we are practicing is not an ordinary place. If we never abandon our impure ordinary perceptions of the mundane world and our mundane lives, we will never break out of our delusion. However, as Vajrayana practitioners we must learn right from the beginning to crack this shell open. So, when taking refuge, you must think that the setting is not ordinary but a pure realm. Then visualize the object of refuge in front of you. It is crucial in Vajrayana to understand that the object of refuge—the guru—is the embodiment of all the buddhas as well as of the Dharma, the Sangha, and the devas, dakinis, and dharmapalas. Basically, all objects of refuge are embodied in the guru.

Now, unless your teacher specifically instructs otherwise, normally one visualizes the object of refuge, the guru, not in his ordinary form. I say this because many of us have received teachings from the great Tulku Urgyen Rinpoche, and in his guru yoga, he instructs us to visualize him in his ordinary form, however we have seen him. That's his instruction, and we have to follow that. I'm sure there's infinite purpose behind it. But, generally, in most of the ngöndro instructions, you visualize the guru in the form of Guru Rinpoche or Vajradhara, not in the form of a human being. This too is a pith instruction, and there are lots of reasons for it, but they all come down to the same point: recognizing the great purity and equality.

In our ordinary human, rational mind, we think that it is much easier to visualize our guru as we remember him or her. Most of us have never seen Vajradhara or Guru Rinpoche. Even if we know what Vajradhara looks like, he is still pretty impossible to visualize: a blue being with thirty-two major marks and eighty minor marks. Thirty-two major marks are incredible, inconceivable, for example, webbed hands and a tongue so long it can reach across his face. So, are you supposed to visualize your guru as a duck or a dog? It sounds silly, and so we would rather simply remember what our guru looked like in the flesh. Besides, that's how we got inspired in the first place. All these fanciful details go against our normal thinking pattern; nevertheless, according to most ngöndro instructions, it is necessary to visualize one's guru not as an ordinary being but rather as Guru Rinpoche.

Our practice is feeble, and we have tarried on the path for so long, primarily because we always see the guru as an ordinary being and not a buddha. We cannot imagine him or her as a buddha. Instead we consider him as a normal person who has similar likes and dislikes to our own.

In his explanation of guru yoga, Jamyang Khyentse Chökyi Lodrö notes the importance of how you approach your guru. Usually we think, "I like him because he's a decent human being; he's kind, he's compassionate, and he's a good man." But, according to Jamyang Khyentse Chökyi Lodrö, the blessing you will receive corresponds to your level of devotion, and in this case, it is not much. You too will become tolerant and a good person, but your aim is wrong. Our aim is not to become a good person or a tolerant person. Our aim is not to become a little bit better than the rest but to attain enlightenment. Enlightenment is beyond good and bad and everything. If you have a high aim such as enlightenment, you have to change your attitude. As Jamyang Khyentse Chökyi Lodrö explains, believing your guru to be a shravaka or an arhat is much better than thinking that he or she is just an ordinary, decent human being. If you think of your guru as an arhat, then you will receive the blessing of individual liberation. If you think your guru is a mahabodhisattva on the tenth bhumi, you will receive an equivalent blessing. If you think your guru is the Buddha himself, not only imagining it but actually seeing him as the Buddha in person, then definitely you will receive the Buddha's blessings. And in Dzogchen and Mahamudra, if you realize that it is actually your own buddha nature that is manifest in the form of the Buddha or the guru, you will receive the blessing of seeing everything as the Buddha, everything as the guru.

So it is important to visualize not only the place as pure and special, but also the object of refuge, your guru, as an extraordinary being. If you think about this, you will realize that many of our spiritual difficulties are ridiculous. Many of our doubts and fears are simply due to a lack of pure perception. We try to see our guru as someone special, but not really as a buddha. You would not necessarily think that it is so difficult to consider your guru as the Buddha. I'm slightly more fortunate than most of you because I have seen numerous great masters. Many of you, especially the younger ones, are quite unlucky, because you have to put up with people like us. It's very understandable if you have difficulty in thinking that we are the Buddha. But if you find it difficult to think that we, the ordinary lamas you know, are the Buddha, this is actually because you lack understanding of the great vastness of purity and equality. Based on the view of great equality and great purity, you can slowly learn to see all ordinary beings, such as many lamas these days, as buddhas. This is quite important to do.

It's actually the same when you take refuge. What you are declaring is, "I accept that I have the buddha nature. I accept that I can be purified. I accept that my being is the great equality and great purity." This is essential as the foundation not only of Vajrayana but also of Buddhism as a whole. Otherwise, we are taking a very theistic approach to our refuge practice. We consider the Buddha, Dharma, and Sangha as saviors, a panacea of sorts, and we take refuge with the expectation that they will solve all our problems, whether mundane or spiritual. That is a very theistic slant.

Refuge can be understood on many different levels. However, I repeat, do not forget to apply pure perception, especially in Vajrayana. Think,

"This place is not an ordinary place but a pure realm. My guru, my object of refuge, is not an ordinary being but a buddha." When you say this, due to a seemingly unstoppable habitual pattern, there is a tendency to think that you are imperfect. But as Jamyang Khyentse Chökyi Lodrö said, "Never forget that this guru who is sitting in front of you, whom you are trying to think of as a buddha, is not as an ordinary being but in fact the manifestation of your own buddha nature." It is a very beautiful path, you know.

Usually when we take refuge, there's a sense of being lower than the object of refuge. You, a pathetic being, need to be saved, and you take refuge in this very wholesome, omnipotent being. Refuge usually feels like that, but if you understand the great vastness, and the prana, nadi, and bindu, and the guru, deva, and dakini of the bigger picture, then you will know they are not a separate thing at all.

A brief summary is in order. Tune your mind, clear the stale air, and think that you are sitting in a pure realm. Next, visualize your guru with all his or her retinue. I guess it can't be helped, but when you start you usually invoke your guru, the human being for whom you have to buy the plane ticket to fly here. Then try to think that this ordinary form is your own perception. But, in reality, this being is not what you see with your eyes and hear with your ears; he is Vajradhara or Padmasambhava, depending on the text you are using. Finally, think that your guru as Vajradhara or Padmasambhava is actually a reflection of your own buddha nature. By doing so, you complete the circle of taking refuge, from the most ordinary level to the highest, which has such a great benefit. It actually makes you familiar with this idea of the great purity and equality, which is the whole purpose. It's really incredibly important.

Nowadays many people have begun to think that the guru is like a dictator, which is a big misunderstanding. Of course, I'm sure that some gurus do act like dictators, but that has nothing to do with the true notion of a guru. Moreover, the Asian concept of a master as a father figure, like Confucius, is also incorrect. I'm bringing this up because I think that as the East and West are now so closely connected, Western Vajrayana students might tend to think guru yoga is another system supporting the roles of master and servant. Superficially, guru yoga can appear almost criminal: Whatever the guru says is right, and even if he says something wrong, you should think that it is right. If you see him do something impure, it is due to your lack of pure perception. My goodness, there is no justice at all! So it is really important not to forget the great purity and equality. This becomes extremely clear at the end of the sadhana when you dissolve with the guru. Confucius never said the servant and the master should dissolve into one. That's a big difference. The whole purpose, the very essence of both the ngöndro and the main practice, is to mingle your mind with the guru's.

When we say dissolve, it does not mean that you are like a bag and the guru's mind dissolves and pours into you. That would still be hierarchical. Instead think of a pot. Inside the pot there is space, and if I break the pot, the space inside it and the space outside it become one. So, whether it's your mind mixing with the guru's mind or the guru's mind mixing with your mind, it's basically the same. That is the Vajrayana approach. Vajrayana students should never forget this.

At the end of your session there is the dissolution stage. This is where we become indivisible from the guru. We know that everything is nondual, that everything is equal and pure from the beginning. When we talk about equality, we are talking about the equality and purity of samsara and nirvana, along with that of the guru and disciple. We can grasp intellectually that the guru is a perception resulting from our merit, devotion, and so on, but when we practice we can't help actually thinking that the guru is out there.

Even at the beginning of the *Longchen Nyingtig* ngöndro, there are many stanzas taken from the various tantras and sutras reminding us why a spiritual companion or master is so important. After that there is a beautiful composition by Jigmey Lingpa, a song of *Calling the Guru*, invoking the guru from the heart, which clearly elucidates that the guru is not an ordinary human being *out there*, nor is the guru someone who is going to dictate how you should live your life. It's not like that at all.

The first stanza of this song invokes the guru from your heart. It is a very beautiful and poetic metaphor: The guru dwells within your own heart. This is totally different from our ordinary perception, whereby we think that the guru is external and separate from us. The heart refers to the buddha nature. And as one of the infinite manifestations of the buddha nature, there is faith, and as a reflection of this, devotion. For instance, when passionate people look at another being, because of their passion, they see a beautiful object. When aggressive people see another being, because of their aggression, they see an ugly enemy. When devoted people see through the devotion manifested from their buddha nature, they see their guru or spiritual companion.

Jigmey Lingpa says, "From the blooming lotus of faith in the center of our heart, kind guru, our only protector, please arise to protect us from misfortunes. We are tormented by intense kleshas and karma; please remain on top of our head." We invoke the guru from our heart and place him above us as if he's a higher, superior being. But please, never forget that in all the Vajrayana practices, and especially the Anu and Ati Yoga practices, one always dissolves the guru, or merges with the guru. This is called receiving the empowerment (abhisheka) or initiation from the guru. Light radiates from his forehead, next from the throat, and then from the heart, and this light dissolves into you. Finally, you or the guru dissolve into the light, and the two of you merge and become indivisible.

I think this aspect should be emphasized because many of our practices seem to have gone a bit off course. We exert ourselves in visualizing the guru in front of us, praising him, supplicating him, begging for his blessing, and so on. But we are content with doing the dissolution and merging for only a minute or two. Instead we should spend an equal amount of time, if not more, on the dissolution phase. My father, Thinley Norbu Rinpoche, would emphasize this a great deal. He told some of his students in Bhutan to practice receiving each of the four empowerments for a year. I think this is good advice because we tend to spend so little time on the dissolution stage.

Dissolve the guru into yourself, like water dissolving into water; then remain in that state of oneness as long as you can. If you prefer, you can visualize the guru instantaneously and repeat the process over and over. In fact, it's encouraged, especially if you have received any Dzogchen instructions from your masters. If you have recognized, of course, train in rigpa, the nature of mind. But because of our habitual tendency, as soon as we watch the nature of the mind, or the state of merging our mind and the guru's mind, we drift into all kinds of distractions. Therefore, it is often helpful to "fence in" the mind. If you have a flock of sheep or herd of cattle that you want to lead in a certain direction, you build a fence so that they go where you want them to go. Likewise continuously visualizing the guru in front of you, dissolving into him, and watching that state of mind is called *fencing*.

It is very easy for us to say, "Rest in the nature of the mind." But who knows whether we really are doing so or are simply in a coma? Are we in the state of experiencing the all-ground (*alaya*), which is like complete numbness? Or are we totally distracted, making plans for the future or rushing after the past? Are we so completely distracted that we don't even realize it? If we continue in that vein, it's all a big waste of time. Instead, repeatedly visualizing the guru and dissolving him into you while watching your mind would seem to be a wise approach. As Longchenpa said in the *Treasury of Pith Instructions*, "Again and again, meditate in short periods but many times." And when finishing the session, of course, never forget to dedicate the merit.

*13*

# VAJRASATTVA

## *Tsoknyi Rinpoche*

Now we will do a meditation on Buddha Vajrasattva. Keep the body straight but relaxed. Remain loose, and leave your breath and mind free, without conceptualizing anything. The mind should be vivid and wide awake. Don't follow any thought about the past, don't invite any thought of the future, and don't think about the present. Leave your mind open and empty, like a blank piece of paper. Within this state, you can keep your eyes either open or closed, as you like.

Now imagine in the sky before you a white lotus flower with eight petals. Upon this sits our teacher, Buddha Shakyamuni, with a body that is golden, as radiant as pure gold. His left hand is in the gesture of equanimity, his right hand in the earth-touching mudra, and he is smiling. He looks upon all sentient beings with the same love that a mother has for her only child. Bring to mind the fact that the Buddha is endowed with inconceivable qualities of enlightened body, enlightened speech, and enlightened mind. Imagining that this remarkable being is present in person, form this resolve: "From now until complete enlightenment, I will rely upon you. I take refuge in you until my view, meditation, and conduct are equal to yours."

From Tsoknyi Rinpoche, *Carefree Dignity* (Boudhanath: Rangjung Yeshe Publications, 1998), "Vajrasatva Meditation."

The form of the Buddha is insubstantial and transparent, visible yet devoid of any solid substance. He is not made of stone or clay but rather is like a rainbow. Remind yourself, "From now until attaining supreme enlightenment, I accept you as my teacher, my guide. I will put the words you have spoken, the Dharma, into practice; I will take the two levels of truth as my path." Until we have fully realized ultimate truth, we will take refuge in the Dharma. Similarly, we take refuge in those who are following in the Buddha's footsteps: the shravakas, the pratyekabuddhas, and all the bodhisattvas. We take refuge with them as our companions.

After that, imagine that rays of light stream forth from the body of the Buddha and dissolve into yourself. Through this, boundless obscurations and negative karma are purified and removed. Imagine that you accomplish the vajra body. Now imagine that from the throat of the Buddha, boundless rays of light shine forth and dissolve into your own throat. Through this, all the negative karma and obscurations created through your past words are purified, and you accomplish the vajra speech. Now imagine that from the Buddha's heart, countless rays of light shine forth and dissolve into your own heart. They purify all negative frames of mind, ill will, wrong view, craving, ignorance, and dullness. Not only that, but the qualities of the enlightened mind—the knowledge that sees the nature as it is and the knowledge that perceives all possible existing things—are fully developed and perfected.

Now imagine that the Buddha melts into light and that this light mingles indivisibly with yourself. The Buddha's body, speech, and mind and your own body, speech, and mind are of one taste. Without following any thought about the past or the future, and even letting go of the thought "I am the Buddha," remain in the state of primordial purity which is unconstructed. *(Rinpoche rings the bell. Period of silence.)*

Don't focus on anything as the meditation, but don't let your attention wander either. Whatever is experienced, all the various different contents—don't hold any of that. Do not conceptualize anything perceived, not a single thing. Like Paltrül Rinpoche said in his *Tsigsum Nedek, The Three Words Striking the Vital Point*:

Nothing whatsoever—totally disengaged.
Disengaged, yet utterly open.
A total openness which is indescribable.
Recognize this as the dharmakaya awareness.

Or like Milarepa sang:

> In the gap between two thoughts,
> Thought-free wakefulness manifests unceasingly.

Now we will chant the refuge three times:

> *Namo* 𑗃
> *Dagsok semchen dugngel dröldön du* 𑗃
> *Jangchub bardu kyabsu zungwey ney* 𑗃
> *Lama dorje sempa könchok sum* 𑗃
> *Yidam khandrö tsokla kyabsu chi* 𑗃

> NAMO 𑗃
> In order to liberate myself and all sentient beings from suffering, 𑗃
> I take refuge in Guru Vajrasattva, the Three Jewels, 𑗃
> The yidams, and all the dakinis; 𑗃
> Until enlightenment, I will regard you as my refuge. 𑗃

Remain free and completely at ease. Within this open state of mind, remind yourself that all sentient beings possess this awake openness as their basic nature. Everyone has buddha nature, yet, unaware of this, they suffer in all sorts of terrible samsaric states. Contemplate how utterly sad this is, and form this resolve: "Through the method of this training, I will remove the delusion of all sentient beings. I will do away with this temporary delusion of seeing things as they are not." Develop that confidence, that courage. Remind yourself that all the confusion of samsara, all deluded experience, comes about through clinging to the notion of me and mine. It all originates from cherishing oneself. Breathe out deeply and slowly, a long deep breath, and imagine that the exhalation carries all your virtue, positive karma, and merit to all sentient beings. Gently breathing in again, gather all their negative karma, obscurations, and suffering. Take it into yourself, and again send them your positive merit. Practice like this for a while. *(Period of silence.)*

Now imagine that all the suffering of sentient beings really does dissolve into yourself, that you really do take it on yourself. When their suffering enters you, it vanishes completely, melting into the state of primordial purity, like snow on water. Imagine that your positive karma, virtues, and merit are truly given away to all sentient beings and that they receive it and it dispels all their suffering.

Let's chant the bodhisattva vow in both Tibetan and English, three times.

*Dagni ngöngyi gyalwey dzepa zhin* 🏵
*Semchen küngyi dönrab tsönpar ja* 🏵
*Semchen magal draldang madröl dröl* 🏵
*Semchen ug-yung nyangen deygö jug* 🏵

Like the deeds of the victorious ones of the past, 🏵
I will endeavor in the ultimate goal of all beings 🏵
To take those across who have not crossed and liberate those who have
    not been liberated. 🏵
I will give assurance to beings and establish them in nirvana. 🏵

*Dronam deden dugnel drelwa dang* 🏵
*Pakpey detob tangnyom laney shog* 🏵

May all beings have happiness and be free from suffering. 🏵
May they achieve the sublime happiness and dwell in equanimity. 🏵

*(Rinpoche rings the bell. Period of silence.)*

Now remain in equanimity without sending out, without taking in, without accepting, and without rejecting. Remember the statement "Seen by merely looking, free by merely seeing." What is seen? The absence of concreteness and all attributes. No center and no edge. Without past, present, or future. Empty, awake mind. *(Period of silence.)*

You don't need to be afraid that a thought may arise. You don't need to be afraid that rigpa will slip away or that you will become distracted. If you nevertheless do think this, simply look into the thinker. When seeing no thinker there, rest evenly in the seeing of this absence. This vivid emptiness, free of center and edge, is the primordially pure dharmakaya. At the same time, we are not oblivious or knocked out. There is a sense of being wide awake. That is the sambhogakaya quality. Within this, any perception can unfold, and while perceiving, nothing is held or fixated upon; it is utterly empty and yet perceiving. There is no barrier between being empty and perceiving. That is the nirmanakaya quality, the seed of nirmanakaya. In this way, in one moment of rigpa, the basic substance, the seed, of dharmakaya, of sambhogakaya, and of nirmanakaya is fully present. We recognize that simultaneously our essence is empty, our nature is cognizant, and its capacity is unconfined. That is rigpa. Now, remain evenly like that. *(Rinpoche rings the bell. Period of silence.)*

Remain without even an atom of a focus being meditated upon and without being distracted for even an instant. Undistracted nonmeditation. Your mind is doing nothing. There is nothing you need to do. However it is, leave it like that, without modifying. However mind is right now, let it be exactly like that. You don't need to improve it or correct it in any way. The five senses are wide open and clear. You don't need to block that. And you don't confine your attention to only one of the senses. *(Period of silence.)*

This kind of rigpa, this kind of awareness, is the ultimate and real guru. The mind of the guru is dharmakaya, by nature. When recognizing that our own nature is dharmakaya, then without supplicating, without effort, but spontaneously and naturally, our minds are indivisible from the mind of the guru. *(Period of silence.)*

Now destroy your meditation. Move a little bit around. You don't need to stand up. Now continue the training, immediately. *(Rinpoche rings the bell. Period of silence.)*

Now destroy the meditation, immediately. Now continue. *(Rinpoche rings the bell. Period of silence.)*

Now destroy your meditative state totally, so that nothing remains. Now get angry. Recognize the essence in that. *(Rinpoche rings the bell. Period of silence.)*

Now continue the training. There is no need to block anything. It is nothing exciting. However it is, leave it naturally as it is. Within this state, remind yourself of the thought "I am Vajrasattva," without losing the essence. You can see the painting of Vajrasattva on the wall over there. In that picture he happens to be single, but you can also imagine him with consort. The Vajrasattva with consort symbolizes experience and emptiness together. It is not that Vajrasattva needs a consort. Rather, it symbolizes the indivisibility of experience and emptiness.

Now, let's chant the Vajrasattva practice.

Our meditation got a little distracted, but that's okay. If you don't feel like imagining yourself as Vajrasattva, you can imagine Vajrasattva in the sky before you. Vajrasattva is an extraordinary deity, the embodiment of all buddhas in a single figure who has the power and ability to remove all negative karma and obscurations.

Imagine that Vajrasattva is seated on a multicolored lotus flower, alive and vibrant, fully present. He has a very awesome presence. He is very beautiful, very handsome, very compassionate. First imagine this radiant form, then recite the hundred-syllable mantra of Vajrasattva. This mantra is unique in that it purifies broken commitments, failings, and conceptual obscurations. Also, it is the dharani-mantra, the syllables that are the life force of the hundred peaceful and wrathful deities, the hundred families of the victorious ones. These deities are present right now within our own bodies and will fully manifest at the time of the bardo. In order to prepare ourselves to realize that the hundred peaceful and wrathful deities experienced in the bardo are nothing other than our own display, we chant this mantra. For these two reasons, the hundred-syllable mantra is extremely profound.

Chanting the hundred syllables gently and slowly, we imagine that countless rays of light radiate from the form of Vajrasattva in all directions. The stream of nectar flows from his body down into the crown of our head, totally purifying our body, like a stream of white milk slowly filling up a hollow crystal ball. All impurities, karmic and otherwise, leave our body from the lower openings. This does not only apply to ourselves. Imagine that a Vajrasattva also sits at the crown of the head of every other sentient being. We are the main chanter, and all sentient beings chant along with us, all of us together. It's like we are all taking a special shower that washes away all impurities. It is best if we can remain in the state of rigpa while imagining that this takes place; if not, simply consider it as being like a magical show, visible and yet empty.

*Om bendza sato samaya, manu palaya, bendza sato tenopa, tita dridho mebhava, sutokayo mebhava, supokayo mebhava, anu rakto mebhava, sarva siddhim me trayatsa, sarva karma sutsamey, tsittam shreyah kuru hung, ha ha ha ha hoh, bhagaven sarva tathagata bendza mame müntsa bendzi bhava maha samaya sato ah ष[28]*

*(Vajrasattva mantra continues.)*

Now imagine that Vajrasattva melts into light—the Vajrasattva above you as well as the Vajrasattva above everybody else—and dissolves into each of you, so that everyone becomes indivisible from the body, speech, and mind of glorious Vajrasattva. One's whole experience becomes the buddhafield of Vajrasattva, so that whatever is seen is divine, all sounds are the hundred-syllable mantra, and all movements of mind are the mind of Vajrasattva. Now we will chant the short version of the Vajrasattva mantra. While being indivisible from Vajrasattva, our form is Vajrasattva, everything perceived is divine, all sound is mantra, and all mind, all thoughts and memories, are the play of luminous wakefulness.

*Om bendza satto ah* ${}^{29}$

Finally, we dedicate the roots of virtue, taking all the goodness that has been created through the meditation and recitation of Vajrasattva and dedicating it to the enlightenment of all beings. On the exhalation, keep this attitude: "Through this, may the age of strife, famine, and warfare be pacified. May all sickness be relieved. May there be peace in the world, and may all beings have happiness. And may I in all future lives always take rebirth in a precious human body, connect with qualified masters, and quickly progress to liberation and complete enlightenment. In all future lives, may I be a male or female bodhisattva endowed with the noble frame of mind of benevolence, acting for the welfare of all sentient beings." Let's do the dedication chant.

*Hoh*

*Lamey yeshe leyjung wey*
*Sönam taye dampa dey*
*Kha-nyam semchen malü kün*
*Dorje sempa tobpar shog*

HOH

Through the pure and endless merit
Arising from unexcelled wisdom,
May all beings equal to the sky
Attain the state of Vajrasattva.

*Gyurwa meypa rang-gi shi*
*Tagching tenpa dorjei ney*
*Rang-rig yeshe yermey par*
*Ngönsang gyepey tashi shog*

109

May there be the auspiciousness of true awakening, 𖣘
Indivisible from the spontaneous awareness-wisdom, 𖣘
The permanent and firm vajra abode 𖣘
Of the changeless innate nature. 𖣘

*(Period of silence.)*

Now it is all right to arise from the meditation state. What we just did here is considered a traditional Vajrayana practice. We start with taking refuge, forming the bodhisattva resolve, and developing the four immeasurables of boundless love, compassion, joy, and impartiality. But each of these has a relative and an ultimate aspect. Relative refuge involves visualizing the object of refuge in the sky before us, with the attitude of placing our complete trust in it. Ultimate refuge involves resting in the state of mind in which we are indivisible from the objects of refuge. Bodhichitta as well has two aspects, relative and ultimate. To send out one's goodness and take upon oneself the suffering and obscurations of others is the basis for relative bodhichitta. The ultimate bodhichitta is simply remaining without any mental constructs, without anything whatsoever formed in one's mind.

After that comes the yidam practice, in this case, Vajrasattva. The foremost way to practice is to imagine that we ourselves are the deity, having the form of Vajrasattva, and at the same time to recognize the nature of mind. The development and completion stages are thus simultaneous and indivisible. This is the unity of means and knowledge. While chanting the mantra, we accomplish the welfare of all beings by means of the four activities with the emanating and reabsorbing of the rays of light. Finally, we experience all sights as the divine deity, all sounds as mantra, and all movements of mind as the play of original, luminous wakefulness. We remain in samadhi like this for some time.

We can also practice by alternating these, reciting the mantra for a while and then resting in equanimity, in the view, and continuing like this. When we get tired of chanting, we simply let be into equanimity. When we get tired of letting be into equanimity, we continue reciting the mantra. At the end, dedicate the merit, make good aspirations, good wishes, and then rest in equanimity as the unconditioned dedication.

This is the traditional way, and if you can practice one session with this structure, it is excellent. Once a day is very good. If you do it quickly, it doesn't take longer than half an hour. If we speed it up, we can do it in five minutes! Practicing very gently and slowly, we can easily spend two or three hours. In general, two or three hours is a good duration for a session. If we do four three-hour sessions a day, that is called staying in retreat. If in a three-year retreat the three-hour sessions are too short, we can do sessions lasting three and a half or four hours. In a normal retreat, three-hour sessions are long enough.

We need to be diligent in the beginning. If you are in doubt about this, read the life stories describing how other practitioners acted in the past, how they trained, and what difficulties they undertook. And especially explore how the masters in the Dzogchen transmission practiced. We can learn from the lives of the Kagyü and Nyingma lamas.

There are two ways to deal with spiritual practice. If you are interested in being totally free, completely liberated, and attaining full enlightenment, you'd better hurry up and practice with great diligence. The other approach is to take spiritual practice as a sort of vitamin or dietary supplement. When you feel a little low on energy or a little upset, you sit down and practice a little in order to feel better. We try to balance ourselves through practice, then later we return into activity. This approach advocates a little dose of spiritual practice once in a while.

Which of these particular ways we want to follow is up to us. I personally feel that it would be better to eliminate confusion from its very root, so that we no longer have to powerlessly take rebirth within the three realms of samsara. On the other hand, if we want to get through life without hurting too much, if we feel that doing business and getting rich or being successful in a career is not quite enough, and we need a little meditative stability to embellish our life or make it a little more beautiful, that is all right too. If we choose to use spiritual practice in that way, it's entirely up to us. It's like giving our life the Dharma-polish!

Some people have this attitude, believe me! We tell ourselves that we need some spirituality in our lives, that we can't be totally materialistic. So we give ourselves a little dose in the morning and evening to give the gloss of spirituality to our normal life. This is also a particular solution or style, and certain teachers—not masters, but teachers—teach in this way. They instruct their students in five-minute meditation sessions. They are trying to make spiritual practice easier, more appetizing or palatable, trying to bend the Dharma to fit people's attitudes. That is not the true Dharma. You might encounter this type of "convenience Dharma." Don't make the mistake of confusing this type of practice for the real thing.

We *can* practice only five minutes and do it in a genuine, true way, in which we establish a sincere attitude, and then train in the main part with genuine focus, then dedicate in a genuine way afterwards. In this case, even five minutes becomes something authentic. Otherwise, you could also just give it up altogether. There are a lot of other things on which we can spend a life. If we try to practice the Dharma but don't really practice it, we do a disservice to the Buddha's teachings. We become an embarrassment to the Dharma, and we waste our lives as well.

Even if you practice just a little bit, try to do it in a genuine way, with genuine view, genuine meditation, genuine conduct. Even if it is for a short while, let it be real. Otherwise, it is better to give it up all together, because not only are we caught up in confusion, but we use the Dharma to tie ourselves up as well. That is really a wrong road, a wrong attitude. To pretend to be a spiritual person and wear a rosary in one hand is useless if it's false. If it happens naturally, it is okay. There's no problem if we really are that way. But if our intention is to be respected by others, to be regarded by others more highly because we meditate or are spiritual, that is a fake or wrong attitude.

Regardless of whether we are new or advanced students, we should always be certain not to fool ourselves. If somebody else fools us, there's not much we can do about it. But to fool ourselves is much worse, isn't it? So try not to do that. Make use of spiritual books that teach authentic practice, not Dharma-polish. The former cuts through confusion and clears up delusion; the other glosses over the confused state. The latter type of spiritual practice can make our deluded state appear prettier, more pleasant. One can advertise the value of spiritual practice, like advertising an exciting machine, "Use it two times a day for three weeks, and it's guaranteed you'll have a flat abdomen and lose five kilos!" In the same way, "Use this practice daily, only five minutes a day, and your confusion is guaranteed to clear up!" It sounds nice, but does it really work? We need to think about this. Let's not fool ourselves.

We need to exert ourselves and persevere. When you get bored, just be bored, but continue the training. I feel that being bored is very good. The more bored one is, the more opportunity there is for progress. Meditation practice is not meant to cater to short attention spans, like TV ads where every twenty seconds there is a new and exciting thing to catch our attention. Something interesting does not happen every twenty seconds in meditation!

You can see this tendency in movies also. Old movies are long, with long conversations and not so much happening. Nowadays the scene changes every few seconds, and there is so much action. People's expectations have become like that. It's a combination of what movie producers believe people need and want, and also that people expect something exciting all the time. It's a kind of mutually reinforced confusion.

People can also be deluded by the movies they see. A lot of young Nepalese, both boys and girls, are really influenced by the role models presented in Indian and American movies. They try to act like that, they try to dress like that, and so forth. They become imitations. This type of delusion is like mutual dependency, a coincidence of factors from both sides.

What we need is to have a natural mind: unconfused, unmistaken, undeluded. We need a natural, fresh, original state of wakefulness to cut through the stream of confusion. Original wakefulness cuts deluded experience into pieces, so that it becomes insubstantial. You can also think of confusion as a knot fashioned of burned rope—something totally insubstantial.

The basis for realization is a happy mind, along with diligence. When we are unhappy and uneasy at root and we try to be diligent on top of that, we might go a little crazy. Don't do that. On the other hand, if we go astray into feeling happy, feeling good, we can become stuck in blissing out. We become like a Hare Krishna practitioner! We get caught up in the emotion of feeling good, being happy and blissed out, singing "Hare Krishna." True spirituality is not a training in being overtaken by bliss, allowing ourselves to get caught up. On the other hand, as long as we retain the innate stability of wakefulness, it's all right to look like a Hare Krishna devotee, to sing loudly and have tears of devotion rolling down our cheeks. As long as the stability of wakefulness within is not lost, it's perfectly okay to behave like that, because we are not getting caught up in the emotion.

Questions?

STUDENT: Could you explain more about this Vajrasattva practice we are doing? It seems quite unelaborate.

RINPOCHE: This Vajrasattva practice is one of utmost simplicity. There are not that many words, but if one personally wants to fill in more of the meaning, one can. In itself, however, it is complete, sufficient. One takes refuge and bodhichitta; then for the main part, beyond concept, you can either see yourself as the yidam or else imagine Vajrasattva in the sky before you. At the end, when you chant OM BENDZA SATTO AH, imagine yourself as Vajrasattva, and feel that whatever is seen has the nature of Vajrasattva, all sounds have the nature of mantra, and so forth. "All sights are the deity" doesn't mean that we literally see Vajrasattva everywhere, holding vajra and bell. It's more that all sights possess the quality of the unobstructed; visible emptiness is itself the form of Vajrasattva.

Among the traditional three samadhis of deity practice—the samadhi of suchness, the samadhi of illumination, and the seed samadhi—what evolves out of the seed samadhi is insubstantial and transparent, with a sort of see-through quality. It is not something solid or concrete, like solid matter. Nor is it like imagining that everything else we normally see becomes empty and disappears and that only Vajrasattva's real, concrete form is left behind. The whole development stage has that insubstantial quality, and that is the form of Vajrasattva.

# 14

# MANDALA AND
# GURU YOGA

## *Tsoknyi Rinpoche*

The purpose of the mandala offering is to relinquish ego-clinging and any form of conceptual attitude that holds on to something as being one's own. Giving away everything, by means of the outer, inner, and innermost mandala offerings, relinquishes all types of clinging. Automatically, at the same time, the accumulation of merit is perfected.

It's said that the first mandala offering was made after the Buddha attained complete enlightenment, when the kings of the gods, Brahma and Indra, requested him to teach the Dharma. Presenting the Buddha with a thousand-spoked golden wheel and a miraculous rare white conch shell that was coiled clockwise, they requested him to begin teaching, to turn the wheel of the Dharma.

Later, when the Tibetan king Trisong Deutsen invited Padmasambhava to Tibet to establish the Buddhadharma in his country, he composed four lines of verse to accompany his offering. As he made the mandala offering to Padmasambhava with the request to teach, he gave his entire kingdom, all three provinces of central Tibet, as an offering. While making the offering of his kingdom, he chanted these lines, which we still recite today:

From Tsoknyi Rinpoche, *Fearless Simplicity: The Dzogchen Way of Living Freely in a Complex World* (Boudhanath: Rangjung Yeshe Publications, 2003), "Salad Dressing."

> The earth is perfumed with scented water and strewn with flowers,
> Adorned with Mount Meru, the four continents, the sun, and the moon.
> Imagining this as the Buddha realm, I offer it,
> So that all beings may enjoy that pure realm.

I am told that it was due to the auspicious coincidence of the king making this mandala offering that the Vajrayana teachings were able to remain for such a long time in Tibet, in a natural and very propitious way.

What is the substance of such an auspicious coincidence? It consists of a complete surrender of ego-clinging. That is essentially what our practice of the mandala offerings is about—laying down everything that could be clung to as being "me" and "mine." Another way to describe this is to say that the king totally opened himself up. He turned over to Padmasambhava whatever he could cling to as being his, and in this way he rendered himself a genuinely suitable recipient for the Vajrayana teachings. By completely surrendering ego-clinging, King Trisong Deutsen established an authentic basis for the Vajrayana teachings in Tibet. Not only was giving away his entire kingdom an incredibly courageous deed; it was also a way to temporarily make a gap in ego-clinging. Of course, ego-clinging cannot be totally and permanently erased from one moment to the next. This is a process that happens through disciplined training. Still, the temporary suspension of ego-clinging is in itself something truly remarkable.

Some people say, "How can you offer Mount Meru, the four continents, the sun and the moon and so on when they don't actually belong to you or to me? How can I give them away? They didn't belong to King Trisong Deutsen either, so how could he give them away?" It's not necessary to be this nitpicky. As a matter of fact, our world does belong to us. Whatever we perceive through our five senses and whatever occurs in our mental field constitutes our world, our life, and as the contents of our own experience it is ours to give. Our personal experience doesn't belong to anybody else. Thus, we are able to give away whatever we perceive as our world.

One purpose of the mandala offering is to eliminate ego-clinging. Another is to perfect the accumulation of merit. Any act of giving is an offering, not just of the object being given, but of the effort that went into creating that object. For example, when giving a single butter lamp, you offer not only the act of lighting the wick, but also the work you put into obtaining the butter or the oil, as well as creating the vessel, providing the metal for that vessel being formed, and so forth. This principle applies to other types of offering as well. Basically, all that energy is what creates the merit.

Some people understand the concept of merit quite readily, while for others it's difficult to comprehend. Merit most definitely does exist. Like everything else in the world, it's formed through causes and conditions. All phenomena come about through causes and circumstance; there is no independent entity anywhere. Everything is dependent on these causes and conditions. For instance, anything material is dependent on the four elements. Especially in the West, with its emphasis on materiality, matters are very dependent. Like everything else, merit is dependent on causes and conditions. Through the accumulation of merit, positive situations can be created. For example, meeting with the Dharma and receiving instructions on practice requires certain favorable circumstances to arise simultaneously. The occurrence of this requires merit.

Mandala offering is a very profound practice, which is why it is one of the preliminaries in the Tibetan tradition. I personally feel that all the preliminary practices are extremely important, but among them, the most profound are probably guru yoga and mandala offering. That doesn't mean the others are not profound, but rather that these are perhaps the most profound. People often come to me and say, "I understand the reason for doing the prostrations, taking refuge. I also understand the purification aspect of Vajrasattva practice. But I just don't get the point of making mandala offerings, and I don't understand guru yoga." This kind of statement shows how profound these practices actually are. Ego is not so easily willing to accept them. Ego is very clever and would like to create doubt for us about anything that undermines it, anything that might prove hazardous to its favorite practice, which is ego-clinging. This is really true—check it out for yourself. Whenever something is harmful to ego, ego will try to raise doubts about it. We need to recognize this trick from the beginning.

Prostrations are easy for people to understand. Some look at them as if they're good physical exercise. They think that they're good for the heart: "Oh, I understand. Prostrations strengthen my legs and back. If I sit for a long time in meditation and I get back pain, then I'll just do prostrations to correct this. I might feel drowsy or lazy, but prostrations will chop up the laziness. I think refuge is very important: Whatever we do, we need a certain type of guidance. So we have the Buddha as our guide, the Dharma as the path or technique, and friends as the Sangha. I completely understand taking refuge. And Vajrasattva is the natural form or the manifestation of compassionate emptiness. I get it. By chanting the mantra and visualizing this thing moving down through me, well, I don't exactly know what bad karma and obscurations are, but I feel less guilty. All this feeling bad about myself goes away, so that's great. Karma, all these things, well, I don't really know, but never mind, I certainly have some baggage, a few emotional patterns. I must clean these out; it makes sense.

"But mandala offering I don't understand. Offering the whole world—it doesn't even belong to me. Mount Meru does not even exist, and what's this about the four continents, when there are actually seven? And why offer the moon and sun? It's ridiculous—really crazy talk. Also that thing about blessings, I don't get it. And why do we have to supplicate the guru, who after all is somebody made of flesh and blood, just like us. What's the point of that?"

These doubts come up because we don't really understand what the "guru" in guru yoga really means. The guru is not just the particular person you met. The guru principle refers to a lot of things. There is the guru as nirmanakaya, sambhogakaya, and dharmakaya, and the essence body, the svabhavikakaya. There is the guru as living lineage master, as well as the guru who manifests as our life situations, and the guru who is the scriptures we read. Then there is the guru who is our intrinsic nature. We should understand all of these aspects as being the guru. If you learn something from a tree, then that is the guru as symbolic experience. You could say, "All right, I'll take support from the tree; I learned something there." If your wife is giving you a hard time and you learn something from that, your wife is your guru in that situation.

The purpose of guru yoga is to receive the blessings of realization of the root and lineage masters. Recognition and stability in the self-knowing wakefulness of one's own nature doesn't take place without direct transmission by a living teacher. Therefore, connecting with a living master and practicing guru yoga is essential.

There is a very good reason the preliminary practices come before the main part of practice. Every single aspect of the preliminary practices is meant to be like a pestle to grind and smash your laziness. Imagine that you are making hot sauce, *achaar*, with a stone mortar and pestle. When making this Tibetan salsa, you successively add garlic, ginger, chili peppers, and spices, grinding them all together into a smooth sauce. It's the same with the preliminaries: You smash your laziness first with prostrations, then with Vajrasattva practice, then with mandala offerings and guru yoga, till all the laziness is gone. If you really go through these practices in an effective, thorough way, there is no room for being lazy, for hanging on to personal comfort—none at all.

After we do all the preliminary practices, we find we can sit for one hour, five hours, six hours in meditation, and it really feels like taking time off. "What I went through before was so hard, but this is nothing—I can easily sit and meditate for hours and hours." This is because the laziness has been relinquished, totally vanquished.

You might think it would be enough to do only 10,000 repetitions, but our tradition is to do 100,000 of each. With this quantity, there's no way to be lazy. You'll never finish unless you really persevere, really push yourself and use a lot of effort. In this way, through doing 100,000 of each practice, the laziness does not dare return. It'll mutter to itself, "I'm just getting a beating if I stay around here. If I dare to come back, I'll probably get 100,000 beatings again, so I'm not gonna hang around this guy any longer." I'm not joking here; it's really true.

For a practitioner who has already recognized self-knowing wakefulness, doing the preliminaries can totally obliterate all laziness so that none remains. At the same time, these practices also perfect the two accumulations and remove all hindrances. The essence of mind is further and further revealed by the steady process of removing that which obscures it. All this takes place through doing the preliminaries.

Sometimes we find that there is just nothing to do: No matter how much we try to be lucid, sharp, bright, and compassionate, it does not work. The twofold ignorance and negative emotions take over repeatedly. That is when we need a practice other than simple mindfulness. The whole accumulation of merit through various practices removes that which causes twofold ignorance to recur and reduces the intensity of emotional states, before the main part of practice. This is in fact the whole point of the ngöndro practice.

By going through the ngöndro, you approach the main part having already accumulated a lot of merit and having already reduced the intensity of the emotions. Afterward, when you try to let be in the state of the Great Perfection, you find that it automatically lasts for a long time. Sustaining rigpa becomes much easier. The preliminary practice is a very effective and pragmatic way of going about training in rigpa. Emotional states are something formed, and therefore the proper remedies can destroy them.

# 15

## GURU YOGA

*Adeu Rinpoche*

No matter which of the three vehicles you practice—Hinayana, Maha-yana, or Mantrayana—from the moment you enter the gate of Buddha Shakyamuni's teachings until you attain complete enlightenment, you must have the support of a spiritual teacher in order to obtain the teachings. The *pratimoksha* precepts of individual liberation need to be given by a precep-tor who possesses the twelve qualities of spiritual training according to the shravaka level. The bodhisattva vow is transmitted by a holder of that vow, someone whose stream-of-being is saturated by bodhichitta and thus worthy of giving the vow to others. Vajrayana teachings must be received from a vajra master, who has earned the title by demonstrating a degree of accomplishment in the stages of development and completion. Only a mas-ter with the blessings of the lineage can transmit the Vajrayana teachings. No matter what level of practice you pursue, you cannot really progress by groping in the dark or trying to figure it out by yourself. Merely trying to use your own intellect to decipher the path to enlightenment lacks the true blessings of the lineage.

Right now, as we are unable to meet the Buddha in person, we must learn from someone who represents the Buddha and teaches what the Buddha taught. From our perspective, in terms of kindness, such a person is superior to Buddha Shakyamuni, for, unlike the Buddha, this is the person we are able to meet and from whom we can receive teachings. So, you must first acknowledge your personal guru's kindness as the communicator of the Buddha's teachings.

If you have already set out on the Buddhist path by taking refuge and are determined to proceed onward to attain complete enlightenment, it does not help to walk blindly, seeking direction by chance, nor does it make sense to follow someone who does not know the path. You need a guide who has traveled the same path and can tell you how to proceed. If you are sincere about attaining enlightenment, then whichever level you want to practice—whether pratimoksha, bodhisattva, or Mantra—it is indispensable to find a capable spiritual guide.

First, be skilled in examining the teacher; second, be skilled in following the teacher; and third, be skilled in absorbing his or her state of realization or wisdom mind. Learn how to evaluate the person from whom you are about to take guidance. Once you feel confidence in this person, study how to follow him or her. Lastly, assimilate or train in his state of realization.

Before following anyone, you need to first examine that person to determine whether he or she is actually competent and possesses the prescribed qualifications according to the pratimoksha, bodhisattva, or tantric level. But once you have decided to follow a particular teacher, it does not help to continue to judge him or her, trying to figure out whether you made the right choice. Such an attitude will only pollute your mind. Instead, after making a positive assessment and choosing to follow a teacher, simply do so. Remember, it is your responsibility to check carefully whether a potential teacher is qualified, holds a lineage, and has received blessings. Only after becoming confident that this is so, and feeling that you can really trust this person and can keep pure samaya with him or her, should you ask for the appropriate teachings.

What if you later find out that you were mistaken, that the teacher is not trustworthy, and that he or she is not guiding you toward liberation but is pointing you in the wrong direction? Someone who guides people in the opposite direction of liberation is, by definition, not a spiritual teacher but a *misleader* and unqualified, and there is no duty to follow blindly merely because you accepted him or her to begin with. It is perfectly all right to find somebody else. Especially today, all kinds of people present themselves as spiritual teachers. If you run into one of these charlatans, you need not stay. On the other hand, if you do have a true teacher but somehow develop a negative attitude and destroy your connection with that person, this is the same as rejecting the Dharma, and it will have severe repercussions.

Not only should you examine the teacher, you should also scrutinize yourself. Even if you have a precious human body possessing the eight freedoms and ten riches, you still need to be truthful about your level of sincerity. Examine yourself honestly. You need to determine whether you are willing to follow a teacher sincerely and do whatever he or she recommends, rather than merely acting as if you are going to. Learn all about the shravaka precepts, the bodhisattva trainings, and the tantric commitments and what they entail. Then ask yourself, "Am I really willing to abide by them?" Check your level of resolve and determination and your level of fortitude and perseverance. Are you prepared to go through with this? Once you connect with a teacher, you should follow his or her instructions. If you are directed to do something, are you really willing to do it? You need to determine this beforehand, to avoid merely pretending that you are going to follow the prescribed path.

The teachings about the necessity of a teacher are well known in all the Buddhist scriptures; for example, there is the statement that one thousand buddhas of this aeon all have spiritual teachers of their own. The word *buddha* would not even appear in the world if there were no spiritual teachers. In other words, a teacher is indispensable.

The connection between you and your spiritual guide is of the utmost seriousness. Your relationship with that person makes or breaks your spiritual development. In fact, as you progress through the vehicles, the relationship between you and your teacher becomes increasingly crucial. For example, the bodhisattva's connection to a teacher is more profound than the shravaka's, and if you want to follow the path of Vajrayana, the relationship is even more vital. In Vajrayana, it is by means of a master that you proceed to enlightenment. Your ultimate root guru introduces you to your innate state of wisdom, pointing it out to you. This is the most significant person you could possibly meet. Attaining buddhahood is due to training in this ultimate wakefulness; and the only way you can wind up in the hell of incessant torment is by destroying the connection with your teacher. So you could say that the highest risk as well as the greatest benefit depends on the person of the utmost importance—your ultimate root guru. That makes him or her a very significant person.

Once you feel confident in your choice, the next step is knowing how to follow the spiritual guide. That is something you can and should learn very carefully. In all the sutras and tantras, how to behave in your relationship with the spiritual master is defined precisely. How to honor, respect, and act around your teacher as well as how to treat your guru and how to request teachings are all explained. You should check whether you are actually adhering to all of these suggestions and then adjust your behavior accordingly.

As I mentioned, when relating to a guru, you should be skilled in three things: first, examining the guru; second, following the guru; and third, absorbing his or her state of realization, the wisdom mind. I have covered the first point. What about the second point?

Following a guru can be done in different ways: The best way is by practice and realization; the next-best is by serving your guru with your body and voice; and the third-best is by offering material things. Each of these ways of honoring your master directly relates to and brings you closer to a particular level of practice.

Milarepa is regarded as Tibet's greatest yogi. He was able, in a single lifetime, to overcome the depths of samsara and attain complete realization. He is the highest example of someone who honored his own master by one-pointedly practicing what he was taught. He is also the foremost example of serving a master with body and speech. He obeyed every command Marpa uttered, without any hesitation or mistrust. No matter how much Marpa abused or scolded him, putting him through severe trials, Milarepa never lost faith for even one instant. When he was refused teaching, instead of turning against Marpa, he blamed himself for not having enough merit. Even though he came to the brink of despair, he never once turned against Marpa. Hence Milarepa is considered the highest example of how to follow one's teacher wholeheartedly.

Another way of serving the guru is by making material offerings. Tsang-Yang Gyatso, a disciple of the first Tsoknyi Rinpoche, exemplifies this. He began as a layperson and later became a monk at my monastery. At the age of forty, he met Tsoknyi Rinpoche. Several times during his life he offered his teacher every single possession he owned, not keeping even a teacup or an extra set of clothes. When he accumulated more possessions, he gave everything away again. After the third time of giving all he had, his guru said, "That's enough. You have completed the accumulation of merit now. I can guarantee you that." He is an example of someone who was able to honor the guru with material things.

Here is another story about serving the guru. Kyobpa Jigten Sumgön, one of the early Drigung Kagyü masters, had tens of thousands of disciples. One day, a group of them wanted to present their realization as an offering to their guru. Not only did they explain their level of realization, they each performed a miracle in front of him to demonstrate their level of practice. Meanwhile, the master's cook thought, "I worked hard here in the kitchen and never had time to do even a single practice session. All I have ever produced is food and tea, so I have nothing to show." He sat there, miserable and depressed. The master knew his thoughts and said, "Hey, cook, stand up! I am sure you have something to show." And sure enough, when the cook stood up, he not only left a footprint in the stone floor, he also levitated. The others complained, "Hey, wait a minute! We did all this practice while this guy only cooked. How can he perform miracles like that without any practice?" Their master replied, "Don't think that serving with body and voice is not practice. Real practice means to surrender and follow the guru's wishes in whatever way one can. So even cooking can be practice. That is probably why the blessings of realization have entered his stream-of-being."

Finally, become skilled in assimilating the guru's state of realization, his or her wisdom mind that is the source of all the qualities the guru embodies. In addition to practicing and serving the guru, following the guru means imitating him or her in all ways: emulating the guru's behavior—how he or she treats others, even how he or she dresses and walks—and trying to adopt the flavor or quality of the guru's being. Now, to assimilate the guru's realization means first to understand exactly who your guru is. Find out how he or she trained, received teachings, practiced those teachings, and developed his or her practice; what kind of experience and realization the guru has and what his or her accomplishment is; and then what qualities have manifested in the guru, what virtues and absence of flaws. You need to know something about all of these.

Once you find out who your guru actually is, then compare yourself in every single aspect. When you have discovered how your guru trained and what he or she learned and realized, ask yourself, "What am I actually doing and what have I really done? What have I learned, what have I practiced, what have I understood and realized?" Examine yourself minutely in comparison with the guru. If you don't do this, you might think, "Well, he is a human being, and I am a human being. He eats and sleeps and dresses, and so do I. We both have needs; we are pretty much alike. Maybe he is a little better, but we are basically the same." In the long run it is not enough merely to feel admiration. That will never turn into profound devotion, and devotion is necessary because it allows you receive blessings. In fact, there can be no blessings without devotion.

Unfortunately, devotion does not come spontaneously. It is not a given that you will automatically have the requisite pure appreciation of your teacher. He may simply be someone you are fond of. Therefore, you may need to work at engendering devotion. Just as it is mandatory to discover what the mind is in order to be able to remain in the natural state, you must know how to give rise to a genuine feeling of devotion in order to receive blessings. There are many teachings that explain how to generate devotion when it is lacking, such as the *Profound Path*, a famous manual of the Drukpa Kagyü school.

To perceive the guru as a buddha in person, it is necessary to reflect upon the guru's superior qualities. In other words, truly understand that he or she is extraordinary. The guru is not at all like us. If you are honest about it, free of all pretense and duplicity, you will become aware of what your stream-of-being usually is: one harmful emotion after another. This bundle of *skandhas* is a continuous stream of negativity. The guru, on the other hand, is someone who realizes the path to complete enlightenment. This difference is immense. If you sincerely understand this difference, then real devotion may arise, and you will begin to yearn to assimilate similar qualities. It is essential to motivate yourself with a strong wish and determination to follow in the guru's footsteps and attain the same level. This is a point of exceptional importance.

So, if devotion is lacking, it needs to be created. Later, when you truly see the qualities of the lama, unfabricated devotion will arise of its own accord. To attain the level of your guru, first you need devotion. If devotion is not there in the beginning, develop it. Once you have trained in devotion and feel it, then it doesn't matter what kind of guru yoga practice you do. It can be done extensively or briefly, but if you lack devotion, the blessings of the Dharma will never enter your stream-of-being.

It is said that if you see the guru as just a person, then when receiving nectar from the vase, you will perceive only water, nothing else. If you perceive your guru as an ordinary human being, you will attain only the state of an ordinary human being. However, if you can perceive your guru as a buddha, you can become a buddha. If you perceive your guru as a siddha, you can become a siddha. The very level you will be able to achieve is whatever level you perceive the guru to be.

When I was in a Chinese prison camp, I met a *geshe* called Gyamtso. He was a follower of a teacher from Drepung named Drayu Dorje Chang, who was the single most important Gelugpa lineage master of his time. Everyone from Sera, Drepung, and Ganden monasteries had received empowerments and teachings from him. Gyamtso had learned a lot from this teacher, and he told me this story. Drayu Dorje Chang was giving teachings to a large gathering of important incarnate lamas, geshes, and senior monks at Drepung, one of the greatest Gelugpa monasteries in central Tibet.

"Today," he began, "I have something important to ask you, and I want you to be honest with me. Will you give me a sincere reply?" He joined his palms, and they wondered what he was going to ask. He then continued, "In this snowy land of Tibet, the four traditions of Buddhist teachings—Gelugpa, Kagyü, Sakya, and Nyingma—are all equal, and all follow the same teacher, Buddha Shakyamuni. There is no difference there; that is for sure. Each of these four schools possesses the complete path of the Sutra and Tantra and the methods on how to attain complete enlightenment. They are all equal, and there is no difference there either. But the last time someone in our lineage attained the celestial realm, (going to the buddhafield in a physical body,) was a very long time ago." The teacher mentioned an early Kadampa master. "Since then I haven't heard of that happening in the Gelugpa lineage. It seems like a very rare occurrence. But in the Kagyü and Nyingma schools, there are numerous stories of people either attaining the rainbow body or going straight to the buddha realms in a physical body, even these days. So tell me frankly, if we have the same teachings and we are following the same teacher, why do some traditions have more, you could say, *visible* attainments and others have fewer? What is the difference?"

He joined his palms and looked at everybody, waiting for an answer, but nobody said a word.

After a while, Drayu Dorje Chang spoke again. "Well, if you are not going to say anything, maybe I can propose an answer, and then you can then tell me if I am correct."

There was a moment of silence. He then quoted two lines from a tantra called the *Tokpa Dünpa*:[30] "Or else the simple-minded person with faith will be closer to enlightenment, while the intellectual who scrutinizes will have no accomplishment." He then said, "As I understand this, no matter how you go about it, trust or faith is the one decisive factor for all these occurrences of accomplishments that you see in the Kagyü and Nyingma lineages. It is because they emphasize guru yoga as the most vital practice, the indispensable entrance door to realization. By supplicating, generating devotion, and receiving blessings, they attain realization. In my humble opinion, this is why the Kagyü and Nyingma lineages have so many practitioners who have attained accomplishments. What do you think?" Again, nobody uttered a word.

This story that Gyamtso, a follower of Drayu Dorje Chang, told us in prison camp, illustrates the extraordinary qualities of guru yoga.

In the writings of the early Drukpa Kagyü masters such as Götsangpa, Lorepa, Yangönpa, Barawa, and many others, you find the statement that single-minded devotion is of utmost importance. They put a lot of emphasis on how to first generate devotion and then, after having given rise to devotion, how to stabilize it. Finally, there are teachings on how, by means of steady devotion, to attain realization by practicing guru yoga.

To begin training in guru yoga, first you need to check yourself to see whether you have any devotion. Next you need to learn how to give rise to devotion in your heart and to cultivate it. Then gradually, as you train more and more, you will receive the compassionate power of blessings in actuality. In all the teachings of Vajrayana, you will find that guru yoga is considered the most important practice. Developing devotion in guru yoga practice alone is sufficient, but without it no path will be successful.

As I said, even though we have connected with a spiritual master, if we take an honest look at ourselves, we must admit that we are merely ordinary people. We need refinement, and the way to improve and nurture ourselves is to go through certain trainings by which we can develop the will to be free of samsaric existence. According to our own disposition, we aim either toward the higher realms within samsara, the definite goodness of liberation, or toward complete enlightenment.

The way to develop true renunciation is described in most of the scriptures, including the *Light of Wisdom* and the *Essential Instruction on the Threefold Excellence*.[31] Start by reflecting on the four mind-changings that comprise the general preliminaries. Subsequently, train in the specific preliminaries, taking refuge, forming the bodhisattva resolve, and so on. Different chants are used in different traditions. The intent and meaning are the same whether the preliminaries belong to the old or the new schools, so use the text that you were given by your own teacher. The key point is to practice and persevere in making yourself a suitable recipient for the teachings. Guru yoga practice is taught in all the Buddhist lineages. Sometimes it is called a preliminary, sometimes the main part, but either way it remains the entrance door for the blessings, the empowerments, and so forth. Guru yoga is the universal practice.

The main part of practice is an extension of the preliminaries. This is equally true for the general preliminaries of the four mind-changings or the special, extraordinary preliminaries called ngöndro. The preliminaries are the common foundation for all schools; whether Nyingma or Sarma, there is no difference. It is the insight you gain during the preliminaries that becomes the main part of practice, and it is within the preliminaries that guru yoga is found in a short, simple form.

Guru yoga opens the door of blessings. There can be no realization without blessings, no blessings without devotion, and no devotion without supplicating. However, supplication does not mean simply chanting but opening up from the core of your heart. When there is devotion in your innermost heart, you receive the blessings, and receiving the blessings makes realization possible. This is the purpose of guru yoga, very concisely put.

The Nyingma and Sarma schools have many guru yoga practices of varying lengths. Look at it this way: When you taste molasses, whether it is a huge amount or a small one, it always tastes sweet. Likewise, however long or short the practice is, the key point remains the same: to receive the blessings.

It should also be noted that in yidam practice, the guru is in the form of a particular deity. It is said that by realizing one sugata, all buddhas are realized. In other words, if you accomplish one guru, you accomplish all buddhas. It is like Guru Rinpoche says in the terma teachings of *Barchey Künsel*, "If you realize me, you realize all buddhas. If you behold me, you behold all buddhas." In other words, you see all buddhas in actuality. You can realize all enlightened ones, all yidams and so forth, by realizing a single one.

Realization of the guru is naturally also realization of the yidam, as illustrated in this story from Marpa's biography. Naropa once manifested the mandala of Hevajra so that Marpa could see the central figure very clearly on the shrine. He then asked Marpa, "Well, now, from whom do you prefer to receive the blessings, the substance of the accomplishment—me or the yidam?" Marpa thought, "I'm with the guru all the time, but seeing the yidam in actuality is a unique opportunity." So, he bowed to the shrine. Naropa then reabsorbed the Hevajra deity back into his heart center and said, "Now whom are you going to prostrate to?" This story shows that every yidam deity is the manifestation of the guru. And remember that you do not receive large blessings from an extensive practice and small blessings from a short practice. In both cases, the blessings are exactly the same.

Tilopa once told Naropa that everything is included within guru sadhana, even removing hindrances and bringing forth enhancement. Tilopa said, "While supplicating, combine the object, thought, and substance into one." The object here refers to the sublime object, the root guru. The thought is the willingness to accomplish whatever your guru commands down to the letter. This willingness to persevere is the brave attitude to continue with the practice no matter what. Finally, the substance is the state of realization and behavior that the guru embodies and that should be assimilated within your own stream-of-being. Ultimately, it is by realizing the guru's mind, the play of original wakefulness, that you truly mingle the guru's mind with your own.

The general advice is to study as much and as broadly as possible. But when combining everything into your own practice, condense it into these three principles: First, be skilled in examining the teacher; next, be skilled in following the teacher; and third, be skilled in assimilating the teacher's realization. All the different levels of Buddhism recommend including everything in a single practice. Here is a story to illustrate this point.

My incarnation lineage is also called Trülshik. The third Trülshik used to chant the supplication to the guru for almost any purpose. The prayer begins, "All sentient beings, my mothers infinite in number, supplicate the nirmanakaya guru," and continues with one line for each of the four kayas. If this lama were called to somebody's house to do *phowa* near the dead body, he would go there, put his hand on the corpse's head, and recite these four lines. After he had chanted them three or four times, there would invariably be some visible sign. For example, people would see a rainbow radiating from the body, or a bit of the hair would fall out.

He would do the same chant for other purposes as well. One autumn, he went with his disciples to collect alms, but they ran into bandits who took everything from them, including their pack animals. How did the guru react? He chanted the same supplication to the guru: "All sentient beings, my mothers infinite in number, supplicate the nirmanakaya guru ..." The disciples were a bit upset, and behind his back they grumbled, "He *never* chants anything else. Maybe he doesn't know any other prayer." Anyway, the next morning, much to everyone's surprise, the bandits came and gave everything back. It seems that while the bandits were cooking parts of one of the animals, they looked in the pot and all of a sudden saw nothing but clear water. There was no meat left. Other strange things occurred as well, and they got very scared and thought, "Wait a minute! Maybe we robbed the wrong guru!" So they went and returned everything they had taken, saying, "Keep this—we don't want any of it!" Then the disciples said among themselves, "Our lama may know only one chant, but at least it works!"

In fact this lama had attained complete mastery, and it did not really matter what he chanted. Based on guru yoga, from within his wisdom mind, his state of realization, he could carry out all activities. He did not have to do specific practices for different purposes.

This is also what Gyalwa Yangönpa, an earlier Drukpa Kagyü master, said: "Among all the different practices that I have taught you, there is only one that suffices for all purposes. I can guarantee that one practice: guru yoga." In both the Nyingma and Sarma schools, guru yoga is considered indispensable and always to be applied. Everything can be included within this single practice—all aspects of both development stage and completion stage, as well as the inner yogas of channels, energies, and essences.

There are various ways to practice guru yoga. There is the way of accomplishing the guru according to the nirmanakaya level, according to the sambhogakaya level, according to the dharmakaya level, and finally according to the level of the essence body, the svabhavikakaya. For example, in the tradition of Ratna Lingpa's termas and also in the Drukpa Kagyü *Profound Path,* when one practices all four levels of guru yoga, it is at the sambhogakaya level that the subtle yogic practices are included. Additionally, in our Drukpa Kagyü tradition, there is a set of teachings called *The Five Command Seals.* These are the view of Mahamudra, the meditation of Naropa's Six Doctrines, the conduct of equal taste, the fruition that manifests as auspicious coincidence, and then the guru yoga that is always vital.

The practice of guru yoga is similar in all traditions. One begins with the outer methods of realizing the guru through guru sadhana, namely, paying respect by bowing down over and over, by making offerings such as mandala offerings, and the various other ways of gathering the accumulations. Next there is the inner practice of guru yoga with the Three Roots as the guru principle. Here the guru embodies the essence of the Three Jewels and Three Roots. After this comes the innermost way, where the main point is to regard the yidam as being the guru in essence and then using the yidam and recitation of mantra to realize the guru's mind.

Whether the sadhana is long or short, it always includes receiving the blessings in the form of the four empowerments. Empowerment, from the

Sanskrit *abhisheka*, means "dispersing and anointing," in the sense of purifying the veils of obscurations and becoming imbued with the enlightened qualities. This is what it all comes down to. What you recite for this can also be either brief or extensive, but what you visualize is always the same: You imagine that the four levels of obscurations are cleared away and you receive the four empowerments authorizing you to practice the four levels of path and implanting the seeds for the ultimate fruition of the four kayas within your stream-of-being.

Please understand that no matter what you chant or visualize, the vital point of guru yoga is to train in repeatedly receiving the four empowerments at the end of the session. This is the entrance door to the blessings for the extraordinary and special teachings. After the empowerments, in some form or other, every text says, "Now settle evenly in the state in which the guru's mind and your own are indivisible as one taste." What does "settle evenly" mean? If you are a beginner who doesn't know what the guru's mind is, then do as the master Karma Chagmey instructs: "Just imagine that whatever the guru's mind is, is also now yours. No more and no less, as if you are stamped from the same mold. Your state of mind is identical with the guru's." Merely feel confident that this is so, and remain without being interrupted by any thought about this or that, past, present or future. After remaining like that for a while, dedicate the merit. According to Karma Chagmey, "That is good enough for a beginner. Just feel confident that the guru's mind and your own are now one."

If you have already been introduced to the state of rigpa, then you can have a different type of confidence. On one side there is the guru's mind, which is identical with that of dharmakaya Samantabhadra, and on the other, there is your own buddha nature that is present as the ground nature of your mind. These two do not differ in the slightest, neither in size nor in quality. Like space mingling with space, your mind mingles with that of the guru, so as to be indivisible, of one taste. Be confident that your realized mind and the guru's are no different, then settle into the state of equanimity.

At this point there are two options: You can imagine either that your entire being dissolves into the guru or that you have now obtained every single enlightened quality that the guru possesses, without a single exception. Whether you think of that as dissolving your normal state of mind into the ultimate wisdom or whether you think of it as the ultimate wisdom being transferred into your own stream-of-being, which is the final transmission, you are able to realize the state of the guru's mind as indivisible from your own. Either of these ways of settling into equanimity is fine.

To reiterate, first you receive the four empowerments and then mingle your mind with the guru's and settle in equanimity—completely and utterly letting go. Continue as you know best, which is an individual matter. Simply feel confident that you have received all the blessings, and then let be.

If you do not have spontaneous trust and devotion from the very start, there is great benefit in trying to develop it. Then as you progress on the path, your devotion will be as steady as your stability in self-existing awareness.

According to Paltrül Rinpoche, "To gauge your level of realization, you could of course go and present it as an offering to a master, but that is not always necessary. Instead you can be your own judge and offer your realization to yourself.[32] Get it authenticated in this simple way: As you go along training in the composure of awareness, if you notice that you have more trust and devotion, more compassion, less attachment, and more renunciation, kindness, and so forth, then I can assure you that you are moving along the correct path. However, if you notice that you are becoming more insensitive, that you do not trust any master you meet, that the more time you spend with your guru the less appreciation you have, and that you don't care whether sentient beings suffer or not and you are more unfeeling and cold, then I can certify that you are moving in the wrong direction. Meditating while continuing along the wrong track will bring no benefit whatsoever, as it is not a direct cause for enlightenment." This is how you can see for yourself whether your practice is going well. In short, devotion and compassion increase as stability in rigpa improves.

Whether you practice guru sadhana on the outer, inner, or innermost level, or as the ultimate manner of simplicity, you should keep the destination—the expanse of naked awareness—clearly in mind. In other words, whether you call your practice Mahamudra or Dzogchen, and whichever level you are at, you are still aiming at the same goal. The guru's mind, having realized rigpa in actuality, is the state of mind you must mingle with. The guru is the vehicle for arriving at the realization that the guru's mind and yours are in nature indivisible. This is the ultimate guru yoga taught in all the different traditions.

Tulku Urgyen Rinpoche's *Ultimate Guru Sadhana of Simplicity* belongs to that type of guru yoga. It is the way to realize the dharmakaya level of mingling the guru's mind and your own mind. In that sense it is identical with the *Tigle Gyachen*,[33] which is the innermost unexcelled level of practice in the Nyingtik tradition. There are many other practices like that, but they are all equal in recognizing that the awakened state the guru has realized and your own state of rigpa are not different in any way. Training in that is called the ultimate guru yoga, the real guru yoga. It has to do with realizing the state of rigpa, which is the guru's mind.

Keeping pure samaya supports your practice of guru yoga. There is a famous statement in the teachings that the best friend is pure samaya and the worst enemy is broken samaya. Once you have received teachings or empowerments from someone, you progress by keeping the samayas. There are many details to this, but in short, maintain the sacred bond in terms of body, speech, and mind. Keeping these ensures progress. On the other hand, if any of these samayas is broken or even damaged, it needs to be mended and purified. If the guru is alive, then whenever you have gone against one of these principles, personally approach your guru and admit to it. If he has passed away, go in front of his remains and apologize. You can also do this in your own practice, since guru sadhana restores the purity of the samayas.

Finally, what is really meant by "root guru"? Whomever you receive teachings from is the root guru for that particular teaching. For example, if you received the details of development and completion stage of a yidam from a specific teacher, then he or she is your root guru for that particular yidam practice. The ultimate root guru, however, is the one who gives the pointing-out instruction so that you recognize the nature of mind. That person is the true root guru because he or she has taught you how to attain complete realization.

# 16

## THE GURU PRINCIPLE

*Sogyal Rinpoche*

When we talk about the lama, the master or the guru principle, it is important to remember that the guru is not merely a person. The guru represents the inspiration of truth; he embodies the crystallization of the blessing, compassion and wisdom of all buddhas and all masters.

Perhaps the most moving and accurate account of the true nature of the master I have ever heard comes from my master Jamyang Khyentse Chökyi Lodrö. He said that although our true nature is buddha, it has been obscured from beginningless time by a cloud of ignorance and confusion. This true nature, our buddha nature, however, has never completely surrendered to the tyranny of ignorance; somewhere it is always rebelling against its domination.

Our buddha nature, then, has an active aspect, which is our 'inner teacher'. From the very moment we became obscured, this inner teacher has been working tirelessly for us, tirelessly trying to bring us back to the radiance and spaciousness of our true being. Not for one second, Jamyang Khyentse said, has the inner teacher abandoned us or given up on us. In its infinite compassion, one with the infinite compassion of all the buddhas and all the enlightened beings, it has been ceaselessly working for our evolution—not

From Sogyal Rinpoche, *Dzogchen and Padmasambhava* (Santa Cruz, Calif.: Rigpa Publications, 1990), "The Guru Principle."

only in this life but in all our past lives also—using all kinds of skilful means and all types of situations to teach and awaken us, and to guide us back to the truth. Everyday we can realize how our life is teaching us. It may often be a teaching that we do not want, but we can not run away from its truth, because life just goes on and on teaching us. This is the universality of the guru.

When we have prayed and aspired for the truth for a long time, my master said, and when our karma has become sufficiently purified, this inner teacher actually begins to manifest more clearly and take shape in the form of the *outer teacher* whom we actually encounter. This encounter is the most important of any lifetime. Who is this outer teacher? None other than the embodiment and voice and representative of our inner teacher. He teaches us how to receive the message of our inner teacher, and how to realize the ultimate teacher within, restoring a belief and confidence in ourselves and thereby freeing us from the suffering that comes from not knowing our true nature.

The outer teacher is a messenger, the inner teacher the truth. If someone wants to reach you on the telephone, for example, they call *your* number. In the very same way, the buddhas call you through your buddha-nature, your inner teacher. He is the direct line, but until you know how to listen and hear, it is your outer teacher who answers the phone. They work through him, to you. It is important not to lose the sense of this connection between the inner and outer teacher. The outer teacher is teaching you how to find yourself, how to find the buddha in you. He is introducing you to yourself, and until you find the buddha within you, he is that substitute.

In the Dzogchen teachings, Padmasambhava embodies this universal principle. He is regarded as the incarnation of the buddhas of the past, the representative of the buddhas of the present, and the source from whom all the future buddhas will come. He is the timeless guru, within whose being all masters are embodied. Many of the great masters of the Tibetan tradition have drawn inspiration from him, and *are* his emanations, like the rays that burst out from the sun. So if you connect with any one of them, they will eventually lead to him. His human connection with you is your teacher. It is through your teacher that you can recognize him.

For whatever you consider Padmasambhava to be, or whatever you consider your master to be, is what Dzogchen is. That absolute state of Dzogpachenpo is the *wisdom mind* of your teacher. So you do not regard him as an ordinary human being. What he embodies is the truth or wisdom that he

135

touches and inspires in you. So for you he comes to embody the wisdom mind, so much so that just to think of him crystallizes all the teaching and practice into an essential flavor. The master is not separate from the teaching; in fact, he is the energy, truth and compassion of the Dharma. He is the embodiment of Dzogpachenpo, so whenever you think of your master or Padmasambhava, it invokes this blessing into your presence. This is the principal source of inspiration for Dzogchen practice.

As Kalu Rinpoche said in his last public teaching: "What we call the buddha, or the lama, is not material in the same way as iron, crystal, gold or silver are. You should never think of them with this sort of materialistic attitude. The essence of the lama or buddha is emptiness; their nature, clarity; their appearance, the play of unimpeded awareness. Apart from that, they have no real, material form, shape, or color whatsoever—like the empty luminosity of space. When we know them to be like that, we can develop faith, merge our minds with theirs, and let our minds rest peacefully. This attitude and practice are most important."[34]

We need to humanize the truth in order to make it accessible to us. Without that how could we possibly understand the absolute? For us, the guru is the human face of the truth. And as Dilgo Khyentse Rinpoche says, "There is no buddha who became enlightened without having relied upon a spiritual teacher." You cannot realize the absolute within the domain of the ordinary mind. And the path beyond the mind is through the heart and through *devotion*. As Buddha told Shariputra, "It is through devotion, and devotion alone, that one realizes the absolute."

Nyoshul Khen Rinpoche points out: "According to Dzogchen, and the special approach of the great Dzogchen master, Shri Singha, there is a way of recognizing the nature of mind solely through devotion. There are cases of practitioners who simply through their heartfelt devotion attained realization, even though their teacher had already passed away or was nowhere near them physically. Because of their prayers and devotion, the nature of mind was introduced. The most famous example is that of Longchenpa and Jigmé Lingpa."[35]

Dzogchen cannot be realized merely with the intellect or the thinking of the ordinary mind, but only through the purity of the heart. For Dzogchen is beyond mind; it is the wisdom of rigpa, which can only be transmitted via a closeness of the heart between master and disciple.

When the master is able to open your innermost heart, and offers you an undeniably powerful glimpse of the nature of your mind, a wave of joyful gratitude surges up in you toward the one who helped you to see, and the truth that you now realize the master embodies in his or her being, teachings, and wisdom mind. That uncontrived, genuine feeling is always rooted in repeated, undeniable, inner experience—a repeated clarity of direct recognition—and *this* is what we call devotion, *mögü* in Tibetan. *Mögü* means "longing and respect": *respect* for the master, which grows deeper and deeper as you understand more and more who he or she really is, and *longing* for what he or she can introduce in you, because you have come to know the master is your heart link with the absolute truth and the embodiment of the true nature of your mind.

So then, it is essential to know what real devotion is. It is not mindless adoration; it is not abdication of your responsibility to yourself, nor undiscriminating following of another's personality or whim. Real devotion is an unbroken receptivity to the truth. Real devotion is rooted in an awed and reverent gratitude, but one that is lucid, grounded, and intelligent.

The more I come to reflect on devotion and its place and role in the overall vision of the teachings, the more deeply I realize that it is essentially a skillful and powerful means of making us more receptive to the truth of the master's teaching. Devotion, then, is in one sense the most practical way of ensuring a total respect for, and therefore openness to, the teachings, as embodied by the master and transmitted through him or her. The more devoted you are, the more open you are to the teachings; the more open you are to the teachings, the more chance there is for them to penetrate your heart and mind, and so bring about a complete spiritual transformation.

Devotion becomes the purest, quickest, and simplest way to realize the nature of our mind and all things. As we progress in it, the process reveals itself as wonderfully interdependent: We, from our side, try continually to generate devotion, the devotion we arouse itself generates glimpses of the nature of mind, and these glimpses only enhance and deepen our devotion to the master who is inspiring us. So in the end devotion springs out of wisdom: devotion and the living experience of the nature of mind become inseparable, and inspire one another.

As Dilgo Khyentse Rinpoche says: "Devotion is the essence of the path, and if we have in mind nothing but the guru and feel nothing but fervent devotion, whatever occurs is perceived as his blessing. If we simply practice with this constantly present devotion, this is prayer itself.

When all thoughts are imbued with devotion to the guru, there is a natural confidence that this will take care of whatever may happen. All forms are the guru, all sounds are prayer, and all gross and subtle thoughts arise as devotion. Everything is spontaneously liberated in the absolute nature, like knots untied in the sky."[36]

This natural confidence, whatever may happen, gives us an innate ability to invoke the warmth and blessing of the truth in times of need. It comes from having seen the view, and from this also comes tremendous compassion. As Nyoshul Khen Rinpoche explains: "Once you realize the true meaning of emptiness or Dzogpachenpo, effortless compassion arises for all beings who have not realized; if tears could express that compassion, you would cry without end." These three: the view, devotion and compassion, are indivisible, one flavor—the taste of Dharma.

*17*

# GURU YOGA &
# YIDAM PRACTICE

## *Mingyur Rinpoche*

The main principle underlying guru yoga is the understanding that your own essence and the guru's essence are indivisible. Recognizing this purifies you of the effects of your harmful actions, negative karma, and obscurations. It also allows you to experience the infusion of blessings that come through guru yoga practice. In a sense, when you train in guru yoga in any formal way, you do so based on accepting that it is ultimately your own basic nature, as a state of original wakefulness that is manifesting externally in the form of a guru or a buddha. By acknowledging this, you can effectively practice guru yoga. On the basis of such an understanding, you can truly appreciate your personal guru to be one with all the buddhas in essence.

This guru yoga principle can be applied to any yidam or dharmapala practice.[37] In Vajrayana we often hear it said that there is an indivisibility of the guru and the deity or the protector. By practicing in such a way, you apply the guru yoga principle to the yidam practice or to a protector practice. That understanding of the essential identity of the guru and the yidam or protector—and ultimately the guru and oneself—is realized in actuality. According to the Vajrayana teachings, that is how the yidam can actually bestow blessings, which bring about not only the ordinary states of spiritual

Printed with permission of the author. © 2004 by Yongey Mingyur Rinpoche. Translated by Lama Chökyi Nyima (Richard Barron).

attainment but also the sublime attainment of enlightenment itself. But if you practice a deity meditation without applying the guru yoga principle, then you merely gain the ordinary benefits of longevity, health, and prosperity. The ultimate attainment of enlightenment through yidam practice is gained only by realizing that the yidam, the guru, and one's own mind are in essence indivisible.

We could say that all aspects of our formal practice to which we bring that understanding are forms of guru yoga. What determines whether a practice is guru yoga is the underlying acknowledgment on the part of the practitioner. In regard to Vajrasattva meditation, whether you are visualizing Vajrasattva in the sky in front of you or above your head, or yourself as Vajrasattva, or whether you are resting in the more general awareness of all forms as the form of the deity, all sounds as mantra, and all thoughts and awareness as the play of wakefulness, it's all yidam practice. If you also apply the guru yoga principle of realizing the indivisible identity of your own essence and the essence of the guru and the essence of the deity, then it becomes effectively a guru yoga practice. It's more a question of your ability to apply the guru yoga principle rather than it being a formal practice of this or that type.

The underlying principle of the yidam practice is that each one of us has a particular predominant affinity for one of the buddha families: *vajra, ratna, padma, karma,* and *buddha.* The wisdom deities of those particular families embody a state in which the latent potential has become completely evident and all obscuration, negativity, and impurity has been removed. Because of our connection to a particular wisdom deity being actualized through meditation upon a deity of that family, we have a very direct avenue to bring about our own purification and attainment in this lifetime. Moreover, it becomes possible to make our latent potential fully evident.

To be really effective, yidam practice must be based upon a significant understanding of emptiness. When we train in deity practice, we are dealing with the way in which our ordinary mind perceives the inanimate universe as a kind of container and the life forms within that universe as its contents. The mind ordinarily perceives the inanimate and the animate universe in an incorrect or impure way; likewise, we experience our physical body, speech, and mind in an impure, distorted manner. The mind in its ordinary functioning is very fixated upon defining things through their mundane characteristics, investing them with a reality that they do not actually have. With yidam practice, we are replacing that way of perceiving things with a new way of perceiving. We train in perceiving the inanimate universe as the pure realm or the immeasurable mansion of the deity and all beings in that universe as the manifestations or mandala of deities. We train in perceiving all sounds as mantra and all thoughts and mental events as the play of enlightened mind.

Practicing in this way purifies a vast number of conceptual thoughts and delusions by purifying the normal mistaken way of perceiving, in the form of the karmic or emotional energies within the body. Purifying these energies leaves room for the pure wisdom energies. In short, this attitude of pure perception clears the subtle energy currents, and hence these energies help the mind to become even purer. To use the analogy of a horse and rider, the subtle energy is like a steed upon which the mind is mounted, and whichever way that subtle energy moves tends to influence the way in which the mind moves.

Another reason for yidam practice is that all the qualities, kayas, and wisdoms of buddhahood are present in all beings, and their nature is pure from the very beginning. The nature of confusion is emptiness and therefore is the dharmakaya of all buddhas. We too possess these spontaneously present kayas and wisdoms. Deity practice is a way to acknowledge and remind ourselves that, since the very beginning, "I am a deity". When meditating, everything we see and hear and all mental events in our consciousness are all naturally the original state of wakefulness, the buddha nature. By doing yidam practice, we are recognizing what is for what it is.

# 18

# THE HEALING

# MEDITATION OF DEVOTION

*Tulku Thondup*

Everything is one in Buddha-nature: the mind, the earth and stars, time and space. Everything is perfect in this oneness, even that which we ordinarily see as imperfection. Buddha-nature is in all living beings, and in the particulars of everyday life. Ultimately, Buddha is beyond images, words, or concepts, which are creations of dualistic mind.

This is what Buddhists believe. So when some Westerners become interested in Buddhism, they could be disappointed to learn about the practice of devotion. They say something like: "This is what we wanted to leave behind, praying to a high authority outside ourselves." What a funny situation, to run away from devotion, only to find belief and prayer waiting around the next corner!

Yes, it's true that the whole universe is a Buddha-nature, and that peace lies within us. So why practice devotion? It is one way we have of letting go of the idea of self. Belief helps us to open. It is the releasing of doubts and fears. Being open and receptive is a way of asking for the help we need.

Certain schools of Buddhism emphasize the act of bowing as a devotional practice. This is a simple way of surrendering self. It acknowledges the belief that grasping and trying to control everything leads us away

---

From Tulku Thondup, *The Healing Power of Mind* (Boston: Shambhala Publications, 1998).

from wisdom. Belief is also possible outside of institutional religion. For example, the Twelve Steps program of Alcoholics Anonymous emphasizes giving up the tight little "I" that tries to control. It acknowledges the need for help from a "higher power," in whatever way that is understood by the individual.

In Buddhism, devotion is the development of trust in the Buddha as guide; trust in the Dharma, the teachings of Buddhism, as the path; and trust in the Sangha, the Buddhist community, as support on the spiritual journey.

Devotion means asking for strength along the path. The fulfillment of our spiritual needs may not always be in the form we desire or expect, according to our timetable. The important point of belief is openness; that is the way to receive blessings and relieve suffering. Quoting Guru Padmasambhava, Paltrül Rinpoche writes:

If your mind is free from doubts, wishes will be achieved.
If you have total trusting devotion, blessings will enter you.
Devotion is like the sun, melting our grasping at self
and allowing our true nature to shine through.

Quoting Drigung Kyobpa Rinpoche, Paltrül Rinpoche writes:

From the snow-mountain-like master ...
Without the touch of the rays of sun like devotion
The stream-like blessing will not flow.
So exert your mind in the training of devotion.

If we do not have trust or devotion, even if the Buddha is standing in front of us in person, we will receive hardly any benefits, for our minds, which are the only key to our spiritual growth, are not ready for the opportunity. That is why a Tibetan proverb says:

From whomever one sees as a Buddha
The blessings are received as from a Buddha.
From whomever one sees as a fool
The effects come as from a fool.

So the Buddha-nature is everywhere, but it is possible to train in devotion by meditating upon the Buddha, for instance in the form of a statue or a mental image. The statue itself will not change our lives; it is our minds that can open through the act of devotion. This is the essence of skillful means.

Spiritual objects can inspire us, but the main factor is not any object. It is the way we see it, positively, and the way we feel, with devotion and trust, that help us along the path.

Relying on any spiritual object or mental image is a way to empower ourselves with the joy that arises from the Buddha within us all.

Untill now, I have emphasized how anyone can meditate upon a source of power of his or her own choosing, such as the sun, the moon, or some personal image. But here I will describe a source of power that is specifically Buddhist, a devotional meditation upon Guru Rinpoche, Padmasambhava, the ninth-century founder of Tibetan Buddhism who embodies all the enlightened ones—Buddhas, divinities, saints, and sages.

There are so many spiritual representations that could inspire us as a source of power. We could, for example, meditate upon Shakyamuni Buddha to help us gain wisdom; or the Medicine Buddha for healing; or Tara, the Buddha in the female form, for pacifying all fears and dangers. I have chosen Guru Rinpoche because of his boundless compassion, which has helped so many people over the centuries who have called upon him, and because I myself trained in his lineage. Guru Rinpoche's majestic presence is the vajra manifestation of absolute Buddhahood, the overwhelming strength and bliss of the universe that pacifies all turmoil.

As background to this meditation, I will go into quite a bit of detail about how we might visualize the image of Guru Rinpoche. Every detail of the iconography associated with a sacred image gives a teaching, and these signs, symbols, colors, and gestures can arouse positive feelings in us that mirror those teachings, both one by one, and as they are seen and felt as part of a whole.

Details can help an experienced meditator rest in awareness of a mental image that is full and rich. But don't worry if you lack experience and skill; simply visualize however much you feel comfortable with. In the following guided meditation, what really matters is the feelings the words attempt to convey. Use the feelings to call up in your mind an image of Padmasambhava that is simple but heartfelt. If you merely feel the warmth and presence of Padmasambhava that in itself can be very healing.

Remember, too, that artistic renderings such as those in my book are meant as an aid. A picture or stature may inspire you, teach you, or help as a starting point for meditation, but don't feel limited by it. What matters in visualization is the image in your own mind, and the warmth and openness that can come through devotion.

## Invoking the Majestic Image of Padmasambhava

Like a flower that blossoms from emptiness, the majestic presence of Padmasambhava arises from the imagination. In an aura of beautiful light, the radiant and youthful Guru Rinpoche sits on a clear, shining moon disc, above a bright, warm sun disc. The moon and sun are resting just above a huge lotus plant, fragrant and perfumed, fresh with moisture. The lotus has thousands of brilliantly colored petals.

The sun, moon, and lotus are symbols of his birth. He was born by "immaculate birth" in the "Lotus Buddha Family" out of the union of wisdom (sun) and compassion (moon).

Guru Rinpoche's face is white with a reddish hue, ever youthful and wise, beyond the realm of change and aging. His smile of joy is beyond suffering. His clear, unblinking, loving eyes bring universal bliss, healing our mind in its every movement and mood and our body in every cell and atom.

His robes radiate light. His white inner robe and red gown symbolize the enlightenment of a bodhisattva, who helps all suffering beings in this world. His blue outer gown symbolizes the perfection of the esoteric attainments, and he wears the shawl of perfect monkhood. A brocade cloak is a symbol that all religious trainings are one in universal truth. This cloak, and his hat and shoes, are also reminders of his mystical powers. They are gifts from a king of Zahora who was amazed at his powers. The king had tried to burn him, but Guru Rinpoche simply transformed the fire into water, now known as Rewalsar Lake in India.

Guru Rinpoche holds the symbols of the teachings. A golden vajra in his right hand symbolizes indestructible skill and power, the masculine principle. In his left hand he cradles a skull, which holds a vase filled with the nectar of immortality. The skull symbolizes the union of emptiness and bliss, which are the feminine principle. The vase and nectar symbolize long life and the timeless truth of the Buddha-nature.

In Buddhism, esoteric masters are often spiritually united with a female consort. The wisdom of femininity is represented here by a trident, which rests in the fold of Guru Rinpoche's left arm. The three sharp points of the trident signify the three true natures of the mind: openness, clarity, and the power of compassion. Three heads ornament the trident, representing the three Buddha bodies: the skeletal head is total openness, the mature image is the pure form of the Buddha as it is, and the youth is the impure image of Buddha as seen by ordinary minds.

Among the other symbols are locks of hair hanging from the trident. These are a reminder of the practice in charnel grounds of meditating upon the dissolution of the body, and the liberation of realizing the truth of living and dying.

In his limitless wisdom, Guru Rinpoche knows every happening in the universe, simultaneously and without distracting from his absolute open nature. His infinite compassion is open to the whole universe and reaches every single being, as a mother showers her only child with love.

Now that we have some familiarity with this image, here is an extended devotional meditation.

## CALLING UPON THE STRENGTH AND COMPASSION OF PADMASAMBHAVA

Visualize that you are sitting at some lofty spot such as a mountaintop, looking at the vast, clear blue sky. Enjoy the view for a few minutes, resting in the openness. The image of being at a high spot raises your mind above your own turmoil. The open sky clears your mind of the images, thoughts, and emotions that constantly crowd it.

From this openness, first imagine the lotus seat with its beautiful petals, then the sun disc, and above it the moon disc. Finally, Guru Rinpoche radiantly appears.

Feel the boundless peace and warmth of this loving divinity, and rest comfortably for some time in those feelings. Allow devotion to melt your heart. As you bring your awareness to the image, give yourself wholly to it, not just as a form created by your mind, but as the true and pure healing Guru.

Now imagine the whole earth filled with all kinds of beings with devotional hearts, cheerful faces, and joyful eyes. All are looking at the loving, beautiful, and powerful face of Guru Rinpoche, the source of all healing. Imagine that you hear them all saying a mantra in one voice, in a thunderous and sweet melody. The mantra is a prayer to Guru Rinpoche, a means of healing our problems, a joyous expression of mental and physical energies, a celebration of the presence of this divinity, a meditation on pure sound that is in itself the nature of oneness.

From the depths of your heart, chant the mantra of Guru Rinpoche, in either of the forms that follow:

*In Tibetanized Sanskrit*

OM AH HUNG BEDZAR GURU PEMA SIDDHI HUNG

*In Sanskrit*

OM AH HUM VAJRA GURU PADMA SIDDHI HUM

A translation of this is: "The embodiment of the body, speech, and mind of the Buddhas, O Padma(sambhava), please grant all blessings."

As a result of the prayers and openness, beams of blessing lights of various colors from Guru Rinpoche touch you, bringing warmth and openness in body and mind. These lights are not just beautiful, pure forms but the energy of peace, warmth, bliss, and openness. Allow this feeling to pervade you, through every pore and door, dispelling all worry and distress, as sunlight dispels darkness. Feel that your whole body is transformed into light and healing energy.

Repeat the mantra many times, giving yourself wholly to the sound. Imagine that your prayers have opened the minds of all beings to devotional joy, and the light from Guru Rinpoche radiates in every direction, dispelling all the confusion, sadness, and pain. All beings are liberated in a mighty chorus of chanting. The chant fills the universe, which becomes one in sound, light, and joy.

Rejoice in this warmth and openness. Allow all concepts and feelings to merge into an ocean of devotional peace, in which there are no distinctions or boundaries, beyond pain and excitement, good and bad, this and that, you and me, but where all are one and the same.

Although the higher purpose of this meditation is spiritual realization, you could also contemplate Guru Padmasambhava as the source of power for ordinary healing of emotional or physical problems, by visualizing any form of healing energy emanating from the image, such as laser-like light. Or imagine healing nectar from Guru Rinpoche's vase flowing into you, first washing away all your mental, emotional, and physical suffering, then filling your whole body and mind with peace and strength. Guru Rinpoche could also be the source of energy during meditations in which another person acts as a healer for you.

Whatever the visualization, you can repeat it during one session as often as it feels comfortable. When you are doing your daily chores, from time to time bring the open feeling of the meditation into your life. You can even chant the mantra out loud, or silently when you are in public.

## MEDITATING IN OPENNESS

In the higher Buddhist view, appearances rise from emptiness and dissolve back again. So we began this devotional meditation by entering the state of openness, letting the visualization arise like a reflection in a clear mirror. After resting in tranquility upon the imagery, we end in openness and oneness again. It is a process like birth, living, and dying, a good way to practice letting come and go. Always, at the end of meditation, simply be in the openness of your state of mind, just as it is, without grasping.

Depending on our state of mind, we may rest longer and longer in the space of openness. We may begin with visualization, and then drop technique and simply meditate in an open way. Then it doesn't matter so much what the experience of meditation is. It may be possible to merge the experience, the experiencer, and the ways of experiencing all into oneness.

Don't try to shape the openness, or see it as one thing or another, or gain anything from it. Just let things be. This is the way to find your center. If you trust your true nature, you do not need to look for another center. Just be open and aware.

As long as we are subject to the possibility of suffering, meditation can deepen and strengthen us. As we realize the nature of openness, meditation melts into everyday life.

Relying on external healing sources is helpful and even essential as long as we are under the control of dualistic concepts and depend on external objects. However, it is important to understand that the ultimate healing is going beyond dependence on external forces. It is securing our own peaceful, open nature so that we can reach all through that peace and openness.

# 19

# SONG TO MANDARAVA

*Padmasambhava*

Listen here a while, Mandarava flower!
Pay heed without distraction, perfect princess!

You have wandered in samsara, in the miseries of existence,
Like an ocean without escape, for so long.
Now is the time to achieve the lasting aim.
You must practice the divine Dharma, young princess!

There's no end to the tasks and deeds of this world,
And you have pointlessly occupied yourself for so long.
Now is the time to think in different ways.
You must reach liberation, young princess!

By the power of attachment, you have yearned for relatives,
And nurtured thankless companions for so long.
Now is the time to train in lucid emptiness.
You must look into your mind, young princess!

From the *Golden Garland Chronicles*, the extensive life-story of Padmasambhava.

By the power of anger, you have raged against enemies,
And brought ruin to yourself and others for so long.
Now is the time to tame your own emotions.
You must soften your selfishness, young princess!

By the power of delusion, you have drifted in samsara's common states
And slept like a shameless corpse for so long.
Now is the time to persevere in the undistracted practice.
You must bring forth your brightest best, young princess!

By the power of conceit, you have taken the high seat of influence,
Giving lofty advice to others for so long.
Now is the time to be a counsel to yourself.
You must repel your own faults, young princess!

By the power of jealousy, you have disparaged others
And engaged in rivalry for so long.
Now is the time to follow in the footsteps of the conquerors.
You must train in pure perception, young princess!

By creating evil karma, you have floundered in the ocean of samsara,
Taking inferior rebirths for so long.
Now is the time to train in the deity's form of empty presence.
Cultivate the development stage, young princess!

Deluded idle gossip promotes only more conditioned states,
And you have given yourself to endless chatter for so long.
Now is the time to chant the essence mantra of empty sound.
Keep this in your mind, young princess!

Through so many thoughts, myriad emotions arise,
And you have submitted yourself to deluded thinking for so long.
Now is the time to capture the kingdom of empty bliss.
Train in the nonarising, young princess!

The profound vehicle is like taking a precious shortcut.
While you have the chance to enter this path,
Now is the time to train in all-pervasive pure perception.
Generate devotion, young princess!

# PART THREE

# THE MAIN PRACTICE

# 20

# CREATION AND COMPLETION

*Jamgön Kongtrül*

Creation stage is mainly for undermining the deluded appearance of
    ordinary reality,
and completion stage for undermining attachment to the reality of that
    creation stage itself.
The actualization of Vajradhara in a single lifetime
will not be achieved if creation and completion are separated.

Even though the unity of creation and completion is the profound
    approach,
until the movement of thoughts arises as meditation,
it is not the real practice of unity, so you should alternate their practice.
Contrived unity is a mental fabrication and should be abandoned.

In the meditation of creation stage there are four aspects
of which you should gain at least some understanding:
the basis of purification, that which is to be purified, that which purifies,
    and the result of purification.
The basis of purification is the eternal, non-composite realm of reality
that fully permeates all beings as the buddha nature.

From Jamgön Kongtrul Lodrö Thayé, *Creation and Completion: Essential Points of Tantric Meditation*, translated by Sarah Harding (Boston: Wisdom Publications, 1996), pp. 36–37, 39–42.

Sentient beings thus also possess the qualities of the Body of Reality, such as
     the marks and signs,
that exist as an integral aspect of awareness: this is the basis for purification.
That which is to be purified is the incidental blemish of delusion
arising from ignorance without beginning, which obscures this buddha
     nature.

An example would be the sun obscured by clouds.
The sunshine is the capacity to manifest inherent qualities.
The clouds are incidental blemishes that could clear away.
Emotional and cognitive obscurations and those of meditative absorption
     are what is to be purified.

That which purifies are the many different form yogas,
such as the creation of the Five Actual Enlightening Factors,
the Four Vajras and the Three Rituals, which purify, respectively,
womb-birth, egg-birth, and moisture-warmth-birth.
Miraculous birth is purified by the instantaneously complete creation.

Although scholars have applied many conflicting explanations,
we could summarize in the knowledge that there is nothing really
     contradictory.
From the initial meditation on the deity visualization up to the dissolution,
each ritual has its own sequence, but to generalize:
the basis on which purification takes place is the buddha nature itself;
that which is purified is the delusion of the infant consciousness from the
     time it enters and is born
through the time of the intermediate state of death.

There are different ritual sequences in the old and new traditions,
but with respect to purifying the blemishes of deluded emotion they are the
     same.
For instance, for disease of the eyes one primarily uses a scalpel,
or orally administers cooling or warming substances for imbalances in heat
     or cold,
the particular remedy depending on the kind of disease.

There are as many methods of purification as there are problems to be
    purified.
For the eyes, whether they are restored with instruments or healed with
    medicine,
for relieving the pain and suffering, it is the same.
Similarly, there are various ritual sequences in the new and old traditions,
but in so far as they all purify the thoughts of afflictive emotions, there is
    no difference.

Whether one meditates on an elaborate or concise version of creation stage,
    there are three main points:
Clarity of form purifies attachment to the appearing object,
recollecting the purity frees one from clinging to corporeality,
and maintaining pride vanquishes clinging to ordinary self.

As to the first, initially visualize each individual part, such as the head,
    hands, feet, and so on,
and when somewhat used to that meditate clearly on the entire form.
When meditation is not stable and thoughts come and go,
focus your awareness on an implement such as the vajra in the hand.

If you are languishing, focus on the crossed legs, and if sinking,
focus on something like a jewel in the deity's crown.
Then if there aren't so many active thoughts but the form is unclear and
    murky,
set before you a picture or statue that is well made and appropriately
    painted,
and without thinking, look at it for a long time.
Then immediately generate your own body in that image.
This will enhance the former meditation.

You may recollect the appropriate purities,
but this mental exercise might just add to discursive thoughts.
For the beginner it will become the cause of unclear, scattered meditation.
It is better to meditate on the deity's form as empty and light, like a
    rainbow,
and to know that the one who is doing that is one's own mind.

Mind itself, intrinsically free of a basis, is emptiness,
and the demonstration of its special qualities
is the arising of forms of faces, hands, and ornaments.

Do not meditate on pride; cut through the root of ego-clinging.
When ego-clinging is destroyed, wherever one's mind focuses, its essence
    arises vividly.

In this way, by meditation on the creation stage with effort,
while actually meditating, the impact of "real" appearances will be
    diminished,
and without meditating, the deity arises.
This is the lesser experience of luminous appearance.

When all deluded appearances, regardless of meditating or not,
arise as the deity and divine palace, it is intermediate luminous appearance.
When you meditate on the deity and form and formless beings see you as
    that deity,
it is the great luminous appearance, called a maturation knowledge-holder
    in the Ancient tradition.

The clear form of the deity is the luminous appearance of your own mind,
and the unclear, dissatisfying experience is also your mind!
So also, mind is the one who desires clarity and tries again,
and mind is the wisdom deity and guru.
Everything is mind's appearance, and yet mind itself is uncontrived.

The beauty of this ultimate essential point of the approach of the two stages
is that no matter which of the many creation stages you do,
if you apply clear awareness and mindfulness that is merely undistracted,
when the meditation is clear, it arises as clarity-emptiness and when
    obscure, as obscurity-emptiness!

In general, creation stage is a contrivance,
but the path of contrivance leads to the authentic natural state.
With the mental conviction of the lack of reality in the root or ground
of deluded grasping to deluded appearance,
resting in a pristine state is completion stage itself, the actual natural state.

The first stage is the provisional meaning and the latter the definitive
    meaning.

It is said that if you understand mind, knowing this one thing illuminates
    everything,
but if you don't understand mind, knowing everything obscures the one
    thing.
The great master Noble Nagarjuna said it this way:
"Where there is appropriate understanding of emptiness, all things are
    appropriate,
and if there is no appropriate understanding of emptiness, nothing is."

All of the various designations, such as
Great Seal, Great Perfection, Middle Path, unembellished, ultimate,
enlightened intention of the victorious ones, intrinsic nature,
perfection of wisdom, view, meditation, and action, and so on,
indicate that mind itself and the true nature of objects
have no true reality whatsoever and are beyond intellect and inexpressible.
This one point could well be the synopsis of all teachings.

In bringing about meditation on the nature of mind in this way,
the power of devotion causes it to arise from within
 and more is really unnecessary.
However, most ordinary people know very little about the meditation
    subject—the nature of mind—
and their meditation could prove ineffectual.

# 21

## THE DEITY AND
## BUDDHA NATURE

*Lama Putse, Pema Thasi*

In the practice of the development stage, the three samadhis are actually the most important aspect. It is said that one should erect the framework of the three samadhis like pitching a tent. The three samadhis are the samadhi of suchness, the samadhi of illumination, and the samadhi of the seed syllable. They are explained in terms of what is to be purified, that which purifies, and the outcome of purification.

The first, the samadhi of suchness purifies the experience of dying. At some point or another, we are going to die. The experiences that occur while we pass away can be purified by means of training in the samadhi of suchness. There are different bardo states, which include the bardos of death, dharmata, and becoming. These states occur from the moment of leaving the body, up till and including taking rebirth within one of the six realms. Some beings remain in the bardo of becoming for a very short period, and some remain for a long time, but generally speaking it lasts about forty-nine days. Training in the samadhi of illumination purifies this bardo state. At some point, we reconnect with a new life in a womb, egg, or such, and this birth process is purified by the samadhi of the seed syllable.

From *Teachings of the 35-Day Practice*. © 2004 by Rangjung Yeshe Publications.

The outcome of the three samadhis is that by the samadhi of suchness we realize the dharmakaya, by the samadhi of illumination we realize the sambhogakaya, and by the samadhi of the seed syllable we realize the nirmanakaya.

The first of the three samadhis, the samadhi of suchness, is necessary as long as there is something to purify when we pass away from this physical body composed of the four elements. During the death process, the power of these four elements begins to dissipate: Earth dissolves into water, water into fire, fire into wind, and wind into space and consciousness. At that point, there is a moment called the dharmakaya of death, which is luminous cognizance. Ordinary people who do not recognize this moment of the basic state of all things, which is empty and free of constructs, fall unconscious. But this is the moment when good practitioners remain in *tukdam,* samadhi after the body dies.

This failure to recognize is exactly what needs to be purified, and it is cleared up by training in something that corresponds to that moment, something that has a similar mode as the dharmakaya of death. You train in the pride or self-assurance that this state of cognizant emptiness, totally free of constructs, is the emptiness of all phenomena, both outside and inside, whatever appears and exists, all of samsara and nirvana. To simply rest your mind free of concepts for a while until you start to think again is called the samadhi of suchness. Understand this to be the basic framework of the entire sadhana practice. The samadhi of suchness also purifies the clinging to the view of permanence—that the world is solid, real, and permanent—which is one of the two extreme views. This view is purified, as is the habitual tendency for taking rebirth in the formless realms.

In short, by training in the state of emptiness free of all constructs, we purify three things: the death state, the view of permanence, and the habitual tendency for rebirth in the formless realms. Moreover, we plant the seed for realizing the state of dharmakaya.

The Secret Mantra path of Vajrayana has two aspects: means and knowledge. Means is the development stage, while knowledge is the completion stage. The development stage entails visualizing the deity and attending to all the other details, such as training in keeping these things in mind, while the completion stage is to see that even the deity is devoid of any concrete identity whatsoever; it too is emptiness free of constructs. In this context, the samadhi of suchness is the completion stage. It is the most vital point. There is nothing more crucial than this.

Suchness is described in the general Buddhist teachings as the three gates of emancipation—emptiness, signlessness, and wishlessness—corresponding to ground, path, and fruition. We need to train in these to purify the moment of death. However, shortly after dying, with its three experiences of whiteness, redness, and blackness, most people fall unconscious. This unconscious, oblivious state usually lasts for three days, although the length of time is not certain. The body is still present, but the mind is in a blank, unconscious state. After several days, one awakens with the thought, "Where am I? What's happening?" Thinking is reactivated, and the bardo of becoming begins. This bardo experience is purified by the samadhi of illumination, which in the tantras is also called the state of magical compassion that illuminates everything.

The second of the three samadhis also acts as a purifier. After dying and the bardo of dharmata begins, there is a spectacle of light rays and colors. Practitioners who have trained in Tögal experience these as deities. Unless you have some training in Tögal, the whole event flickers past and there is nothing more than just a shimmering of lights and colors, which are intensely bright and overwhelming. For more details, you can read Padmasambhava's *Liberation through Hearing in the Bardo.*

At this time, there also appear the soft, cozy lights of the six realms that more readily attract one's attention. These soft-colored lights seduce you back into the realms of the six classes of beings. To purify this experience, train in the samadhi of illumination. How do you do this? Within the state of great emptiness devoid of constructs, direct your attention toward all sentient beings who do not realize their own basic nature of emptiness. Filled with compassion and loving-kindness, think, "How sad that sentient beings have not realized this!" Let your compassion be like the sun emitting rays of light into all directions. It is said, "The moment of realizing emptiness is the same moment as manifesting compassion." This compassion is the second of the three samadhis.

The samadhi of illumination purifies the bardo state, and it has two aspects: the main part and the subsequent part. The main part is simply to remain without any concepts in emptiness filled with the light rays of compassion. Yet, when we begin to think again, the first thought that should arise is the assurance that the purity of the bardo state is the sambhogakaya. Besides the bardo state, this samadhi also purifies the habitual tendency to hold the view of nihilism, as well as the habitual tendency for rebirth among the gods in the realms of form. Finally, this training plants the seed for realizing the sambhogakaya, the form of the deity adorned with the major and minor marks of excellence. This second samadhi that relates to sambhogakaya is also called magical compassion.

The third is the samadhi of the seed syllable. Here the object to be purified is the moment before taking rebirth, when one is just about to enter one of the six classes of sentient beings. The seed syllable is that which grows into or gives rise to the deity. The deity could be an unelaborate form of a single figure or an elaborate form with many faces, numerous arms, and so forth. These are all produced out of the seed syllable. We should first visualize the seed syllable, as the natural manifestation of nondual compassionate emptiness, in the middle of space like a radiant moon.

The seed syllable is the source of the entire mandala of deities. At the very outset of the development stage, visualize the seed syllable again and again until it becomes clear. Whenever the seed syllable is not clear, return to imagining it until it becomes so. This purifies the mind-energy principle, which takes rebirth. To visualize the mind-energy principle in the form of a seed syllable purifies this tendency to take rebirth. It also establishes the basis for realizing the nirmanakaya. This explains the samadhi of the seed syllable.

No matter what yidam you practice, a further set of three aspects should be complete: distinct appearance, firm pride, and recollection of the pure symbolism.

Distinct appearance means imagining the complete form of Padmasambhava or whatever yidam it is, including the hue of his complexion, his attributes, his garments, even down to the black and white of his eyeballs. Everything should appear very distinct, not blurry or mixed together. If some detail does not appear clearly in your mind, simply train in visualizing this repeatedly until it becomes distinct. Whatever is visualized should not be flat and two dimensional, like a painting, but three dimensional, like a statue. In the beginning, visualize the appearance clearly and distinctly, yet empty like the reflection in a mirror or the moon in water. It is visible but devoid of self-nature like a rainbow, transparent and insubstantial.

Next is firm pride. Mundane pride is to think, "I'm great, greater than others. I'm rich. I know this and that. I'm special." This is the normal type of conceit or pride, but that is not what is meant here. Here we are dealing with the pride of self-assurance, the confidence that one's sugata-essence is identical with that of all the buddhas. Our buddha nature too is endowed with the qualities of the fourfold fearlessness, ten strengths, and so forth.

Yet we ourselves are at the stage of the ground. In the case of the Buddha or Padmasambhava, they are at full-fledged realization, the stage of fruition. Nonetheless, we should have the assurance and pride that our own buddha nature is in fact identical with that of Padmasambhava himself in the state of complete buddhahood. That is the kind of confidence meant here.

Lastly, recollecting the pure symbolism is a matter of utmost importance. Recollecting the purity can be applied to any deity, regardless of whether it is peaceful or wrathful, two-armed or six-armed. In short, every single detail means something, and you should learn this meaning.

As I just mentioned, it is our basic awareness that is visualized in the form of the deity. This buddha nature that is present in all sentient beings, down to and including the tiniest microbes or insects, is no different from the nature of all the buddhas who are endowed with the twofold purity. There is no difference whatsoever in its size or quality.

This twofold purity is the purity of the primordial essence and the purity of having removed the temporary defilements. We possess the first of these two; therefore we are the buddhas of the primordially pure essence. But the real buddhas also possess the second purity: the purity of having removed the emotional and cognitive obscurations. Our nature is exactly the same as that of all fully enlightened buddhas, but our buddha nature does not function as a fully enlightened buddha because it is still enveloped by obscurations.

In order to remove these obscurations, according to the general path of Mahayana we train in the five paramitas of means: generosity, discipline, diligence, patience, and remaining in the equanimity of meditation. We also cultivate discriminating knowledge. According to Vajrayana, we train in the path of unifying means and knowledge, in which the development stage is the skillful means aspect and the completion stage is the knowledge aspect. As we train in these practices, the covers are gradually removed until that which is realized is not a new achievement but a realization of what was already present to begin with.

How can we know we have buddha nature? There is evidence to prove that the buddha nature is definitely present within our stream-of-being. It is proved by the very fact that we are able to feel loving-kindness and compassion for others, that we can feel devotion, renunciation, and disenchantment with samsara, and that we take delight in virtuous actions and regret misdeeds. This is possible only because we possess the sugata-essence. Otherwise, these feelings would not arise. The scriptures say that if this potential were not present, we would never feel weary of samsara, nor would we have the desire to become liberated and fully enlightened.

Among the synonyms for buddha nature are *potential* and *element*. A poisonous snake has the potential to be poisonous; when it bites, it can instantly inject the poison. In the same way, we possess the potential for or basic element of enlightenment, and that is why we can awaken to it.

Right now, we have the basic element of disturbing emotions because we have not abandoned the emotional obscuration. Since we have this potential, when we encounter difficult circumstances we become angry, attached, or proud. Nevertheless, we also have the potential for enlightenment. If we remove the obscurations, we can immediately realize the awakened state. This is like extracting gold from gold ore. The ore possesses the basic element of gold, so if it is smelted, the gold will appear. Similarly, milk has the basic component of butter, and if it is churned, the butter will appear. Water, however, does not have the potential to yield butter. We can churn water for as long as we want, but it will never produce any butter.

Buddha nature is unformed, which means that it is not created due to causes and conditions. It is like space—changeless. If you praise space, it doesn't feel delighted; if you blame space, it doesn't feel sad. Our basic nature does not improve when we become enlightened, nor is it worsened when we are deluded in samsara. It is it unchanging because it is unformed.

We should really understand and acknowledge that all of us possess this basic awareness, the sugata-essence, and it is this basic awareness that is visualized in the form of the deity. We should not think of the buddhas as always up there in the enlightened state while we sentient beings are always down here far, far below, so that the difference between us is as vast as heaven. In nature, we are identical with the buddhas. It is only that in our case, this nature is presently veiled by obscurations. Nonetheless, these obscurations can be removed, and that is exactly what we do when we practice a sadhana.

# 22

## VAJRAYANA MIND TRAINING

*Padmasambhava*

*The Unexcelled Mind Training of Secret Mantra; Instructions on Practicing a Deity with Attributes* ࿇

NAMO GURU DHEVA DAKINI HUNG

The great master Padmakara had gained accomplishment in development and completion and had obtained the empowerment of natural awareness-display. He had reached the siddhi of abiding in the bodily form of Mahamudra. Within the space of manifestation, he played with the whole of appearance and existence. For the benefit of the present king and the princes as well as for the beings of future generations, he gave Lady Tsogyal, the Princess of Kharchen, these real instructions, the Unexcelled Mind Training of Secret Mantra.

Lady Tsogyal said: Emaho, great Master! I request from you the oral instructions on the practice of the deity with attributes. Since one does not attain the siddhis without relying on the yidam deity, how should we practice a yidam deity?

From Padmasambhava, *Dakini Teachings* (Boudhanath: Rangjung Yeshe Publications, 1999), "Vajrayana Mind Training."

The Master said: The meditation on the yidam deity with attributes is of two types: the gradual meditation by a person of lesser mental capacity and the meditation on the nondual body by a person of greater capacity.

## THE PERSON OF LESSER MENTAL CAPACITY

The person of lesser mental capacity should train in the precious mind of enlightenment, bodhichitta. To begin with, you, the practitioner, no matter where you dwell, should rinse your hands, mouth, and face and so forth with secret nectar or the water of the vase and sit down in the fully or half crossed leg position on a comfortable seat.

Then you should direct your mind toward sentient beings of the three realms of samsara who are enmeshed in suffering and the causes of suffering. First, form the bodhichitta of thinking: In order to take them all out of samsara, I shall practice the form of the yidam deity! Next, cultivate the compassion of feeling pity for all sentient beings, the love of wanting them to be free from suffering, the joy of wanting them to meet with happiness, and the impartiality of wanting them not to be apart from happiness.

Following this, utter the three syllables OM AH HUNG and then assume the pride that you are the yidam deity, visualize the particular seed syllable upon a lotus, a sun, and a moon in the yidam's heart center.

Next, imagine that through the rays of light issuing forth from the seed syllable, all the buddhas and bodhisattvas abiding in the ten directions as well as all the gurus, yidams, and dakinis are present in the sky before you. Make prostrations and offerings to them, confess misdeeds, rejoice in their merit, take refuge in the Three Jewels, request them to turn the wheel of Dharma, beseech them not to pass into nirvana, arouse the mind set on enlightenment, and dedicate the roots of virtue. Request the masters and the others to depart and let your visualization subside or dissolve into yourself, whichever is suitable. These steps are all aspects of gathering the accumulation of merit.

Following this, in order to gather the accumulation of wisdom, let your entire body become the nature of light by means of rays of light shining from the seed syllable in your heart center. Also radiate light in the ten directions through which all worldly things as well as all beings become the nature of light. This light is then blessed by all the buddhas and bodhisattvas of the ten directions.

As to absorbing the light back into yourself, the world becomes light that is absorbed into the beings, they dissolve into yourself, and the light of your own body dissolves like the vapor of breath on a mirror. That dissolves gradually into the lotus seat, then into the sun and moon, and then dissolves into the seed syllable. The seed syllable then gradually dissolves into the crescent and the bindu. The light of the bindu is of the nature of mind, the size of one part of a hair tip split one hundred ways. Imagine this again and again.

When your visualization is unclear, utter the Shunyata mantra and so forth, after which you let the visualization vanish.

The fruition of the two kayas results from perfecting these two types of accumulation.

From within the state of emptiness, imagine that your mind-essence is present as the seed syllable of the yidam deity, or imagine that the seed syllable is transformed into a symbolic attribute marked with the seed syllable. From the transformation of this, create the complete head, attributes, and so forth of your particular yidam deity and then the seed syllable upon a sun or moon disc on the lotus in its heart center.

The rays of light shining forth therefrom invite all the sugatas, gurus, yidam deities, and dakinis of the ten directions in the sky before you. Present them then with the five kinds of offerings. Summon the wisdom deities and request them to be seated.

Imagine that the sugatas confer the empowerments upon you and seal you with the lord of the family. Request them then to take leave.

Following this, visualize the three seed syllables upon sun discs in the three centers of your crown, throat, and heart. Consecrate them as being Body, Speech, and Mind. Focus your mind one-pointedly on the yidam deity.

When you then feel weary of meditating, do the recitations.

1. The whispering vajra recitation is to recite so that only your collar can hear it.

2. The melodious vajra recitation is to recite with a tune as at the time of a great accomplishment practice.

3. The secret vajra recitation is to recite mentally.

4. The wheel-like recitation is to imagine that it emerges through your mouth, enters the navel, and dissolves back into the heart center.

5. The garlandlike recitation is to spin the mantra garland around the seed syllable in the heart center and recite one-pointedly while focusing your mind on the syllables.

6. The recitation focused on sound is to recite while focusing your mind only on the sound of the mantra.

## PRACTICES DURING BREAKS

Lady Tsogyal asked the Master: What should we do in the breaks between meditating on the yidam deity?

The Master advised: When you cannot do recitations, then offer tormas and make praises after sounding the bell. Having requested the wisdom deity to take leave, remain as yourself with your ordinary conceptual thinking.

When you, the practitioner, then wish to make offerings for accomplishment, place a painting, statue, or scripture in front of you and make a mandala with scented water strewn with flowers. In one instant, assume the pride of being the yidam deity and send forth rays of light from the seed syllable in your heart center. Invite the dharmakaya and all the form kayas dwelling in the ten directions. Request the dharmakaya to remain in the shrine object and scripture. Request the form kayas to remain in the painting and statue.

Imagine that unfathomable assemblies of the buddhas and bodhisattvas, masters, yidams, and dakinis who dwell in the ten directions are remaining before you. Presenting them with any offerings you have, perform the seven purities in front of them.

At this point you can offer tormas to the yidam deity. To the Dharma protectors, give water tormas, make *tsa-tsa* (clay images), or do other such practices.

Then, if you wish to read the words of all the sugatas, imagine that in an instant your tongue becomes emptiness from which appears a HUNG and from that a one-pronged vajra. Imagine that the reading issues forth from your seed syllable through the tube of the vajra. Innumerable replicas of your body fill the billionfold universe, each one having a vajra in its mouth. Imagine that the reading is heard by all sentient beings and that they are liberated from samsara. That was the ritual for reciting the sutras.

All these steps are Dharma practices to perform during the breaks or when doing your daily activities.

## SEALING THE DEVELOPMENT STAGE

Lady Tsogyal asked the Master: How should we seal the development stage with the completion stage?

167

The Master advised: Practitioners who wish to practice the completion stage should, having visualized themselves in the form of the deity, request the wisdom deity to take leave. The samaya being melts into light and becomes the seed syllable of the deity or a HUNG. The HUNG gradually dissolves and becomes the bindu. The bindu grows smaller and smaller and then becomes clear emptiness. From within this state, remain in the "thatness of all phenomena," empty, nonconceptual self-cognizance beyond the extremes of existence and nonexistence. Alternately, remind yourself again and again in accordance with the oral instructions on the completion stage you have received from your master.

If you, the practitioner, do this, practicing three or four sessions daily, you will, within this life or without being interrupted by other rebirths, rest in the great yoga during the intermediate state and attain the Mahamudra form of the yidam deity. Even if the power of your development stage is not fully perfected, you will in the next rebirth abide in the great yoga state and without a doubt attain the vidyadhara level of Mahamudra.

All these steps were advice in progressive stages of meditation for people with simple mental capacities.

## The Person of the Highest Mental Capacity

Lady Tsogyal asked the Master: How should a person with the highest mental capacity practice?

The master replied: When those of the highest mental capacity meditate on a deity, they do not visualize it step by step. Simply by uttering the essence mantra or a sentence, or simply by wanting to and thinking of the deity, he visualizes it vividly, instantaneously, and as self-existing, like a bubble emerging from water. This is itself the invitation of the deity from dharmadhatu.

To visualize yourself as the deity is space, and that the deity is visible while devoid of self-nature is wisdom. Thus it is indivisible space and wisdom.

The relative is to appear unceasingly as the deity, while the ultimate is to realize that the essence of the deity, devoid of self-nature, is empty. Thus it is the indivisible relative and ultimate.

The deity manifesting as male is means, and when manifesting as female it is knowledge. Thus it is indivisible means and knowledge.

The deity manifesting in the form of the deity is bliss, and its lack of self-nature is emptiness. Thus it is bliss and emptiness indivisible.

The deity manifesting in the form of the deity is awareness, and its appearance devoid of self-nature is emptiness. Thus it is indivisible awareness and emptiness.

The deity manifesting in the form of the deity is luminosity, and its lack of self-nature is emptiness. Thus it is indivisible luminosity and emptiness.

Visualizing yourself in that way as the deity, the body aspect is visible yet devoid of self-nature and is therefore beyond age and decline. The speech aspect is unceasing and thus the essence mantra is beyond cessation. The mind aspect transcends birth and death and is thus the continuity of dharmata.

Not being apart from the deity during the four aspects of daily activities—walking, moving about, lying down, or sitting—that is the path of the person of the highest mental capacity. It is extremely difficult and is the domain of someone who possesses the residual karma of former training.

## THE STAGES OF VISUALIZING

Lady Tsogyal asked the Master: Please give advice on how to keep the deity in mind when meditating on the yidam deity.

The Master replied: First, the oral instructions on visualizing the deity: Whether you meditate on the deity in front of you or meditate on yourself as the deity, after you have received the master's oral instructions, the master should have given you, the disciple, his blessings and protected you against obstructing forces.

Next, sit on a comfortable seat and be physically at ease. Take a well-made painting of the yidam deity and place it in front of you. Sit for a short time without thinking of anything whatsoever, and then look at the image from head to foot. Look again gradually at all the details from the feet to the head. Look at the image as a whole. Sometimes rest without thinking about the image and refresh yourself. Then in this way, look again and again for a whole day.

That evening, take a full night's sleep. When you wake up, look again as before. In the evening, do not meditate on the deity but just rest your mind in the state of nonthought.

Following this, the deity will appear vividly in your mind even without your meditating. If it does not, look at its image, close your eyes, and visualize the image in front of yourself. Sit for as long as the visualization naturally remains. When it becomes blurry and unclear, look again at the image and then repeat the visualization, letting it be vividly present. Cut conceptual thinking and sit.

When meditating like this you will have five kinds of experiences: the experience of movement, the experience of attainment, the experience of habituation, the experience of stability, and the experience of perfection.

1. When your mind does not remain settled at this time and you have numerous thoughts, ideas, and recollections, that is the experience of movement. Through that you approach taking control of the mind. This experience is like a waterfall cascading over a steep cliff.

2. Then when you can visualize the deity for a short time with both the shape and color of the deity remaining vivid and clear at the same time, that is the experience of attainment. This experience is like a small pond.

3. Following this, when the deity is clear whether you meditate upon it from a long or a short distance, and when it remains for a sixth of your session without any occurrence of gross thoughts, that is the experience of habituation, which is like the flow of a river.

4. Next, no thoughts move and you are able to maintain the session while clearly visualizing the deity. That is the experience of stability that is like Mount Sumeru.

5. Following this, when you can remain for a full day or more without losing the vivid presence of the deity's arms and legs even down to the hairs on its body and without giving rise to conceptual thinking, that is the experience of perfection.

Practitioner, apply this to your own experience!

If you sit too long with an unclear visualization of the deity, your physical constitution will be upset. You will become weary and consequently unable to progress in your concentration. You will have even more thoughts, so first refresh yourself and then continue meditating.

Until you attain a clear visualization, do not meditate at night. In general it is important to visualize in short sessions. Meditate while there is sunlight, when the sky is clear, or with a butter lamp. Do not meditate when you just have woken up or when you feel sluggish or hazy.

At night, get a full night's sleep and meditate the next day in eight short sessions.

When meditating, if you leave the session abruptly, you will lose concentration, so do it gently.

When your visualization becomes vivid the moment you meditate, you can also practice at nighttime, during dusk, and at early dawn.

In general do not weary yourself. Focus your mind on the visualization, grow accustomed to it with stability, and visualize the complete form of the deity.

## PROLONGING THE VISUALIZATION

Lady Tsogyal asked the Master: For what duration should we remain visualizing the deity?

The Master replied: After you have attained some clarity and a slight degree of stability as explained above, the duration of remaining can be prolonged. Usually the recitation determines the length of the sessions. But since the time for recitation has not yet arrived, the duration of your sessions should be according to your ability to remain visualizing.

For the inner measure of sessions, the intervals of breathing are the most important. However, for the outer measure, time and number of sessions are most important.

The measures for sessions can be determined by keeping four sessions each day and night, for as long as possible. The purpose of measured sessions is to not upset your physical constitution, to keep a balanced practice, to enhance your concentration, and to be able to visualize for a long time.

As for counting, do not count verbally but use a mental rosary. Following this, gradually increase the number; take rest for one period and meditate one period.

For the shadow measure, divide the day into sixteen or eight sessions and meditate for every second part of the lines of the shadow. Rest for each part in between. In short, meditate in eight short sessions and alternate by resting in eight.

When you have become stable in this, meditate in two short sessions and gradually prolong them. Then you will be able to remain for a day, a day and a night, half a month, a full month, and so forth.

In short, no matter how stable your session is, the main point is to not weary yourself. So keep proportional sessions, and naturally prolong the duration of unmoving clarity free from thought activity.

These were the oral instructions on prolonging the visualization of the deity.

## CORRECTING FAULTS

Lady Tsogyal asked the Master: When meditating on the deity, how should we correct the faults of transfiguration?

The Master said: In order to correct the faults of transfigurations, there are two aspects: identifying the faults and correcting the faults.

Regarding identifying the faults, there are two kinds: general and particular.

The general faults are forgetting the visualization, laziness, apprehension, dullness, agitation, too much effort, and lack of effort.

1. Forgetting the visualization is becoming distracted from the meditation.

2. Laziness is indolently thinking, "I will do it later."

3. Apprehension is fearing that you will fail to accomplish and be sidetracked.

4. Dullness is feeling dull because of circumstances, incidentally or naturally.

5. Agitation is feeling naturally agitated, due to either circumstances or a deliberate activity.

6. Too much effort is being discontent while the visualization of the deity is clear and giving rise to further thinking by visualizing it again.

7. Lack of effort is remaining indifferent while the visualization of the deity is unclear.

Concerning meditation on the deity, there are the following twelve particular faults: haziness and cloudiness, up and down reversed, the proportions of the body changing, the attire changing, the shape changing, the number changing, the posture changing, the body colors changing, appearing as just color, appearing as just shape, sitting sideways, and gradually vanishing.

Now to explain the methods for correcting these faults: For the seven general faults, you should adhere to the eight applications that remove them.

Apply mindfulness when forgetting the visualization. Apply faith, determination, and diligence as the antidote to laziness. Apply right thought as the remedy against apprehension. As the antidote for dullness, develop enthusiasm, take a bath, and walk about. When agitated, develop sadness for samsara, tie your mind with the rope of mindfulness, and bind it to the tree of the visualization. In short, for dullness and agitation, use the watchman of alertness. Apply equanimity when you desire to use too much effort. Visualize diligently when you lack effort.

As for correcting the particular faults of the deity, look at the image in detail when hazy, murky, or cloudy, and practice having meditated on nonconceptual emptiness. Alternate between nonthought, looking at the deity, and meditating.

When the proportion of the body or the attire, posture, or shape changes, imagine that the body is of material substance and extremely huge and steady. Imagine that pigeons fly in and out of the nostrils, and that birds, sheep, and deer frolic on the arms and legs. Imagine that it remains of solid matter like a statue.

If the number changes, confine the visualization to one or two deities. When it appears as just color, visualize its shape. If it changes color to red or yellow according to the heat of your physical constitutions of blood or bile and so forth, take rest. If it gradually vanishes, focus your mind clearly on the face and arms. For the fault of incompleteness, meditate vividly on the body in its entirety with all the ornaments and attributes.

In short, practice without becoming weary from any of the faults that may arise. Following this, meditate upon nonconceptual emptiness. Then practice while looking at and focusing on the form of the deity.

These were the oral instructions on correcting the faults when meditating on the deity.

## TRAINING WITH THE DEITY

Lady Tsogyal asked the Master: When training with the deity, how should we train?

The Master advised: The oral instruction on training with the deity is to visualize the deity through meditating on nonthought until you are free from these faults. Meditate while alternating the deity and nonthought. When you can visualize the deity without faults, depart from nonthought and meditate exclusively on the deity.

Now for training with the deity: When you can visualize the deity without faults, visualize it as standing upright or sitting or lying on its back or face down, on a plain or a mountain peak, close by or far away, in the center of a rock or at the bottom of water. Train in visualizing the deity in any of these ways whenever you wish to practice.

## Mingling with the Deity

Lady Tsogyal asked the Master: When mingling with the deity, how should we mingle?

The Master advised: Once you have trained in the deity and grown accustomed to it, dissolve it into yourself. Visualize it whether you are a single deity or a mandala with a buddhafield. Then in order to connect the deity to the ultimate, the deity is visualized by your own thoughts and then stabilized. Your mind and the eight collections of consciousness are what manifest as bodily form and the wisdom of the deity. Ultimately, it is the awareness of enlightened mind, the great self-existing wisdom, the essence of fruition. The deity does not appear from elsewhere. No matter how it appears, it is devoid of a self-nature and is therefore a nondual form. To appear in the form of the deity is beyond attachment as its vajralike body, speech, and mind are manifest while devoid of self-nature.

Although your mind manifests as the deity, it has no self-nature. Since it cannot be examined or demonstrated as being such and such, it is dharmakaya.

You, the practitioner who has thus trained in this meaning, should observe and abide by the six samayas of the practice. You should not break off your devotion for the master who has given you the oral instructions. Apply what is conducive to samadhi and avoid what is not conducive. Do not let your concentration dissipate during daily activities. Carry on to perfection without abandoning the yidam, keep the particular deity you practice secret, and do not meditate with the frame of mind that rejects one deity in order to accept another. Any deity you practice is the same as meditating on all the buddhas. The buddhas are nothing to be meditated upon besides realizing your own mind. Even the visualization of the yidam deity is a mental manifestation. Apart from that, there is nothing to accomplish or meditate upon. The buddhas and bodhisattvas are embodied within your yidam deity. Although you may meditate on many yidam deities, they are still manifestations of your mind. If you meditate on just one, that also is a manifestation of your mind.

These were the oral instructions on mingling with the deity and connecting it to the ultimate.

# How to Accomplish the Deity

Lady Tsogyal asked the nirmanakaya Master: How does one take a deity as the path and accomplish it?

The Master replied: To accomplish a deity, first visualize the deity in front of you. Then stabilize the visualization of yourself as the deity. Up to this point, avoid doing the recitations.

Now, when about to practice the deity, arrange a mandala for accomplishment and set out offerings. Place the shrine objects in front of you and, having refreshed yourself, sit down on a comfortable seat.

Invite your master and the assembly of yidam deities; make prostrations, offerings, and praises; and perform the eight branches. The deities then melt into light and dissolve into yourself, by which method you visualize yourself as the yidam deity. Draw the boundary lines for retreat and sanctify the offerings.

By means of the three samadhis and so forth, visualize the mandala together with the deities. Perform the consecration and empowerment. Invite and absorb the wisdom deity and make homage, offerings, and praises.

Again, visualize the wisdom deity in front of you, separate from yourself, and do the recitation. When you have finished reciting, make praises.

Absorb the deity separate from yourself back into yourself and go to sleep while retaining the pride that you are the deity.

Visualize the deity instantly the next morning and make recitations following your sadhana text as above.

Sanctify your food and drink and offer it as a feast.

In this way, whether you train with the yidam deity to be an assembly of mandala deities or a single form, you will still accomplish it.

This was the oral instruction for accomplishing the deity.

# The Signs of Accomplishment

Lady Tsogyal asked the Master: When one is accomplishing a deity, what signs and indications of accomplishment will appear?

The Master advised: There are four kinds of signs: marks, dream omens, indications, and actual signs.

The four types of marks are like smoke, a mirage, fireflies, and a cloudless sky. These are explained as being examples for progressive stages of experience.

175

The five types of dream omens are as follows: seeing the buddhas and bodhisattvas as different from oneself, seeing the buddhas and oneself as equal, seeing oneself in the form of the deity without front and back, seeing that all the buddhas and bodhisattvas pay homage and make offerings to oneself, and dreaming that all the buddhas impart and explain profound teachings.

Moreover, to dream repeatedly that one is naked is a sign of having purified habitual tendencies. To dream of ascending a staircase into the sky is a sign of having entered the path. To dream of riding on lions and elephants is a sign of having achieved the bhumis. Dreaming of a smiling apparition and so forth is a sign of receiving a prophecy.

Even if you do have such excellent dreams, do not be exhilarated.

There are outer, inner, and secret indications of practice.

1. The outer indications during meditation are: to see material objects such as subtle particles, seed syllables, mind attributes, subtle bodily forms, and so forth; or to see coarse perception-spheres of five colors such as of fire and water and so forth.

2. The inner indications are that when meditating on the deity you do not notice the outward and inward movement of your breath, that your body is buoyant like cotton wool, and that you are free from old age and decay.

3. The secret indications are that when you practice the deity as a mere illusory apparition, wisdom is naturally present. You feel equal compassion for everyone, and your field of experience dawns as wisdom.

Actual signs are the outer and the inner signs. The outer signs are that lights appear, the image of the deity smiles, a great sound or a sweet fragrance appears, a butter lamp lights by itself, your skull cup levitates, and you are without any physical discomfort. The inner signs are that your compassion grows greater than before, your attachment diminishes, you are free from prejudice, you have pure samaya and love for your master and Dharma friends, and you have no fear of samsara and are not intimidated by Mara.

When many such signs occur, do not become exhilarated but be diligent.

These were the way in which the indications and signs of practicing the deity appear.

## THE RESULTS OF PRACTICE

Lady Tsogyal asked the Master: Which qualities will result from practicing a deity?

The Master said: The qualities resulting from deity practice are that you purify your obscurations and gather the accumulations.

Since your conceptualization is brought to an end by meditating on a deity, you will purify the obscurations of karma, disturbing emotions, and places of rebirth.

As for the gathering of the accumulations, there are five types of result: the path results, which are the four vidyadhara levels and the ultimate result.

The vidyadhara levels have two aspects: qualities and essence. The qualities are the six superknowledges and the four magical powers. The essence is the four vidyadhara levels, which are the vidyadhara level of maturation, the vidyadhara level of life mastery, the vidyadhara level of Mahamudra, and the vidyadhara level of spontaneous presence.

The ultimate result is that when your meditation of the deity becomes pliable, even if you have few qualities and little intelligence, you will without a doubt attain the state of perfect buddhahood.

## THE FIVE PATHS

Lady Tsogyal asked the Master: It is taught in the system of prajñaparamita that one must proceed through the paths. How should we combine the five paths with practicing the mandala of the deity to perfection?

The Master replied: The path of practicing the mandala of the deity has four aspects: the path of joining, the path of seeing, the path of cultivation, and the path of consummation.

These gradual paths can be connected to the four aspects of approach and accomplishment in that approach is the path of joining, full approach is the path of seeing, accomplishment is the path of cultivation, and great accomplishment is the path of consummation.

## THE PATH OF JOINING

The path of joining has four aspects: Practicing the suchness and the magical samadhis is heat. Practicing the subtle concentration and the single form is summit. Practicing the full manifestation and the elaborate form is acceptance. Practicing the assembly on the uninterrupted path is the supreme mundane attribute.

1. Through the samadhi of suchness, decide that all phenomena are your own mind and practice nonthought in the unfabricated nature of mind. Practice until you realize it.

The magical samadhi is the self-display of nonarising space. That is to practice the cognizant and yet nonconceptual indivisibility of manifestation and emptiness. It is like space permeated by light, being cognizant while manifesting and nonconceptual while being cognizant.

When you have realized this after attaining pliancy, you will cross the boundary between the affinities of the greater and lesser vehicles after which the eleven signs of attaining the heat will appear:

▸ Insects do not live on your body.
▸ Your outer and inner defilements are purified.
▸ You are free from the illnesses of the four compositions.
▸ You attain physical patience.
▸ You overcome your own conceptual thinking.
▸ Free from material food, your radiance and majestic brilliance is beyond waning.
▸ You do not give rise to ordinary desire.
▸ You are free from the five disturbing emotions.
▸ Your habitual tendencies of feeling inclined toward the view and conduct of the lesser vehicles are exhausted.
▸ You are free from the eight worldly concerns.
▸ You attain the acceptance of the profound Dharma.

These were the eleven signs of being beyond falling back.

2. To practice the single form and the subtle concentration at the summit stage is to meditate on the subtle samadhi and the single form until it becomes manifest in the three fields of objects.

The signs of the concentration of the summit are that your five inner disturbing emotions do not arise toward outer objects and that you cannot be harmed by the five outer elements. Those are the signs that your mind has mingled with appearance.

3. Practicing the yoga of the elaborate form at the acceptance stage is to train yourself in the peaceful and wrathful deities as either three families, five families, or a given number of groups of families.

You have reached perfection in this when, having grown accustomed to it, you can send forth light with an instantaneous samadhi and your natural awareness can visualize a mandala of even one thousand buddhas.

The signs that you have attained the stage of acceptance and have become pliant in disclosing appearances are that you can transform sand into gold, make water appear in a dry place, make a sprout grow forth from charcoal, and control all perceptible things as you wish. These are the signs of having attained mastery over mind.

4. Accomplishing the assembly on the uninterrupted path at the stage of supreme mundane attribute is to practice the meaning of the great bliss of dharmata. When you have become extremely stable, you are endowed with the five articles and so forth, and you commence the sadhana at an auspicious time.

If your power of concentration in this is strong, you attain the vidyadhara level of life mastery, and thus you will, within six, twelve, or sixteen months, reach the attainment of the sacred family of mastery. Your life force will equal the sun and the moon, and you can extend your life span one hundred years at a time.

If your power of concentration is weak, you attain the vidyadhara level of maturation. Having left your body behind, you attain the complete form of the yidam deity in the bardo. That is the result of stability in the development stage.

## THE PATH OF SEEING

Now I will explain the full approach as the path of seeing: After you have realized that your residual body is a mental body, your defilements are exhausted and you attain the changeless vidyadhara level of life mastery beyond birth and death, without even leaving your physical body behind. Having attained the five superknowledges and four magical powers, you realize the characteristics of the ultimate. Although you transform yourself into myriad things through three incalculable aeons, display your magical powers on the path of seeing, and act for the welfare of beings, you engage in actions without attachment and receive teachings from the nirmanakaya in person. You will be beyond falling back from the paths.

## The Paths of Cultivation and Consummation

Now to explain the accomplishment as the path of cultivation: The path of cultivation is to put the characteristics of the ultimate into practice having reached the Mahamudra level of the rainbowlike body.

Although your state of mind during meditation is not different from that of the buddhas, you still retain the state of consciousness of the postmeditation and must therefore deliberately rest in meditation. Because you now abide in unshakable concentration, it is the vidyadhara level of Mahamudra. This is the experience of being unshakable from Ati Yoga. Without moving from the meditation state, you send forth myriads of magical apparitions and accomplish the welfare of beings. Mentally or by means of symbols, you can receive teachings from the sambhogakaya.

As for the path of consummation of the great accomplishment, the vidyadhara of spontaneous presence, your qualities are almost equal to the supreme qualities of the buddhas. The difference is whether or not the meditation state brings forth enhancement. The vidyadhara level of spontaneous presence possesses instantaneous enhancement.

Gathering regents and giving teachings, you attain the consummation, the vajralike samadhi, and accomplish the welfare of self and others through effortless magical powers. This is the action of the expression of wisdom. Meeting the dharmakaya face to face, you receive teachings through blessings and purify the subtle obscuration of dualistic knowledge.

These were the gradual path of how to attain the four aspects of approach and accomplishment, the five paths, and the four vidyadhara levels.

## Skipping the Grades

Lady Tsogyal asked the master: When explaining the short path of Secret Mantra, is it possible to journey the path by skipping the grades?

The Master replied: It is also taught that there is a path that skips grades. It is possible that some people reach consummation, progressing through the paths of joining, seeing, and cultivation simultaneously. Without having to journey step by step, some people attain enlightenment from the path of seeing, some reach buddhahood from the path of cultivation, and some journey progressively to the end and then reach the state of buddhahood. People are divided due to their degree of power of intelligence and concentration.

These four ways of practicing the path according to the levels of the four types of people do not depend on following a path after taking rebirth in a future life. The resultant system of Secret Mantra holds that you are freed from the illness of samsara within this very lifetime, and, having attained the level of samadhi beyond rebirth, you spontaneously accomplish the three kayas.

In order to reach the bhumi of Indivisibility and attain dharmakaya within a single lifetime, intelligent people are taught to train in the path of dharmakaya, grow accustomed to it, and take thatness as the path.

In order to reach the bhumi of Unexcelled Wisdom and attain the kaya of great bliss, passionate people are taught to train in the path of great bliss, grow accustomed to it, and take bliss as the path.

In order to reach the bhumi of the Great Assembly Circle and attain the form kayas, angry people are taught to train in the path of deliverance and grow accustomed to it. People who hold attributes are taught to take the deity as path.

In this way you purify the realms of the three kayas and grow accustomed to the three bhumis. Since all these results are contained within your own mind, decide that buddhahood does not exist elsewhere.

These were the supreme qualities of the path that skips the grades.

## THE KAYAS AND WISDOMS

Lady Tsogyal asked the Master: How do we attain the fruition of Secret Mantra, the five kayas and five wisdoms?

The Master advised: In connection with the different types of capacity just mentioned above, when you have proceeded in the manner of the four ways of taking as the path, you attain the ultimate fruition, the spontaneously present result of the five kayas and five wisdoms.

The dharmadhatu wisdom is the fact that this general form of all buddhas, your innate nature devoid of constructs, a primordially unconditioned essence, is the unproduced, unborn, and original purity beyond arising and ceasing.

The mirrorlike wisdom is the fact that although dharmadhatu is devoid of concrete substance, it is by nature luminous, and all phenomena appear like reflections in a mirror while having no self-nature and are cognized while having no conceptual thinking.

The wisdom of equality is the fact that unceasingly, dharmadhatu is self-existing awareness, and this awareness wisdom is devoid of constructs; perception is unborn, nondual, and the great equality.

Individually discriminating wisdom is the fact that without leaving this nondual state of equality, the general and individual characteristics of phenomena are unmixed and utterly complete, while the habitual tendencies of ignorance are relinquished and omniscient wisdom arises without possessing the misery of conceptual thinking.

The wisdom of the persevering action[38] is to rest while remaining cognizant as just mentioned. This inseparable wisdom is to accomplish and to perfect the welfare of self and others spontaneously and with perseverance.

These five wisdoms manifest separately as the unceasing expression of your awareness, but they are never apart from the basic wisdom of dharmadhatu. The basis of all, this dharmadhatu wisdom, is primordially present in yourself; throughout the three times the practitioner is never apart from it.

Now follows how the five kayas are present:

Dharmakaya is the unfabricated innate nature, a profound naturalness, beyond arising and ceasing and devoid of constructs.

Sambhogakaya is the enjoyment of the self-existing wisdom of awareness because the kayas and wisdoms are present within the continuity of the innate nature of your mind.

Nirmanakaya is compassion born out of wisdom, magically displayed and manifest in all ways.

The great bliss kaya is the unborn bliss of enlightened mind.

The essence kaya is the fact that these four kayas are inseparable as the essence of the innate enlightened mind.

Since the five kayas and five wisdoms are spontaneously present, this is called possessing the general form of all buddhas. The practitioner meditates gradually on the essence of these five kayas at the time of the path as being the nature of his own mind. When the practitioner parts with the enclosure of the physical body, he attains these five kayas and five wisdoms in a way that transcends attainment and perceives them in a way that transcends perception.

Here is the explanation of how buddhahood acts for the welfare of sentient beings. Numerous reflections of the sun appear on the surface of many waters without leaving behind the single circle of the sun. Similarly, the truly and completely Enlightened One, the dharmakaya, without leaving behind the equality of the innate nature, magically appears, through the sambhogakaya and nirmanakaya, in accordance with the particular inclinations of those to be tamed in a number as great as the infinite space.

Although acting for the benefit of beings, the dharmakaya holds no conceptual thinking.

For example, the sunlight does not conceive of benefiting beings. In the same way, the two kayas hold no concepts of acting for the welfare of beings. The welfare of beings results from the power of aspiration.

The Master advised: Tsogyal, when the five-hundred-year cycle of the dark age arrives, most followers of Mantra will only utter the words rather than practice their meaning. They will let the Secret Mantra stray into shamanistic incantations and will misuse the samaya substances for hollow rituals. They will build their hermitages in the center of the village. Claiming to be practicing union, they will indulge in ordinary desire. Claiming to be practicing deliverance, they will indulge in ordinary anger. Confusing good with evil, they will barter the oral instructions, and even the teachers will sell them to the disciples. They will turn the Secret Mantra into speculation and will practice with political incentive and self-centered ambition.

In this final period, the Secret Mantra will be obscured by words. The blessings of the Secret Mantra will diminish because of lack of understanding its meaning. Since only few attain siddhi, there will come a time when the Secret Mantra is close to vanishing. For the sake of a destined person endowed with the residual karma at that time, write down this hearing lineage and conceal it as a treasure.

*In the High Soaring Cave at Yerpa, on the twenty-second day of the last autumn month in the Year of the Monkey, I, Lady Tsogyal, wrote down this jewel garland of oral instructions, the Mind Training of Secret Mantra, and concealed it as a treasure. After meeting with a destined person endowed with the residual karma, may these words purify the obscurations for his wisdom and may he attain the vidyadhara level.*

*Treasure seal.*
*Concealment seal.*
*Profundity seal.*
*Entrustment seal.*

# 23

## THE UNITY OF DEVELOPMENT
## AND COMPLITION

*Tulku Urgyen Rinpoche*

According to the inner tantras, all development stage practices begin with the samadhi of suchness. Suchness means the real, that which truly is. What is real? It is the primordially pure state, also known as Trekchö. The ultimate point of completion stage is the primordially pure state of Trekchö, which is the dharmakaya, here called the samadhi of suchness. In other words, you begin with dharmakaya. The natural quality of that dharmakaya state is called sambhogakaya. Or, said in another way: essence is dharmakaya; nature is sambhogakaya.

The great state of dharmakaya is spacelike emptiness. The expression arising out of the state of primordial purity is a spontaneous presence, which includes the two form kayas—sambhogakaya and nirmanakaya. There is a poetic saying:

> Within the all-pervasive space of dharmakaya,
> Sambhogakaya manifests distinctly, like the light of the sun,
> While nirmanakaya, like a rainbow, acts for the welfare of beings.

What that means is that our essence, which is a primordially pure emptiness, is dharmakaya. Indivisible from that is the natural cognizance, the

From Tulku Urgyen Rinpoche, *As It Is*, Volume I (Boudhanath: Rangjung Yeshe Publications, 1999), "Unity of Development and Completion ."

spontaneously present basis for experience that is the sambhogakaya aspect. Without departing from dharmakaya, the sambhogakaya aspect unfolds. It is like the shining of the sun and moon. They do not come from or go other places to shine; they do so from within space. When the conditions are right, when there is moisture in the air and the sunlight meets the shade provided by the clouds, a rainbow automatically appears. In the same way, nirmanakaya manifests for the benefit of beings out of the unity of emptiness and cognizance.

The training in the development stage follows this exact same principle. Space is primordial purity, the samadhi of suchness, dharmakaya. From this expanse arises experience, sambhogakaya, which is like the sun shining. When the two of these converge there manifests a rainbow, the nirmanakaya. In this way, the three kayas are like a natural progression.

There is no way to practice development stage separate from the completion stage. In fact, to genuinely and authentically train in development stage, according to the inner tantras, it is necessary to receive the pointing-out instruction. Lacking this, one does not identify exactly what the samadhi of suchness is, which is the basic nature of mind. Without that recognition, the second samadhi of illumination is not present because there is no recognition of the cognizant quality. Then the unity of the two, the third samadhi, which naturally takes the form of the seed syllable and thus is called the samadhi of the seed syllable, will not naturally happen.

Without the recognition of the samadhi of suchness, of mind essence, each of the three steps—the samadhi of suchness, of illumination, and of the seed syllable—becomes a mental fabrication. The meditation becomes an attempt to imitate the three samadhis, using a mantra to dissolve everything into emptiness, while the visualization is constructed as a mental fabrication. This is not the actuality of the three samadhis.

The samadhi of suchness, the dharmakaya principle, is great emptiness, and it is indivisible from your natural cognizance, from the quality of experience. This cognizance is comparable to light or clarity, and therefore it is called the samadhi of illumination. And yet it takes place without moving away from the samadhi of suchness, without leaving that behind. Please understand that these two are indivisible. This indivisibility of emptiness and cognizance, often called luminosity, is what naturally manifests as the seed syllable. In other words, allow this indivisibility to take the form of a seed syllable, like the sun or the moon rising in the sky. That is the third samadhi, the samadhi of the seed syllable.

That third samadhi is termed 'seed' because it is the source, the seed out of which the buddhafield, the palace, and the deities all unfold. By letting this seed syllable in the middle of the sky emanate E YAM RAM LAM BAM and SUM, one syllable after the other, each transforms into the mandalas of space, water, fire, earth, and wind, and finally Mount Sumeru. On the top of Mount Sumeru appears the celestial palace and so forth. This is the sequence.

In other words, you evolve the development stage within the structure of the three samadhis. Never visualize the yidam as being in your own room, in your little house, in your own country, or even within your concept of this world. Even this is still too narrow, because in actuality there is not only this world. In Buddhist cosmology, one world system is counted from the vajra hell up to the Summit of Existence, the highest god realm. In between there is Mount Sumeru, the four continents, eight subcontinents, and so forth. All this makes up one world system, while one thousand of these are called a first-order world system. If you take each thousand as a single unit and multiply it a thousand times, that is called a second-order world system. Multiply these again a thousand times, so it becomes one billion, and that is the extent of the sphere of influence of one supreme nirmanakaya buddha. His spiritual reach is such that one billion simultaneous buddhas appear in all these worlds at the same time. Thus, there is no need when practicing development stage to narrow the scope down to being only in one's room or one's house.

The basis out of which development of a deity takes place is primordial purity. From this unfolds the manifest aspect, the spontaneous presence. This spontaneous presence is sometimes called magical compassion, as the luminous cognizance is identical with the compassion. There isn't a single buddha lacking compassion.

The essence is primordial purity beyond mental constructs, while the nature is a spontaneously present compassion. The indivisibility of these two, emptiness and experience, is the seed samadhi. Once again, the first, the essence, the empty, is the samadhi of suchness, dharmakaya. The second, the nature, the cognizance, is the samadhi of illumination. The third, the indivisibility of emptiness and cognizance, the compassion, the nirmanakaya, is the seed syllable from which the celestial palace and the deity arise.

I am trying to give you a hint as to how the three kayas actually are. Dharmakaya is like space. You cannot say there is any limit in space in any direction. No matter how far you go, you never reach a point where space stops and that is the end of space. Space is infinite in all directions. So is dharmakaya. Dharmakaya is all-pervasive and totally infinite, beyond any confines or limitations. This is so for the dharmakaya of all buddhas. There is no individual dharmakaya for each buddha, as there is no individual space for each country. You cannot say there is more than one space, can you? It is all-pervasive and wide open. It's the same with the dharmakaya level of all buddhas. That is the dharmakaya sphere within which sambhogakaya manifests. No world anywhere in the universe takes form outside of the three kayas—it is simply not possible. The three kayas are the basic dimension within which all mundane worlds manifest and disappear.

This basis is also known as dharmadhatu. Out of this the sambhogakaya appears. The greater sambhogakaya is described as the Five-Fold Immense Ocean Buddhas. In the middle is Buddha Immense Ocean Vairochana. To the east is Immense Ocean Akshobhya. To the west is Immense Ocean Amitabha. To the south is Immense Ocean Ratnasambhava, and to the north Immense Ocean Amoghasiddhi.

The size of these greater sambhogakaya buddhas is described as the following. The buddha Immense Ocean Vairochana holds in his hands, in the gesture of equanimity, a begging bowl of pure lapis. Within this there is an immense ocean. Within it a lotus tree grows and puts forth twenty-five fully opened lotus flowers. The thirteenth of these blooms at the level of his heart, while the twenty-fifth is at the level of his forehead. We ourselves, our world, are somewhere in the thirteenth lotus at the level of the heart center. This lotus has thousands of petals and hundreds of thousands of small anthers. Within each atom in each of these anthers are one billion universes, each group being the sphere of one supreme nirmanakaya buddha.

According to the general Mahayana system, this is as far as the sphere of influence for each of the thousand buddhas of this aeon extends. Their influence is like only one of the particles within the thousands of places within one of these lotuses. Also, in each pore in the body of Buddha Immense Ocean Vairochana, there are one billion world systems. And he is merely one of the five greater sambhogakaya buddhas: In the other four directions are Ratnasambhava, Akshobhya, Amitabha, and Amoghasiddhi. Now you see the immense dimensions involved, as well as the difference between the sphere of a nirmanakaya buddha and a sambhogakaya buddha.

Padmasambhava once explained this to Yeshe Tsogyal, who begged him, "Please show me in actuality what it really looks like." He said "All right, I won't show you the whole thing, but I will show you one fraction." And he showed her the one billion world systems that fall under the influence of Buddha Shakyamuni. Yeshe Tsogyal fainted from this vision—it was too much. Guru Rinpoche threw water on her and revived her. Then he said, "If you can't even grasp the extent of the one billion universes of a nirmanakaya buddha, there is no way you can experience the extent of the greater sambhogakaya realm."

Within these Immense Ocean buddhas is an uncountable number of billionfold universes of nirmanakaya buddhas. In each of these, countless billions of nirmanakayas appear. Whenever there is the opportunity for anyone to be influenced, emanations manifest in whatever way or form is necessary. All these are within one sphere of a nirmanakaya realm that is for one buddha. The other worlds don't necessarily exist in the same way. While one universe or world system is being formed, another one might be dissolving, and a third is in the middle of existing. This is a small hint about the extent of the world systems.

Again, one world system begins with the eighteen hell realms at the bottom of the six classes of sentient beings. The gods are at different levels: First are the gods in the desire realms which have six abodes. Above that are the sixteen abodes of the realms of form, and above that again are the four spheres of the formless realms of infinite perception. All that taken as one is called one world system. If you multiply that a thousand times, that is called the one thousandfold world-system, or the first-order world system. If you count these one thousand as a single unit and multiply them a thousand times, that is called a second-order world system. If you take that resulting one million again as one and multiply it a thousand times, you have the third-order world system, which is one billion. That is what is talked about when you say the third-order thousandfold universe or the billionfold universe. It is one billion world systems counted as one. That is the extent of nirmanakaya buddhas like Shakyamuni or Padmasambhava. Their sphere of influence is one billion world systems.

These buddhas do not have bodies of flesh and blood; they have bodies of rainbow light. Try to count exactly how many worlds there are all together! The three kayas of the buddhas are amazing and their benefit inconceivable. When we practice development stage, starting with the samadhi of suchness, there is no need to narrow it down to our own little area of the world. If possible, at least take the dimension of one billion world systems.

Actually, if you want the real truth, a supreme nirmanakaya buddha's sphere of influence is not just one billion! It is a hundred times a hundred billion, however many that is. Usually in the general Sutra system you only talk about the universe being one billionfold world systems, but according to Vajrayana, it is a hundred times a hundred times a billion in each pore of the body of a sambhogakaya buddha. The Vajrayana system views things straightforwardly, exactly as they are, without limiting their scope. There is a difference in depth between Sutra and Tantra. In Tantra, nothing is held back. Buddha Vairochana has in his body a hundred times a hundred billion pores, each of which has a hundred times a hundred billion universes. That is the kind of extent we are talking about.

We may wonder why the Dzogchen teachings are available in this particular world. It is because our world is situated at the heart level of Buddha Immense Ocean Vairochana. Our world system is only one among the hundred times hundred billion, upon one of the thousand pistils in the thousand-petaled lotus. In each of these universes or world systems are one billion or more worlds with sentient beings. There is an unfathomable number of sentient beings!

For sentient beings in general, there is no end to samsara. But for each sentient being individually, there is an end. Because when we recognize mind-essence and become stable in that, the very root of further samsaric existence has been exhausted. For the individual sentient being, samsara does end. But for sentient beings as a whole, there is no end to samsara.

Dharmakaya is all-pervasive and infinite like space. Sambhogakaya is as vast and unfathomable as just mentioned. It is within all these billionfold universes that the nirmanakaya buddhas appear, in order to benefit and guide sentient beings. It is possible for sentient beings to be enlightened, because both samsara and nirvana are pervaded by the three kayas. All worlds and all beings dissolve and unfold within the sphere of the three kayas; nothing takes place outside it. Therefore, everything is originally and still utterly pure. Yet, what help is this, if individual sentient beings do not recognize the fact that everything is utterly pure? If one is deluded and confused, it doesn't help much. Nevertheless, while one is deluded and confused, one's nature is never separate from the three kayas. Even though we wander in samsara, the essence of our minds is the three kayas. By recognizing the essence, training in it and attaining stability in this, we can become enlightened. When thinking of this, there is a point in practicing the Dharma, isn't there?

It is said in one tantra, "All beings are in fact buddhas, but they are covered by temporary obscurations. When these are removed, they are truly buddhas." What does it mean that all beings are buddhas? It means that within every single sentient being the enlightened essence, sugatagarbha, is present as their nature. It is not that there is some principal buddha nature that we have to somehow get back to and find. It is not like that. The buddha nature is present, at hand, within everyone already.

Buddha nature is empty in essence; it is also cognizant. There is some ability to know; we can perceive and experience. This is not something way above our heads; we can understand this. We can also understand that being empty and cognizant are indivisible, not two different entities. Isn't it clear by now that the three kayas are intrinsically present in ourselves?

Here's an example. Buddha nature is not the same as space, because obviously space doesn't know anything. Yet we have to use the example of space as a way to point at how buddha nature is. Here in the Kathmandu Valley are thousands of houses. In each house there is space. This space in itself doesn't really differ in quality from one house to another. Let's say that this space is lit up by the rising sun. When there is light, there is no darkness. In the same way, cognizant space is the nature in each sentient being, and yet they are separate, like individual houses with sunlit space in daytime. Still, there is space; the cognizance or clarity is like space suffused with sunlight. Can you separate space and sunlight in the daytime? Can you separate the dharmakaya, which is like space, from the cognizance, which is sambhogakaya? This is how the nature of each sentient being is already. Please understand the meaning of this analogy. It becomes quite obvious when you train in the recognition of mind-essence. While being empty, everything is vividly and distinctly experienced, not by the senses but by mind.

The scriptures of the Great Perfection clearly and exactly describe the basis or origin of samsara and the main essence of nirvana, exactly as it is. These scriptures also explain that which is all-pervasive throughout all states, whether samsara or nirvana. This is not taught in any of the other vehicles. In Dzogchen there is the outer Mind Section, the inner Space Section, and the secret Instruction Section. Only in the fourth of the four parts of the Instruction Section, the Innermost Unexcelled Section, is this fully described.

The way to train in the unity of development and completion is without leaving behind the samadhi of suchness. Having been introduced to the nature of mind, the state of emptiness, there is a natural cognizance. This natural cognizance is the samadhi of illumination, sometimes called magical compassion. Allow this compassion indivisible from emptiness to manifest in the form of the seed syllable that emanates the other letters, E YAM RAM LAM BAM. After this, Mount Sumeru, the celestial palace, and the mandala of the deities unfold. This is called practicing development stage within the completion stage, meaning without leaving the continuity of the completion stage. Without ever parting from the samadhi of suchness, allow all of the visualization to take place.

If we have not been introduced to the natural state of nondual awareness, we must create the visualization through thought. First we imagine emptiness, then the illuminating light, then the seed syllable, and we try to picture the palace, the deities, and so forth. This is not the authentic development stage; rather, it's an imitation of the real development stage. While it's definitely better than nothing at all, it's not the authentic way. The authentic way of practicing development stage is to allow the visualization to unfold as the natural expression of rigpa.

There is another way to unify development and completion: Include the completion stage within the development stage. While trying to imagine oneself as the deity, palace, and so forth, at some point remember to recognize mind-essence: "What is it that imagines this? What is it that thinks this?" In the moment of recognizing mind-essence, development and completion stage are a unity, because the empty quality of that which visualizes is and always was dharmakaya.

Whichever particular way we choose to practice, we should always unify development and completion. It's only intelligent to do so. If one is deluded, one will sit and try to construct something with thoughts. The best case is when the development stage naturally unfolds from the completion stage—when the natural expression of awareness is the development stage. Let the natural expression dawn as knowledge, as *sherab*, so that it is liberated and the essence is not lost. The true development and completion stages are always interconnected. It is not particularly intelligent to try to solely practice development stage without the completion stage, since this leads neither to liberation nor to enlightenment.

I'm going to talk a little more about practicing the development stage as an imitation of the real thing, as a mere resemblance. At some point in a sadhana there is the mantra OM MAHA SHUNYATA JÑANA VAJRA SVABHAVA ATMA KOH HANG. The syllable OM is the nature of all form, and it expresses that everything perceived is Buddha Vairochana, the emptiness of all form. MAHA SHUNYATA means great emptiness. JÑANA means original wakefulness, emptiness and cognizance indivisible. In essence, when one recites the mantra, one is saying, "I am of the nature of indestructible wakefulness in which everything perceived is a great emptiness."

Then, after a few seconds, one says, "From this state of emptiness, in one instant, I appear in the form of the deity." Imagining this is called the resemblance of the actual development stage. This moment of remembering emptiness is necessary, because to start and finish without emptiness is like the development stage having no head and no tail. Following this, within the state of emptiness, in one instant, the syllable E manifests the mandala of space. Then YAM becomes wind, RAM becomes fire, and so forth; SUM becomes Mount Sumeru, and BHRUNG the celestial palace on the summit of Mount Sumeru.

Development stage is not something false; it is not self-deception, because primordial purity is naturally endowed with spontaneously present qualities. These are the qualities of rigpa, of nondual awareness. If our nature was merely empty, there would be no qualities at all. Instead, it is empty while being an original wakefulness, and the qualities of this wakefulness are inconceivable. This wakefulness aspect means that original knowing is never really lost, even though for us original emptiness may seem to be without such wakefulness.

Right now we are still ordinary sentient beings within the three realms, among the six classes, and life may be hard. We undergo a lot of trouble and experience a lot of misery. It is in our interest to aim in the direction of enlightenment. Enlightenment is what we actually need. Suffering is what we already have. We have already gone through the suffering of taking birth; we may not remember this now, but we have. We now know the suffering of getting older and of falling sick. Ahead of us is the suffering of dying, which we cannot avoid no matter what we do. People can try to soothe themselves by saying there is nothing after death, but that is an idea they have, an assumption. Total extinction is impossible, really, because mind is not something that *can* die. Remember, it is mind that experiences, not the body that is left behind after death. A corpse doesn't suffer; neither does it feel pleased. You can chop a dead body up into a hundred pieces and it won't feel a thing. You can stick all sorts of weapons into it or shoot it, and it doesn't react at all. You can burn it over and over again; it doesn't feel that either. Only mind feels. That which feels suffering is mind and mind only.

Unless this mind attains some stability in the recognition of its own natural state, its nature of original wakefulness, there will be no end to its suffering. What we should kill is dualistic mind, but there is no way to do that. You can kill its temporary dwelling place, but the present houseguest that is mind is impossible to kill. Without attaining liberation or enlightenment, there is absolutely no way to avoid experiencing further suffering. The mind cannot die—but it *can* recognize its own nature, which is the three kayas.

An important principle in Vajrayana is that the confused state of mind is its own best remedy. In other words, when being angry, attached, or closed-minded, you need to recognize the nature of the disturbing emotion. At that moment, it vanishes completely. Nobody else can do it for you. You can ask someone to please take away your disturbing emotions, your three poisons, but there is nobody who can do that. The only solution is to recognize your own essence.

You could, of course, try another method and counsel yourself very sternly, saying, "You have been so bad in the past, chasing after the three poisons, getting involved again and again, roaming through the ocean of samsara. Now don't do it any more!" Will your mind listen? Or you could remind yourself, "I have been through so much, suffered so much, all caused by my disturbing emotions. I resolve that this is the end—I won't ever do it again." But will you truly listen to yourself?

Isn't it better to recognize the nature of mind? To see that there is no "thing" to see, which is dharmakaya? That which sees the dharmakaya is the sambhogakaya quality. Its indivisibility of being empty and cognizant is the nirmanakaya. In the very moment of looking, it is seen. In the moment of seeing, it is liberated, free. That is the best solution, isn't it, because that perpetually cuts through the three poisons. When the three poisons are absent, what is left over but the three kayas? Train in this, and you will capture the throne of the three kayas. You will take hold of your real heritage, your true legacy.

Ordinary human life means neglecting this most precious thing and roaming around chasing after what is utterly futile and pointless. We make ourselves the slave of good reputation, food, and clothing. This is what most people pursue: a comfortable life. If we never died, it might be worthwhile to do that! We could go on trying to achieve and achieve, amassing more and more. What happens, though, is that while we may achieve these aims, there is no time to really enjoy them. Sooner or later, tomorrow or the day after, we die, and other people take our possessions away. Maybe our friends will enjoy them, maybe our enemies. After we die, others say, "He had no chance to enjoy everything he had—oh well, now we will!" And they will spend your money and have a good time. They will say, "He has no use for this because he is dead! Now we can use it. He took so much trouble to achieve this, but now we're enjoying it." How useless it is to spend a lifetime accumulating things!

Meanwhile, the spirit of the dead person perceives this whole situation from the bardo and becomes furious. He thinks, "I took all this trouble so that my descendants could enjoy my wealth, but now other people are taking it. I'm so angry!" That wealth was difficult to gather and difficult to protect. First you had to work hard in order to make money and make it increase. Later, you had to be constantly careful that nobody took it away by theft or by force. After death, through clairvoyance, you can see very clearly exactly what happens. It would be better not to see anything! You would at least be free from stinginess and anger at that time.

The state of samsaric affairs is really sad. It would be better not to know anything. However, the spirit in the bardo has conditioned clairvoyance and pays attention to what happens to his possessions—who is taking them and what they do with them. This creates miserliness and resentment, and these two feelings are a direct cause for falling into the lower realms. If we knew this beforehand, and if we recognized mind-essence, there would be no getting involved in stinginess and anger. In original wakefulness, those feelings cannot remain. The five poisons become the five wisdoms. But without recognizing, existence is only miserable. There is nothing but one painful state after another.

Please understand the necessity of recognizing mind-essence when practicing development stage. To omit the samadhi of suchness is like having a body with no head. How much use is somebody without a head? How many people do you know without heads?

The most important point in Dharma practice is the samadhi of suchness, knowing mind-essence. We can examine this entire world as scrupulously as sifting through a bag of flour, but we won't find anything more important. You have to identify the real starting point, and the real starting point has to be *real*—that is the samadhi of suchness. Begin with the actuality of rigpa, because rigpa is not blank or vacant. It has a natural cognizance out of which the development stage can take place.

On the other hand, when your starting point is thought and you want to include the completion stage within that, that completion stage undermines the thought-constructed development stage by dissolving it. You could call this dissolution the "dismantling phase." After building up a lot of stuff, the whole setup vanishes the moment you recognize who thinks this. It's like a child building a sand castle on the beach. A wave comes, whoosh, and everything is gone. The name for this is not development stage; it is dismantling stage! This approach is not pointless thought, of course; it is fine. But it is not the unity of development and completion. It is not training in rigpa as the samadhi of suchness.

Rigpa is not a state of being oblivious. In it is a vibrant, cognizant quality that can unfold as the development stage. That is the way of letting the development stage unfold within the completion stage. There are four types of visualization practice, including the fivefold true perfection, the ritual of the four vajras, and the threefold visualization ritual.[39] The most profound is instantaneous recollection. Out of the samadhi of suchness, whatever should be brought forth is brought forth instantaneously, without your having to think of it. That doesn't mean that the state of rigpa somehow gets lost—not at all. This is not the same as when you try to bring completion stage into development stage, which then destroys the development stage, like throwing a bucket of water on a sand castle.

While all four of these approaches are definitely beneficial, the one I discussed is the one to train in. Start with what is real: the samadhi of suchness. There is a reason all sadhanas have a text. Simply chanting the lines is called using words to bring the meaning to mind. Take a short sadhana of Padmasambhava, for example. There is one line for the samadhi of suchness, another for the samadhi of illumination, and a line for the samadhi of the seed syllable. Without leaving the state of rigpa, continue the chanting. Each line helps unfold a part of the visualization. That is how to train. That doesn't make the previously mentioned way of recognizing the one who imagines useless at all. However, it is not the perfect development stage, which is the luminosity of rigpa. If you start the sadhana with thought, you have by definition already lost the samadhi of suchness.

Let's use a clear, bright mirror as an example for the samadhi of suchness. Then the other two samadhis are like its brightness and the reflection appearing in the mirror. Does that reflection in any way influence or affect the mirror? Does it even change the mirror? If a white reflection appears, it is not that the mirror becomes white, is it? It's the same principle when truly training in development stage. A complete *tangka* can be instantly reflected in a mirror, can't it? The mirror doesn't have to reach out to reflect the tangka; nor does the tangka have to get up and move toward the mirror.

The reflection appears instantaneously, fully and completely. The whole image appears, not just the faces and the arms without the legs.

This approach is different from conceptually trying to see a deity reflected in one's mind. When we do that, we think of one thing and forget another. Instead, everything is reflected all at once. This is possible because the brightness of rigpa is like a clear mirror. That is the completion stage, where all the things are reflected simultaneously. The development stage is like the tangka.

Right now, when we think of the legs, we forget the head. When we think of the left hand, the right is forgotten. This is a process of destroying what you have made. The real development stage should unfold within the samadhi of suchness, like a reflection appearing in a bright mirror. Then the samadhi of illumination is like a reflection of a tangka appearing, and the mirror doesn't lose its brightness when the reflection occurs. In other words, don't leave the completion stage behind in order for the development stage to take place. Otherwise, development stage becomes construction work, like making something out of clay or wood. Can a tangka be reflected in a piece of wood?

When practicing the samadhi of suchness, you have to be somewhat familiar with the state of rigpa. When there is a steadiness in rigpa that is the completion stage, development stage is not a problem, because it can manifest as the display or expression of the completion state. In this context, the unity of development and completion is the same as the unity of appearance and emptiness. It's like a reflection in a mirror. A mirror doesn't have to chase after the object. The object is reflected in the mirror.

Please understand this principle of development stage. Development stage that is initiated by conceptual thought is not the real development stage. It becomes a process of merely replacing one thing with another, because when you think of something new, the former instance is supplanted or replaced; it is destroyed. Better to be like a mirror, letting reflections occur in the state of rigpa without fixating on anything. That is the state of suchness. The quality of experience unfolds just as the tangka is reflected, naturally and easily, in the mirror. When you hold a tangka in front of a mirror, it is not that the mirror somehow chooses what part to reflect. Rather, everything is reflected. To reflect the pure development stage, first be a bright mirror. First understand, then experience, then realize. Try first of all to be a good mirror: a mind-essence mirror, a rigpa mirror. A drawing of a mirror is like the mirror of dualistic mind. The real mirror is the rigpa mirror. We can draw a mirror. But can the drawing of a mirror reflect?

*24*

# DEVELOPMENT AND
# COMPLETION UNIFIED

*Tsoknyi Rinpoche*

There are two ways to carry out the development stage: either to imagine ourselves in the form of the deity in a single instant of recollection or to gradually build up the visualization. In the beginning especially, building up the visualization can be a gradual process, proceeding through first one detail, then the next. It doesn't always have to be done like that, however. In one instant you can remind yourself of being the deity. In fact, if it's not done like that, it is only conceptual, meaning with conceptual attributes. It is then known as "development stage with conceptual attributes."

When, for example, we who live in Nepal hear the name "Boudha Stupa," we immediately have a picture in our mind of the stupa. It's not like we first have to remind ourselves that there is the ground underneath and on top of that is the stupa, that it's surrounded by a wall, that people are walking around it, and so on. Rather than thinking all these thoughts one by one, we have an image of the stupa that arises in a single moment.

The development stage should be like that, so that in one instant I visualize myself as the physical presence of the Buddha Vajrasattva. This can occur because our minds are not only empty essence; there is also some sense of knowing, a natural cognizance, out of which the visualization takes place.

From Tsoknyi Rinpoche, *Carefree Dignity* (Boudhanath: Rangjung Yeshe Publications, 1999), "Development and Completion Unified."

Of course there are a lot of details to a visualization in the traditional development stage, as when one unfolds the structure of the three samadhis: the samadhi of suchness, the samadhi of illumination, and the samadhi of the seed syllable. These three are a necessary part of the right framework for the practice. The samadhi of suchness is a sense of complete quiet. In certain seasons when there is no wind at all, the prayer flags at Nagi Gompa hang there completely calm and quiet. This is a good image for the samadhi of suchness. When we experience this, we are completely open to the fact that the nature of all things is emptiness.

From this total quiet, a subtle breeze starts to move, and the prayer flags begin to gently wave. This is the image for the samadhi of illumination, which is a compassionate frame of mind toward all sentient beings. The samadhi of suchness becomes compassionate, like a gentle breeze starting to move the prayer flags. The third, the samadhi of the seed syllable, is when the wind blows more strongly, and all the different-colored prayer flags flap in the breeze, creating a sort of spectacle, a drama. All forms seen are the divine forms of the deity, all sounds are mantra, and all movements of mind are the play of original wakefulness.

All of that is activated out of the first, the samadhi of suchness. Without departing from that, the samadhi of illumination arises, with its compassionate breeze. Finally, the stronger wind of the seed samadhi gives rise to all the different details of the visualization. This process is called unfolding the structure of the three samadhis.

Another way of explaining it involves three aspects, called identity, power, and display—in Tibetan, *ngowo, tsal,* and *rölpa.* The first, identity, is like a horse, a beautiful, strong, well-trained thoroughbred horse. So a strong, fully developed horse is the identity, the horse *itself.* The expression is the capability or the strength of the horse. Its prowess or capacity, its strength and ability to race, is the second aspect. The third, display, is when the horse actually uses its power for racing. A television camera can show a horse running in slow motion, revealing how it actually puts its strength to use and makes a display of its power. So, all phenomena have these three aspects of ngowo, tsal, and rölpa—identity, power, and display. Power and display can have an impure and a pure aspect, but the identity is simply what it is in itself.

Development stage is simply training in the pure aspect of tsal and rölpa, the pure aspect of the strength and the display—the form of the deity, the palace, and so forth. All of what unfolds or takes place is a way in which rigpa as identity shows its capacity to be cognizant, to manifest, and to take on all different forms. It is a way of displaying the capacity of rigpa without leaving its identity, itself. It does not leave behind the unbroken continuity of rigpa, the samadhi of suchness, nor is it interrupted by thoughts of the past, future, or present.

Within this continuity, there is a natural knowing that is unobstructed and can unfold itself. This is the samadhi of illumination, the compassionate energy, a capability that is not separate from the essence itself. Without leaving behind the continuous state of rigpa, which is empty in essence and cognizant by nature, the unobstructed display can manifest as all the other manifold details of the visualization. All phenomena, whatever takes place as arising and ceasing, unfold without really arising and without really ceasing within a backdrop or continuity that doesn't arise or cease. All feelings of joy and sorrow, whatever appears, are all seen as a display of this state.

This description makes it sound like we have three aspects, but actually all three are embodied within rigpa itself. Rigpa is empty in identity, yet has a power, a strength of natural knowing, which can manifest unobstructedly, display in all different ways. The three samadhis that give rise to all the various details are part of one single identity of rigpa.

Remember, rigpa is empty in essence, cognizant by nature, and unconfined in its capacity. From the perspective of *instantaneousness,* the quality of rigpa is the single, sufficient king that is all-embodying. Of course, in the beginning one starts out by practicing these different aspects in a sequential order, but we shouldn't let it remain like that always. At some point, all of it becomes different ways of expressing one identical nature of rigpa.

What I am speaking of here is the best type of development and completion stage. In essence the two are indivisible. Within the state of rigpa, the development and completion stage are fully present. It is not like you always have to first invoke one, then the other, after which they have to be fused together and united as one. As a matter of fact, they are a natural unity. In addition, the two accumulations of merit and wisdom can be perfected within the single continuity of rigpa. Remaining in the samadhi of suchness, never leaving that behind, and forming no concept or constructs in mind whatsoever perfects the accumulation of wisdom. In the same way, the power and the display of rigpa can be allowed to unfold unimpededly in any way, without leaving behind the state of suchness. All of that display perfects the accumulation of merit. In this way, within the continuity of rigpa as indivisibly embodying the three samadhis, we can perfect the two accumulations of merit and wisdom.

Through the realization of empty essence, we perfect the dharmakaya and realize it fully. Through the training in the power and display of the cognizant nature and unconfined capacity, we perfect the rupakaya, the form body that includes both sambhogakaya and nirmanakaya. In this way both dharmakaya and rupakaya are perfected within the state of the continuity of rigpa. Within the genuine, authentic practice of rigpa, of Trekchö, both development stage and completion stage are fully contained. To be absolutely truthful, we can realize the dharmakaya of all buddhas in this very lifetime exclusively through the training in rigpa.

Rigpa here means the rigpa in completeness, not a fragmentary version of what rigpa is. It is not training in a little aspect or corner or facet of rigpa, but rigpa as it really is, in actuality—all-embodying, complete, and full. Training in that type of authentic rigpa is enough in itself. Rigpa is endowed with natural strength, natural sharpness, intrinsic steadiness. One is continually getting caught up in something other; the attention will always stray whenever an object is perceived, unless there is some innate steadiness, some real stability.

When a strong wind comes, a piece of straw bends toward where the wind is blowing, regardless of how thick it might be. A needle, on the other hand, may be extremely thin, but no matter how strong the wind is, it remains exactly as it is. In the same way, any act of deliberate paying attention in some direction, no matter how virtuous or good it is, is easily influenced and bent in some direction. The effortless moment of awareness that is rigpa is always innately stable; it doesn't bend in any direction.

For example, in the practice of shamatha, your attention is quietly fixed on one particular object. Even if you feel like you are utterly undistracted and totally focused on the nowness, still, when something bad happens, the apparent concentration falls apart and you get carried away. Rigpa is not focused on anything. It is like wide-open space. Anything can move through space freely, without hurting or harming the space in any way. Thus, authentic rigpa is unassailable by distraction.

You can compare the focused attention of shamatha to a pillar of concrete reinforced with iron. It may appear quite sturdy, but a bomb can cause it to fracture and fall apart. On the other hand, rigpa is like unformed space, not made out of anything whatsoever. No matter how many bombs you blow up in midair, it doesn't ruin or change the space in any way whatsoever. Bombs only explode themselves, they don't explode space. In this way, rigpa is more like the basic space within which everything can unfold and vanish again, arise and cease, come and go. Rigpa itself is not subject to any of that.

That is why when I started out showing us how to train in rigpa, I said, "Be free of reference point." Rigpa is not a thing that we can focus our attention *on*; it is not an object to be held in mind. That explains the "not meditating" part. In addition to that, we need to be undistracted. *Trying* to be undistracted is not enough by itself, because willing oneself not to let one's attention wander involves holding a focus in mind. It becomes just another deliberate thought, which is not good enough. Remain without meditating on something, and yet without being distracted.

Any questions?

STUDENT: How does visualization fit into this context?
RINPOCHE: There are two ways of practicing visualization or development stage as the means, and completion stage or knowing rigpa as the knowledge aspect. The first way is that you don't combine or unify the two. You practice the development stage, and then at some point you give it the stamp of the completion stage. In other words, you try to adorn or embellish development stage with completion stage during the session. The other way is when you allow the visualization or development stage to unfold out of the completion stage indivisibly, without separating means and knowledge. Whether one practices the first way or the second depends entirely on the individual.

For instance, at the beginning of a sadhana you recite OM SVABHAVA and so on, and you imagine that all phenomena dissolve into a state of emptiness. From within this state of emptiness, something manifests. That is called giving the seal of emptiness at the beginning. After a lot of visualization, you may say HUNG HUNG HUNG, and the celestial palace and the surrounding deities dissolve into the chief figure, the chief figure dissolves into the seed syllable in the heart center, the syllable dissolves from the bottom up, and finally everything is the state of emptiness. You remain like that for a while, and thereby conclude by giving another "stamp of emptiness" onto the visualization. Then, you may say AH AH AH, and from this state of emptiness you again manifest in the form of the yidam deity.

There's also a way to combine Ati Yoga with the development stage, with the visualization. Within the framework of the three samadhis, first comes the samadhi of suchness, which means recognizing rigpa and remaining like that. The second is the samadhi of illumination, which means the radiance of rigpa is allowed to unfold as compassion. The third samadhi is the samadhi of the seed syllable, which is in fact the indivisible unity of being empty and compassionate. This unity is allowed to manifest in the form of a seed syllable from which the deity and the palace and so forth all manifest.

Basically, there are two ways of practicing development stage: through gradual, progressive visualization and through instantaneous recollection, in which everything is brought to mind in one instant. What happens if I ask you to think of your room back home? Your room and your house come to mind in a single instant, don't they? It's not a gradual thing. You could visualize being Vajra Kilaya, for example, in the same way. Without losing that presence of being the deity, you don't have to stray from the continuity of rigpa, either.

When we're chanting the text, we recite from the state of emptiness: "I appear in the form of Vajra Kilaya standing on such-and-such seat. In my three right hands I hold three vajras, and in the three left hands I hold such-and-such." You can say all these things aloud, without losing the vivid presence of the deity and without straying from the state of rigpa. It's perfectly all right if, from the first moment of the emptiness mantra, you appear spontaneously as the form of the deity. Even though you chant all the details, it doesn't have to be itemized piece by piece in your experience. You can be the deity fully perfected from the beginning.

If you're practicing the visualization using dualistic mind, then when a new thought arises the previous one is replaced. The thought of the left hand replaces the thought of the right hand, and when you think of the head, the body is then gone.

When you think of home, you don't have to think of all the details one by one, do you? It all comes to mind at once. You don't have to first imagine the front door, then the hallway, then the living room, then the bathroom and so forth. Instead, "my home" is immediately and vividly present in the mind.

It's quite helpful to combine development stage and completion stage, and you can use the yidam practice as the structure. If, for instance, you are using the *Trinley Nyingpo* sadhana as the framework, vividly imagine yourself as Padmasambhava, and, in all the directions, imagine the twelve manifestations and so forth. The whole environment is the buddhafield of Padmasambhava. You chant the mantra of Padmasambhava. If you are unable to practice the unity of development and completion, simply practice the development stage, chanting the mantra 108 times or 200 times. Then take a break and recognize rigpa. Remain like that. After a while it gets a little boring; you get a little tired. So again you imagine yourself as Padmasambhava, and recite the mantra OM AH HUNG BENZA GURU PEMA SIDDHI HUNG. When you get tired of that, remain in rigpa. You can shift from one to the other.

# 25

## THE VAJRA MASTER AND
## THE YIDAM DEITY

*Padmasambhava*

*The Teachings to Lady Tsogyal: Oral Instructions on the Secret Mantra;
Questions and Answers on the Characteristics of a Master and How to
Meditate on a Yidam Deity* ৪

NAMO GURU

First, Padmakara, the great master from Uddiyana, was born from a lotus flower. Next he accomplished the vidyadhara level of life.[40] Finally he
reached the supreme attainment of Mahamudra.[41] He could perceive as
many sugatas as there are stars in the sky and was skilled in compassionate
means.

Because of his compassion for Tibet, a Dharmaless country shrouded in
darkness as if in a dense fog, he went there. He constructed Glorious Samye
at Red Rock in order to fulfill the wish of Trisong Deutsen, a bodhisattva
on the eighth bhumi.

He practiced sadhana in the Dregu Cave at Chimphu and remained in
meditation. During this time he was attended by King Trisong Deutsen,

From Padmasambhava, *Dakini Teachings* (Boudhanath: Rangjung Yeshe Publications,
1999), "The Vajra Master and the Yidam Deity."

who served him well. Lady Tsogyal of Kharchen also served him and was his personal attendant. Vairotsana of Pagor translated all the Dharma teachings from the language of Uddiyana into Tibetan.

Learned and virtuous Tibetans requested teachings from the master. In particular, Lady Tsogyal, the Princess of Kharchen, persistently requested advice on the oral instructions concerning practice and on how to clear away her doubts about the Dharma.

Lady Tsogyal asked the Master: Great Master, the master and teacher is of the greatest importance when entering the door of the Secret Mantra teachings. What should be the characteristics of the master whom one follows?

The Master replied: The master and teacher is of sole importance. The characteristics of a master are these: He should have trained his mind, he should possess many oral instructions, and he should have vast learning and experience in practice and meditation. He should be stable-minded and skilled in the methods of changing the minds of others and also have great intelligence and care for others with compassion. He should have great faith and devotion toward the Dharma. If you follow such a master, it is like finding a wish-fulfilling jewel; all your needs and wishes will be fulfilled.

Lady Tsogyal asked the Master: Without receiving empowerment from one's master, will one attain accomplishment or not?

The Master replied: Exerting yourself in study and so forth without attending a master and without having received the empowerments, you will have no result and your efforts will be wasted.

Empowerment is the entrance to the Secret Mantra. To enter the Secret Mantra without the empowerments being conferred is pointless, since it will yield no result and your stream-of-being will be ruined.

Lady Tsogyal asked the Master: If a master himself has not been conferred empowerments and he gives them to others, will they receive the empowerments or not?

The Master replied: Although you may be appointed by a charlatan to the rank of a minister thus entrusted with power, you will only meet with misfortune. Likewise, although you may have an empowerment conferred upon you by a master who himself has not received it, your mind will be ruined. Moreover, you will destroy the minds of others and go to the lower realms like cattle yoked together falling into an abyss. Carried away within an iron box with no exits, you will be sent to the bottom of hell.

Lady Tsogyal asked the Master: Isn't the offering of a gift when receiving empowerment just something you yourself have invented?

The Master replied: All the teachings and tantras explain that at this present time when you have obtained the fortune of a human body after being on errant paths for innumerable aeons, you should, free from the three spheres of concepts, offer your body, life, and spouse to the master who shows the path of unexcelled enlightenment.

Lady Tsogyal asked the Master: How severe is the misdeed of breaking the master's command?

The Master replied: The misdeeds of the three levels of existence do not match even a fraction of the evil of breaking the command of your master. Through this you will take birth in the Unceasing Vajra Hell and find no liberation.

Lady Tsogyal asked the Master: How should we regard the master possessing the oral instructions from whom we request teachings?

The Master replied in verse:

You should know that the master is more important
Than the buddhas of a hundred thousand aeons,
Because all the buddhas of the aeons
Appeared through following masters.
There will never be any buddhas
Who have not followed a master.

The master is the Buddha, the master is the Dharma.
Likewise the master is also the Sangha.
He is the embodiment of all buddhas.
He is the nature of Vajradhara.
He is the root of the Three Jewels.

Keep the command of your vajra master
Without breaking even a fraction of his words.
If you break the command of your vajra master,
You will fall into the Unceasing Vajra Hell
From which there will be no chance for liberation.
By serving your master you will receive the blessings.

Lady Tsogyal asked the Master: Which is more important, the master or the yidam deity?

The Master replied: Do not regard the master and the yidam as different, because it is the master who introduces the yidam deity to you. By always venerating the master at the crown of your head, you will be blessed and your obstacles will be cleared away. If you regard the master and yidam as being different in quality or importance, you are holding misconceptions.

Lady Tsogyal asked the Master: Why is it important to practice the yidam deity?[42]

The Master replied: It is essential to practice a yidam deity because through that you will attain siddhis, your obstacles will be removed, and you will obtain powers, receive blessings, and give rise to realization. Since all these qualities result from practicing the yidam deity, then without the yidam deity you will be just an ordinary person. By practicing the yidam deity, you attain the siddhis, so the yidam deity is essential.

Lady Tsogyal asked the Master: When practicing a yidam deity, how should we meditate and practice in order to attain accomplishment?

The Master replied: Since means and knowledge are to practice the spontaneously present body, speech, and mind through the method of a yoga sadhana, they will be accomplished no matter how you carry out the sadhana aspects endowed with body, speech, and mind. They will be accomplished when the sadhana and recitation are practiced in a sufficient amount.

Lady Tsogyal asked the Master: How should we approach the sugata yidam deity?

The Master replied: Realize that you and the yidam deity are not two and that there is no yidam deity apart from yourself. You approach the yidam deity when you realize that your nature is the state of nonarising dharmakaya.

Lady Tsogyal asked the Master: Which yidam deity is better to practice, a peaceful or a wrathful one?

The Master replied: Since means and knowledge are practicing the spontaneously present body, speech, and mind through the method of a yoga sadhana, all the countless sugatas, peaceful and wrathful, chief figures and retinues, manifest in accordance with those to be tamed in whichever way is necessary—as peaceful and wrathful, chief figures and retinues. But as they are all of one taste in the state of dharmakaya, you can practice whichever yidam you feel inclined toward.

Lady Tsogyal asked the Master: If we practice one yidam deity, will that be the same as practicing all the sugatas?

The Master replied: The body, speech, and mind of all deities are manifested by the three kayas in accordance with the perception of those to be tamed. In fact, no matter how they appear, if you practice one, you will be practicing them all. If you accomplish one, you will have accomplished them all.

Lady Tsogyal asked the Master: Is there any fault in practicing one yidam deity and then practicing another?

The Master replied: Although the sugatas manifest as various kinds of families and forms, out of skillful means to tame beings, they are in actuality inseparable, the state of equality. If you were to practice all the buddhas with this realization of their inseparability, your merit would be most eminent. But if you were to do so while regarding the yidam deities as having different qualities that should be either accepted or rejected, you would be immeasurably obscured. It is inappropriate to regard the yidams as good or bad and to accept or reject them. If you do not regard them like that, it will be excellent no matter how many you practice.

Lady Tsogyal asked the Master: Through performing the approach[43] to one *tathagata*, will we accomplish the mind of all sugatas?

The Master replied: By practicing with a vast view and remaining in the innate nature, you will attain stability in a yidam deity. When you complete the recitation, you will accomplish the activities of all the victorious ones without exception by simply commencing them.

Lady Tsogyal asked the Master: If one's view is high, is it permissible to dispense with the yidam deity?

The Master replied: If you attain confidence in the correct view, then that itself is the yidam deity. Do not regard the yidam deity as a form body. Once you realize the nature of dharmakaya, you will have accomplished the yidam deity.

Lady Tsogyal asked the Master: How should my body appear as the mandala of the deity, and how should I train in the two families?

The Master replied: To visualize your body as the mahamudra[44] of the deity's form is to visualize your mind-essence in the form of the deity.

Since your mind-essence manifests in various ways, as chief figures and retinues, however they may appear, they are all the magical display of the enlightened mind of buddhahood.

Lady Tsogyal asked the Master: Wrathful deities trample noble beings such as Brahma, Indra, and the guardians of the world-corners beneath their feet. Will meditating like that not result in transgressions?

The Master replied: That is shown as a symbol or indication in order to relinquish the clinging to self and others, to trample thoughts into dharmadhatu, and to outshine the arrogance of conceited beings. To regard them as being used as concrete seats is ignorant and confused.

Lady Tsogyal asked the Master: Is there any difference in the degree of virtue of meditating on wrathful deities with three heads and six arms and so on, or with just one head and two arms?

The Master replied: When wrathful deities have many heads and arms, their three heads symbolize the three kayas, and their six arms symbolize the six paramitas. The four legs symbolize the four immeasurables, and their various attributes symbolize the annihilation of vicious beings as well as numerous other qualities. In actuality these forms do not have any substantial nature.

When the deities have one head and two arms, their single head symbolizes the unchanging dharmakaya and their two arms symbolize accomplishing the welfare of beings through means and knowledge. Their two legs symbolize space and wisdom, both manifest and abiding, for the benefit of beings. However you visualize the deities, dharmakaya is beyond any difference in quality and size.

Lady Tsogyal asked the Master: What should we do to have a vision of the yidam deity?

The Master replied: Do not regard the yidam deity as a form body; it is dharmakaya. The meditation on this form body as manifesting from dharmakaya and appearing with color, attributes, ornaments, attire, and major and minor marks should be practiced as being visible while devoid of a self-nature. It is just like the reflection of the moon in water. When you attain mental stability by practicing like this, you will have a vision of the deity, receive teachings, and so forth. If you cling to that, you will go astray and be caught by Mara. Do not become fascinated or overjoyed by such visions, since they are only the manifestations of your mind.

Lady Tsogyal asked the Master: If we have a vision of one yidam deity, will that be the same as having a vision of all the sugatas?

The Master replied: If you have a vision of one yidam deity, it is the same as having a vision of all deities because dharmakaya is beyond quantity.

You will have a vision of whichever deity you are practicing because your mind is becoming pliant. Since the deity is a manifestation of your mind, it does not exist anywhere else.

Lady Tsogyal asked the Master: When it is said that one attains the level of a vidyadhara through practicing a deity, what does "vidyadhara" mean?

The Master replied: Through meditating on your body as being the sublime bodily form (mahamudra) by means of self-cognizant intelligence, you will attain the deity of your realized mind-essence endowed with major and minor marks and superknowledges. It is a mahamudra form belonging to whichever family you have practiced. That is called vidyadhara.

Lady Tsogyal asked the Master: Where do the vidyadharas dwell?

The Master replied: It is your own mind that is dwelling in the form of a deity, and it dwells in the manner of nondwelling. Yet it is said that once you reach a vidyadhara level, you will be beyond falling back.

Lady Tsogyal asked the Master: How should we venerate the yidam deity?

The Master replied: You should venerate the yidam deity by not giving up the yidam deity even at the cost of your life, by not holding doubts about the yidam deity, by not separating yourself from the yidam for even an instant as long as you have not attained the unexcelled mind of enlightenment. By visualizing the deity when you walk, lie down, or sit, you will automatically receive the siddhis and blessings.

Lady Tsogyal asked the Master: Is it necessary to practice the yidam deity continuously? Once you accomplish one method, is it still necessary to practice?

The Master replied: When first practicing a yidam deity and following a sadhana text, even if you have a vision of the yidam deity and receive teachings, it will be a major transgression if you then discontinue the practice. It is therefore essential to practice continuously.

Lady Tsogyal asked the Master: How should we continuously practice the approach and accomplishment of the yidam deity?

The Master replied: When practicing a yidam deity, you should practice the development stage in each session. Perform the recitation in each session, make offerings, give tormas, make praises, and request the fulfillment of your wishes. Seal the practice in emptiness with the completion stage.

At best do eight sessions a day, as second best do four sessions. At the least, do one session a day. Any less is not permissible. Through that your samayas are fulfilled, and you will receive the siddhis.

When you attain stability in development and completion, without discarding your body it will be matured into a deity. That is called the vidyadhara level of maturation. Although your body remains as an (ordinary) human being, your mind is matured into a deity. This is like an image formed in the mold.

When leaving your body in the bardo state, you become that particular deity just like the image coming out of the mold. That is called the vidyadhara level of mahamudra. The body of a practitioner is called an encasement, and the moment the body is discarded, the practitioner becomes the form of the yidam deity.

Lady Tsogyal asked the Master: Why are some deities shown as having the heads of animals on bodies of deities? Isn't that meditating on the deity as having substantial existence?

The Master replied: The deities manifested with heads of animals symbolize the particular quality which that animal possesses. It is not the case that real and substantially existent deities with animal heads are to be accomplished from somewhere else; they are the manifestations of your own mind.

Emanated from the deities in union are the offspring alloys (*tramenma*) with animal heads, such as the Eaters and Killers of Kilaya or the eight alloy goddesses (*tramenmas*) of Yangdag. Just as a mixture of gold and silver is called an alloy (*tramen*), these are emanated as having the body of a deity with the head of an animal. They are emanated through the compassion of the male deity and the knowledge of the female deity; or from the male deity who is the nature of means and the female deity who is the nature of knowledge. Symbolizing the particular activity they fulfill, they are manifested as having the head possessing that particular quality.

Lady Tsogyal asked the Master: Isn't it conflicting to place supramundane and mundane deities together such as when the chief deity who is supramundane is surrounded by a retinue of mundane deities?

The Master replied: The chief figure who is supramundane is a wisdom deity. Like a powerful king, he brings conceited beings under his command. The visualized retinue of mundane deities are the deities who carry out his commands and consequently liberate enemies, obstructing forces, and so forth. Supramundane and mundane are like a king and his attendants, so there is no conflict.

Lady Tsogyal asked the Master: Is concentration or recitation most important for daily practice?

The Master replied: For the accomplishment of the supreme siddhi of Mahamudra, when your mind is pliable your concentration will be pliable, and then in actuality you will meet the form of the deity. When you recognize that the deity is your own mind, the three kayas will dawn within you.

For the accomplishment of common siddhis, the countless activities of pacifying, increasing, magnetizing, subjugating, and so forth, the mantras are most important. Consequently, complete the set number of recitations. Until you finish retreat, it is essential not to interrupt your practice with ordinary talk. No matter what task you may accomplish, you should persevere in the mantras; be very persevering.

Lady Tsogyal asked the Master: If one accomplishes the yidam deity that is naturally present, is there any accomplishment?

The Master replied: The yidam deity manifests as the unobstructed activity of the compassionate means of all the sugatas. Therefore in the perception of the sentient beings to be tamed, they appear as peaceful and wrathful, mandalas and buddhafields, male and female, chief figures with retinues and single figures. The palace of the deity, the chief figure, the retinue and so forth, in the abode of Akanishtha, are therefore unlike other abodes of gods. The form kayas manifest from the state of nonarising dharmakaya for the benefit of beings and are perceived in accordance with their particular inclinations.

Lady Tsogyal asked the Master: In regard to making offerings of tormas and so forth to the deity, if the deity accepts the offerings and is pleased by the praises, it is the same as a substantially existent mundane god. If not, what is the use of performing those deeds?

The Master replied: The wisdom deity is not delighted by praises or pleased by offerings. In order to purify your mind, you visualize and invite the deity, make praises and offerings, and so forth. When you do so, your devotion purifies your mind. Due to the unceasing compassionate means of the sugatas, you will receive the blessings and siddhis. This is like the following example: When offerings are made to a wish-fulfilling jewel, it will fulfill the needs and wishes of sentient beings even though it has no intention to benefit them.

Tsogyal, Tibetan practitioners set aside the deity present in themselves and seek the buddha in Akanishtha. Without even an atom of concentration, their activities stray into shamanistic incantations. Not knowing how to naturally purify their three poisons, they offer tormas of flesh and blood. Without practicing for accomplishment of the supreme siddhi, they desire magical powers, offspring, and wealth. Misapplying the Secret Mantra, they divulge its secrets. Bartering the oral instructions like merchandise, they busy themselves with magic and evil spells. Many of them will be reborn as people with wrong views, *rudras*, *yakshas*, and *rakshas*. So perfect the power of the view, practice with concentration, engage in the four activities as your conduct, and accomplish the fruition, the supreme siddhi of Mahamudra.

*This ends the oral instructions on the Secret Mantra taught by the Master Padmakara to Lady Tsogyal, the Princess of Kharchen, in the form of questions and answers.*

*Treasure seal.*
*Concealment seal.*
*Entrustment seal.*

# 26

## RECITATION

*Tulku Urgyen Rinpoche*

After visualizing the deity, you proceed with the recitation of the various mantras. Recitation includes the *approach*, then the *full approach*, the *accomplishment*, the *great accomplishment*, and finally the *application of the activities*.

There can be different mantras for each of these in a sadhana, or all aspects of approach and accomplishment can be completed within the recitation of a single mantra. The first of the four is the "moon with a garland of stars": the syllable HRIH surrounded by a garland of stars in Guru Rinpoche's heart center, for example, in a Guru Rinpoche sadhana. Then, as the mantra starts to circle and revolve, there is the second intent or visualization that is called the fire brand. These refer to approach and full approach. The moon with the garland of stars is generally considered the intent of the approach, and the fire brand the intent of the full approach. These represent the first two of the four types of recitation intents, approach and full approach.

The third, "the messenger of the king," begins with the emanation of light rays. Upwardly one makes offerings to the mandala of the victorious ones; downwardly, the rays of light are the generosity that purifies all the

---

From Tulku Urgyen Rinpoche, *Vajra Heart* (Boudhanath: Rangjung Yeshe Publications, 1988), "Recitation."

obscurations and negative karmas of sentient beings. This radiating upward and downward while making offerings and purifying sentient beings is called the intent of the king's messenger and belongs to the third aspect of recitation, the accomplishment.

The fourth, great accomplishment, includes all four: approach, full approach, accomplishment, and great accomplishment. At the time of pursuing the great accomplishment, there should be an individual for each of the deities in the practice. For example, for a convocation of the peaceful and wrathful deities, one needs a hundred people for the hundred deities. Then such a practice can truly be called great accomplishment.

In the Guru Rinpoche practice of *Barchey Künsel*, the recitation of the HA RI NI SA mantra fulfills the pacifying, enriching, magnetizing, and subjugating activities embodied by the four gatekeepers. Each of the four types of activities has its own particular mantra for whatever action one has to complete. If one needs to magnetize, there is a magnetizing mantra; if one needs to subjugate, there is a subjugating mantra. Through the supreme mantra, which is the spontaneously accomplished activity, one can accomplish the supreme action. In this case then, there are five activities: pacifying, enriching, magnetizing, subjugating, and the supreme activity, which is the spontaneously accomplished activity, the samadhi action of self-existing wakefulness.

In the *Barchey Künsel* sadhana, when practicing mantra recitation, one first visualizes the buddha mandala of one's body, then practices the approach, accomplishment, and applications of the activities simultaneously, like bees swarming from the hive. One's body is visualized as the nature of deity, the deity's body; all sounds are of the nature of the deity's speech; all thoughts are of the nature of the deity's mind.

# 27

## CAPTURING THE LIFE
## FORCE OF ALL DEITIES

*Tulku Urgyen Rinpoche*

The different schools of Tibetan Buddhism vary in how they regard the practices of the yidam deity. In the new schools, the Sarma schools, particularly the Sakya, one has to keep the link to the yidam alive through daily recitation of the mantra. Although the link is obtained through empowerment, you must maintain it by keeping up daily samaya practice; otherwise the link vanishes. While it's never said that one who misses daily practice will go to hell, the Sakya tradition insists on daily practice in order to keep the link to the yidam deity. That is why some Sakya lamas have a thick book of daily practices. It's not the same in the Kagyü and Nyingma system, where the emphasis is placed on "condensing all into one." In this approach, if you practice one deity, all the others are automatically included within that. If you realize one buddha, you automatically realize all other buddhas at the same time.

The statement "Realize one buddha and you realize them all" means that all buddhas are one within the expanse of original wakefulness. It is like the immensity of space, the expanse of the sky: We cannot say there is one sky for one part of the world and another sky for another. The entire expanse is the same space. Likewise, the spacelike enlightened mind of all buddhas

From Tulku Urgyen Rinpoche, *As It Is*, Volume I (Boudhanath: Rangjung Yeshe Publications, 1999), "Capture the Life Force of All Deities."

is identical, although they show themselves in different forms. Still, the essence of what they really are does not consist of different entities.

The fact that all buddhas are one in the expanse of original wakefulness is not merely my invention. This is taught by the buddhas themselves. If you can feel confident in that, you will also understand that all the different forms of the buddhas are not like different people that you have to keep in close contact with. It is not as if there were thirty people and you had to maintain a good friendship with each and every one of them. Wisdom beings like buddhas don't have any thoughts, and they don't discriminate as to whether someone likes them or doesn't like them. They are not like normal people. All the many forms of the buddhas have the same identity. By practicing one of them, you automatically keep the link with all of them. Feel confident that that is how it is.

Although all the buddhas are in essence the same, they show themselves in a variety of different ways. In this respect it's the same with us; in essence, we all have buddha nature. With respect to our buddha nature, there is no difference between us; we are all basically the unity of empty cognizance. But there are definitely differences between us in how this buddha nature expresses itself as thoughts. While I am happy, another person might feel sad; we don't feel the same. Still, in essence, we are the same.

Deities don't have thoughts, they don't discriminate, and in terms of identity they are like the single expanse of space. Imagine the space within each room in all the houses in Nepal. Although these houses are separate from each other, still the space itself is not different from one house to another. In terms of basic essence, all buddhas are identical. Therefore, if you realize one, you automatically realize all of them.

Whenever you visualize a deity in the development stage, please understand that the basis of that is completion stage. If you can visualize after recognizing mind-essence, simply allow the form of the deity to manifest, to take place, within that state. Then there is basically no difference no matter which deity you practice, because you are simply allowing the form of the deity to be displayed while you are still in mind-essence. If you don't practice like that—if you practice with ordinary dualistic thought—then all the deities are definitely different: The thought of one automatically excludes the thought of another.

When it comes to realizing a certain yidam, the most important points are: recognize emptiness, do the practice out of compassion for all sentient beings, and be free from hope and fear. If you practice in that way, you are certain to realize the deity; there is no doubt about that. But if you do the practice out of a materialistic motivation—"I wish I could obtain such-and-such"—then this expectation postpones the accomplishment. You will never realize the deity through hope and fear. First of all, recognize mind nature; next, engender compassion for all beings; then, give up hope and fear. By training in this way, you will definitely accomplish the deity.

You can begin to visualize a deity by looking at a tangka. It gives you a visual impression, a visible form, but the real deity is not exactly like that, because a tangka is tangible; you can take hold of it with your hand. The form of the deity you imagine is visible but not tangible. It is empty, and yet you can see it. It is like the reflection in the mirror, in that you can see it but you cannot take hold of it.

There are four major schools of Tibetan Buddhism: Kagyü, Sakya, Nyingma, and Gelug. In all four of these traditions, when we practice development stage, we need to start with the samadhi of suchness, as I explained in detail previously. Suchness means the innate nature of your own mind. It is not some other suchness from some other place. That suchness is simply the completion stage. The *complete* in completion means what is completely present as your own nature, which is the dharmakaya nature of mind. To recognize that is called completion stage. While recognizing mind-essence, while remaining in the samadhi of suchness, one allows the visualizations of the development stage to take place without leaving the natural state behind. Out of the expanse of the three kayas, the practice of sadhana takes place for the benefit of beings. Both samsara and nirvana always manifest out of the expanse of the three kayas.

The first of the three samadhis, the samadhi of suchness, means primordial emptiness. It is actually the essence of the kayas of all buddhas. The empty essence is the quality of enlightened body. The cognizant nature is the quality of enlightened speech. The unconfined capacity of awareness is the quality of enlightened mind.

The body, speech, and mind of all buddhas are also expressed as follows: The unchanging quality is body, the unceasing quality is speech, and the unmistaken quality is mind. In the deluded state of being, a manifestation of these three qualities becomes the body, voice, and mind of sentient beings.

Thus, in these three qualities you have both samsara and nirvana, the body, speech, and mind of all buddhas and the body, speech, and mind of sentient beings. In this way, the nature of the three kayas permeates both samsara and nirvana. It may sound like there are three separate things, like one is dharmakaya, another is sambhogakaya, and the third is nirmanakaya, but actually it is one indivisible identity. That is the svabhavikakaya, the essence body, which is no other than the nature of your own mind. This pervades or is present throughout all samsaric and nirvanic states.

The body, speech, and mind of all sentient beings is nothing other than the expression or the manifestation of the body, speech, and mind of all the buddhas. They don't come from anywhere else. If we fully recognize the identity of this, we become totally stable. That is called "awakening to the enlightenment of the body, speech, and mind of all buddhas." But if we fail to recognize our own nature, we are bewildered and continue to roam about in samsaric existence, just as we are doing now.

To quote from the tantra, "All sentient beings are buddhas, but they are covered by temporary obscurations. When these are removed, they are truly buddhas." Although the very identity of all buddhas and beings is the same, when we don't recognize it we continue in samsara. It is a case of one identity with two aspects. We can be enlightened and are able to attain buddhahood because we already have the very essence of enlightenment—buddha nature. Without that, there is no way that we could attain any enlightenment.

Of completion stage and development stage, completion stage is the most important. It's like the very life force in that we already possess it; the innate three kayas are the nature of our mind. Completion stage is the three kayas of the awakened state. While we already have these and don't need to work to create them, we *can* develop their manifest quality. Development stage is what we imagine, what we allow to play in the field of our mind.

There is mind and mind-essence. Mind is different from essence. That which thinks and imagines is dualistic mind, while in the essence there is nothing thought of or imagined. The three kayas are naturally present in the essence, and in one way they become manifest in form through the act of visualization. We do this in order to gain the accomplishments and to purify obscurations. The foremost way to do this is to allow all the different aspects of the development stage to take place while one recognizes mind-essence. That is first class, the best way. However, even if one does not know mind nature and practices development stage, development and completion are still a unity, since mind-essence is an unconfined empty cognizance. It is essential to understand the basic principles of yidam practice with regard to these points.

In order to outwardly manifest the qualities of the three kayas—the yidam's body, speech, and mind—we go through a variety of different steps during sadhana practice: We make offerings, recite the mantra, imagine light rays being radiated out and absorbed back, make praises and apologies, request to turn the wheel of Dharma, beseech the buddhas not to pass away into nirvana, and dedicate the merit. All these steps are different ways of removing the clouds in the sky. Together, they constitute what is traditionally called purifying the obscurations, the gathering of the accumulations of merit and wisdom. They are the skillful and compassionate means of the buddhas and, as the expression of wisdom, are incredibly effective. Never regard development stage as meaningless, pointless, or unimportant.

The most vital point in development stage is described as "capturing the life force of all buddhas." In other words, if you realize the completion stage, there is no way you can avoid realizing all buddhas and yidams. Without the completion stage, all the buddhas and yidams are only something we imagine. When you recognize well that mind-essence is beyond achieving, the deity is automatically accomplished. Really, there is no other profound technique than this to realizing the deity.

The ultimate aim of yidam practice is to recognize the nature of the three kayas as indivisible from your own mind. The visible aspects that can manifest are automatically accomplished within recognition of our mind-essence. Though they manifest outwardly, inwardly one is not creating anything whatsoever.

Completion stage is like having an electric lightbulb in the center of your heart, while development stage is like painting an image of a lightbulb on the wall. The painted light can never really be switched on, but it will remind you that there actually is a *real* light, and you can thus recognize it more easily. This is the difference between the two.

We need both development and completion stages. While we are not yet stable in samadhi, in the completion stage, the visible aspects of the development stage help us to purify obscurations and gather the accumulations of merit and wisdom. These have a great and deep significance in that they remove the obscurations. Never think that the development stage is unnecessary. Often the phrase "identifying the deity to be accomplished" is mentioned. It means we should identify that the ultimate deity is actually the completion stage, the very nature of our mind. That is what we should acknowledge as the deity to be accomplished.

The buddhas never teach that we can attain enlightenment only by means of the development stage. One attains enlightenment by the unity of development and completion. But the real, vital force in attaining enlightenment is the completion stage. It's possible to attain enlightenment only through the completion stage, but not only through the development stage. Still, the swiftest way to attain enlightenment is by unifying means and knowledge.

Means is the development stage and knowledge is the completion stage. You may have knowledge in the form of a person who can put an entire airplane together, but if you don't have the means, which is all the parts, you can keep that person as long as you like, but you'll never have an airplane. Conversely, you can have every single part of an airplane, all the means, but if there is not the know-how of a person who can assemble them, there is no way that those pieces will fly by themselves. It is only when you put the knowledge together with the means that it is possible to have an airplane that can actually fly.

The reason the Secret Mantra, Vajrayana, is said to be a swift path to enlightenment is simply because of unifying means and knowledge, development stage and completion stage. Vajrayana practice involves combining the visualization of a deity together with the recognition of mind-essence; that's why it's a swift path.

Here's another example for "realizing one deity, you realize all of them." Let's say that you have one thousand electric bulbs. You wire them, but you haven't switched on the electricity. What good are those thousand bulbs going to do in terms of illuminating anything? But if you turn on the electric switch, the one thousand bulbs will light up at the same time. Even though they are individual and distinct, the light that shines through them is the same in identity. In essence it is the same light. No matter where in the world you have electric light, that light shines and illuminates in exactly the same way, although it may vary according to the condition of each bulb. The main force, like the electricity that lights the bulbs, is what we call original wakefulness, *yeshe*. And that is the most important thing. If you realize that, you've realized the light in every single one of the bulbs, not just one of them.

Or maybe the bulbs are different colors, so that when the light shines through them, one bulb is yellow, the others blue, green, or red. This is an example for the lights of the five wisdoms. While the colors or the specific qualities of each emanation may differ, the light that shines through them is the same original wakefulness. Please understand this.

If this wasn't so, we would be able to argue whether development or completion stage was best. It would be like development stage and completion stage getting into a fight. Please understand that the means is development stage and the knowledge is completion stage, and that they are both important. It is the union of the two that is most vital.

Don't think that there are no real deities, that they are nothing but our imagination. There are deities intrinsic to our buddha nature, which are wisdom deities. In the same way, no matter what color the bulb is, whether blue, red, white, or green, the light that shines is exactly the same. You may have ten thousand or a hundred thousand bulbs, but without electricity to shine through them, they're useless. In the same way, we need completion stage together with development stage.

You may succeed in visualizing 10,000 or even 100,000 different yidams as clearly and distinctly as if they were present in person, but your practice still needs to be combined with the completion stage. If not, it's like having all the parts of an airplane but lacking the knowledge of how to put them together.

Without knowing mind-essence, one is forced to practice Vajrayana as an imitation of how it really is. That is a second-rate development stage. One needs first to say a mantra, such as OM SVABHAVA SHUDDHO SARVA DHARMA SVABHAVA SHUDDHOH HANG, and imagine that everything becomes emptiness. Out of this state of created emptiness, the seed syllables for space, wind, earth, water, fire, and the celestial palace gradually appear, followed by the deity, and so forth. These are all something that one imagines. Honestly, saying that the mantra makes all things become emptiness is not really true, because all things were *already* emptiness. It is not that they all of a sudden become emptiness because you think it. If one hasn't recognized mind-essence, one doesn't see that. The thinking of one thing after the other then becomes an imitation of the true development stage because of not really knowing the completion stage.

On the other hand, you may have been introduced to the nature of mind and recognized the samadhi of suchness. Suchness means how it really is, not merely how one imagines it to be. While not departing from this state of suchness—while recognizing mind-essence—one can then allow the different aspects of development stage to be played out or displayed, without leaving the state of suchness behind. That is the real unity of development and completion. There is a real way and a simulated way, and without recognizing mind-essence there is no chance that one can practice the real way.

The real way of practicing the unity of development and completion means that you have been introduced to the view of Trekchö, cutting through, the real samadhi of suchness. It is like the example of a blank mirror. Anything can be reflected, and when reflected, the reflection has no substance or materiality whatsoever. And yet it is clearly visible.

The seed samadhi, the third of the three samadhis, is like the reflection appearing, while the brightness and the mirror itself are like the first two samadhis, which are emptiness and cognizance. The samadhi of suchness is emptiness, and the samadhi of illumination is the cognizant or bright quality. These two are indivisible, and out of this indivisible unity of emptiness and cognizance, also called emptiness and compassion, any reflection can take place; any form of development stage can take place freely. Whatever unfolds as development stage indivisible from completion stage is experienced, but it has no material nature. This is only because of recognizing completion stage. Without that, development stage is like the building work going on outside my room. It becomes construction work, which means that something is visible but also tangible.

Let's say that you've received all the empowerments for the *Rinchen Ter-dzö,* the *Treasury of Precious Termas,* a cycle of teachings with many, many deities. It takes four months to receive all the empowerments. If your style of practice is according to the new schools, you would have a huge stack of daily practices, all of which you have to chant. You'd have to be chanting continuously from morning to evening in order to get through these and say the mantras. At the end, you'd think, "Whew, today I made it, I got through this. I still have the sacred bond to all the deities; they haven't left me." Then perhaps one day you forget one of them or you are not able to do the practice. You think, "Oh, no! Now I've broken the sacred link to this yidam; I've broken my samaya, and for sure I will go to hell." Then you're really in trouble. The trouble comes because there are so many different forms of yidams that it becomes very difficult to keep the bond to each of them individually.

You can also take the approach that every yidam and every buddha is identical in the expanse of original wakefulness. Then you can keep the bond to all of them very simply, for example, by chanting the three syllables for the body, speech, and mind of all the buddhas, OM AH HUNG. OM is the essence of Vairochana, the Manifester of Forms, the enlightened body of all the buddhas. AH is the essence of Amitabha, Boundless Light, which is the speech of all buddhas. HUNG is the essence of Akshobhya, the Unshakable, which is the nature of mind free of conceptual thinking. The HUNG syllable is the essence of the mind of all buddhas. Actually it would be perfectly fine to chant OM AH HUNG … OM AH HUNG while recognizing mind-essence. You are then keeping the samaya with every possible aspect of the yidams and buddhas, because all of them are included within enlightened body, speech, and mind.

Now think of all the teachings given by the buddhas. In this world, the Tripitaka, the Kangyur, and the Tengyur—the words of the Buddha and the treatises that are the commentaries upon them—fill hundreds and hundreds of volumes in incredible detail. Then there are all the tantras. However, the very essence of all these teachings is development and completion stage. When seeking to perfect comprehension, you can go into great detail, but when it comes to applying this comprehension to your experience, you should condense everything and simplify it. In other words, these three syllables, OM AH HUNG, contain the body, speech, and mind of all buddhas, all teachings, and all samadhis.

Similarly, the body, speech, and mind of the victorious ones are contained in a single instant of recognizing mind-essence. OM is the essence of Vairochana, which means "manifest in form." The form of the deity is something visible, something manifest in form. For example, in the bardo state we meet the sounds, colors, and lights, the major and minor spheres of light, the peaceful and wrathful deities, and so forth. Everything we meet here is something perceptible, which is manifest in form, and that is the body aspect of all buddhas. Next is AH for speech. Speech is Amitabha, Boundless Light, which is all the unending infinite teachings all contained within one syllable. The HUNG for mind is Akshobhya, which means unperturbed or unshakable—the state of nondual awareness, free of any conceptual thinking whatsoever. In this way, the three syllables OM AH HUNG embody or include the body, speech, and mind of any buddha form in any way whatsoever. You can go into all of this in great detail when trying to comprehend, but when applying it in your own experience, condense everything into the essential.

The essence of the body, speech, and mind of all the buddhas is called deity, mantra, and samadhi. The way to condense that into the essential is that the deity is something you visualize, rather than something you make by hand. It's not a big construction. It is the recollection "I am such-and-such deity." At that moment you have imagined yourself as being a certain deity, so that is very simple. With your speech, which is mantra, say OM AH HUNG.

With your mind, which is the samadhi aspect, recognize mind-essence. Everything is included within this simple approach.

Unless we train in the three principles of deity, mantra, and samadhi, as sentient beings our minds are always carried away by the three or five poisons. For example, look at this cup. You think this is a nice cup—well, that is desire. When you look at this used handkerchief, you don't like it. That is anger or aversion. This unused toothpick is neither good nor bad, right? When you look at it, you don't feel attracted to it, you don't get angry at it, you just feel neutral. Any thought that we think is like one of those three. There is no state of dualistic mind that is not mixed with the three poisons. When we see something nice, we like it. If we see something ugly, we dislike it. Something in between, we feel indifferent, right? Also, when we hear something nice, when we smell something sweet, when we taste delicious food, we like it. If it tastes foul, we dislike it. We all have the three poisons. When something appears in our mind that is pleasant, we like it; if it's painful, we dislike it. We do have pleasure and pain, don't we? But anything in between we don't care much about, we dismiss. Whatever appears to our six senses, we always react to with the three poisons.

Development stage is simply changing this pattern into white thoughts, by imagining the celestial palace, the form of the deity, the offerings. When we imagine Mount Sumeru after the five syllables, the celestial palace on top of the vajra cross, the deity and offerings, all this purifies our habitual thinking. We chant the invocation, and the wisdom deities appear in the sky and dissolve into ourselves. "I myself am a deity; I emanate rays of light turning into offering goddesses who turn around and present boundless offerings and praises to myself as a deity." All this is something we imagine, and it changes our thought pattern into white thoughts. That was about the deity, for the body aspect.

Next we imagine the three *sattvas*: samaya-sattva, jñana-sattva, samadhi-sattva, which are the triple beings called the samaya being, wisdom being, and samadhi being. The samadhi being is a seed syllable in the center of our heart encircled by the garland of the mantra, which spins and shines out rays of light. There are a lot of different activities and functions related to the recitation of mantra that belong to the speech aspect. When it comes to the samadhi or mind aspect, you simply recognize what it is that imagines all this. Experience the state of indivisible, empty cognizance.

The development and completion stages are taught by the buddhas out of skillful means and great compassion. These teachings are extremely precious and effective. The whole purpose of the development stage is, first, to transform black thoughts into white thoughts. The purpose of the completion stage is to let the white thoughts dissolve tracelessly. When you recognize mind essence and see the state of indivisible empty cognizance, that dissolves even the whitest of thoughts, so that no trace is left behind.

People sometimes say, "I want a vision of the deity." They expect that after they recite a certain number of mantras, the deity will arrive in front of them and they will see it. Actually, that attitude externalizes the deity. The real deity is the unity of emptiness and cognizance, the nature of your own mind. Instead of ringing the bell and beating the drum, expecting the deity to appear up there in the sky before you, you should simply recognize what it is that imagines all this. At that time you see the state in which emptiness and cognizance are indivisible. That is being face to face with the real deity. Isn't that much easier than hoping a deity will appear from the outside? The real vision of the deity is to recognize the nature of your mind.

Even if you look for a billion years into the nature of your mind, you will never see that it is any concrete thing other than being empty. That is the dharmakaya deity, and when you look, you see it. No matter how you investigate, analyze, and scrutinize this nature of mind, you will never find it to have any sort of concrete, material substance. That's why it's called unconstructed emptiness. To recognize this is to be face to face with or have a vision of the dharmakaya buddha. What is it that sees that mind is empty? There is some cognizant, aware quality that can see that it is empty. This is unlike space; space doesn't see itself. Mind, on the other hand, is cognizant as well as empty. The empty quality is dharmakaya, the cognizant quality is sambhogakaya, and their unity is nirmanakaya.

This is the easiest way to have a vision of the deity, as well as the real way. The superficial way is to expect a deity to appear as coming from outside, after ringing the bell and beating the drum. Actually, though, the easiest way is to have a vision of the deity as the completion stage. That is also the true way. If you only practice the development stage by feeling "I wish the deity would come, I wish the deity would come," that is training in hope and fear. It only pushes the true deity farther away.

Recognizing mind-essence captures the life force of thousands of buddhas. When you take hold of the life-force, they cannot escape you. Through the power of the genuine state of samadhi, you capture the life force of all the deities, without having to conjure them up as being somewhere over there in the distance.

There is another way as well, in which one tries to please a deity in a solid, rigid sort of way, thinking that the deity really exists somewhere up there. This kind of attitude thinks, "I must put offerings out, otherwise he will get angry. If I put nice offerings, he will be pleased. If I chant the mantra, I make him happy, and if I forget, he will be upset. If I break the bond with him, it will make him feel very bad." That attitude is also called training in hope and fear, and it is not the genuine way.

It is much simpler to practice like this: First, remind yourself with the thought of being the deity, for example, "I am Vajra Kilaya." Then, recite the mantra, OM BENZA KILI KILAYA, or simply OM AH HUNG. Next, recognize what it is that imagines the deity and what it is that chants the mantra as being nothing other than your own mind.

Without this mind, there would be no visualizing the form of the deity. Without mind, there would be no chanting the mantra. When you look into what it is that imagines or recites, recognizing your own mind, you see that it is an indivisible empty cognizance, and not in some roundabout way. For example, if you want to touch space with your finger, how far do you need to move your finger in order to touch space? Doesn't it touch it the moment you first stretch your finger out? In the same way, the moment you recognize, you come in contact with the completion stage—the empty and cognizant nature of mind. It is recognized immediately. Thus, while seeing the nature of mind, you can carry on chanting the mantra.

When beginning your practice session, don't neglect to imagine the form of the deity. If you don't look in the mirror, the face is not seen. Visualizing the deity means the mind mirror is allowed to think, "I am Vajra Kilaya." It is all right to remind yourself that you are the deity, because your five aggregates and five elements from the very beginning are the mandala of buddhas.

In this way, with the single thought "I am the deity," visualization takes no more than an instant. This instantaneous recollection, bringing the deity vividly to mind in an instant, is the highest and best form of visualization. With your voice, chant the mantra, and with your mind, recognize. If you can decide that this type of practice is sufficient and all-inclusive, that is perfectly all right. It's not like we have to please the wisdom deity, who has no thoughts anyway. Wisdom deities don't get pleased or displeased, so it is really more a matter of making up your own mind and practicing in this simple, all-inclusive way. This is my opinion. Maybe I'm being too simple here. On the other hand, maybe it is true.

The wisdom deity represents what is called *rangjung yeshe* in Tibetan, or *swayambhu jñana* in Sanskrit: self-existing wakefulness. In this way, the wisdom deity is indivisible from the nature of our own mind. The wisdom deity has no thoughts, and thus it doesn't discriminate and is not pleased or displeased by our actions. However, a text states, "Although the wisdom deity holds no thoughts, still, its oath-bound retinue sees the faults of people." The wisdom deity itself is not made happy by offerings or displeased if one forgets. Its total realization acts like a magnet to attract all sorts of mundane spirits. These mundane spirits do have shortcomings, they do have thoughts, and they do see the faults of people. They can either help or harm. The retinue of the wisdom deities includes the *mamos*, the *tsen*, the *dü*, and all the different earth, fire, and water gods. Whether or not you make offerings does make a difference to them. But for wisdom deities themselves, it makes no difference, because they have no thoughts.

To reiterate, carry out whatever yidam practice you are involved in while practicing it within the structure of the three samadhis and while recognizing mind-essence. If you practice like that, I can guarantee that within this one lifetime you can accomplish both the common siddhis and the supreme siddhi of complete enlightenment.

Let me tell you a story to illustrate this. Sakya Pandita was not only an extremely learned master, but he was accomplished as well. He had developed clairvoyance based on sound. Traveling through a place along the Tibetan border, he listened to a stream running down the mountain. Through the water he heard the mantra of Vajra Kilaya mispronounced OM BENZA CHILI CHILAYA SARVA BIGHANAN BAM HUNG PHAT. He thought, "Someone must be saying the wrong mantra up in the mountains; I'd better go up and correct him." He went up there and found this insignificant little meditation hut with a lama sitting inside. Sakya Pandita asked his name and what he was doing, and the lama replied, "My yidam is Vajra Kilaya and that is what I'm doing." Sakya Pandita asked, "What mantra are you using?" and the lama said, "OM BENZA CHILI CHILAYA SARVA BIGHANAN BAM HUNG PHAT." Sakya Pandita said, "Oh, no! That's the wrong mantra; it's supposed to begin with OM BENZA KILI KILAYA. That's where the real meaning lies, in the words 'Vajra Kilaya with consort, the Ten Sons and all the Eaters and Slayers.' They are contained within the sounds of the mantra." The meditator replied, "No, no, the words are not as important as the state of mind. Pure mind is more important than pure sound. I said CHILI CHILAYA in the past, and that's what I will continue to say in the future. No doubt about that! You, on the other hand, will need my phurba." And the meditator gave Sakya Pandita his kilaya dagger, saying, "You take this with you." So he did.

Some time later, in Kyirong, which is on the Tibet-Nepal border, Sakya Pandita met with Shangkara, a Hindu master who wanted to convert the Tibetans. The two had a big debate, with the winner of each round getting one parasol or umbrella as a symbol of his victory. Each had won nine, and there was one left. At that point Shangkara flew up into the sky as a magical display of his siddhis. While he was levitating there, Sakya Pandita took his dagger and chanted "OM BENZA CHILA CHILAYA ... " Shangkara fell straight to the ground, and Sakya Pandita won the tenth parasol. It's said that Buddhism in Tibet survived because of that.

An old saying has it that "Tibetans ruin it for themselves by having too many deities." They think they have to practice one, then they have to practice another, then a third and a fourth. It goes on and on, and they end up not accomplishing anything, whereas in India a meditator would practice a single deity for his entire life and would reach supreme accomplishment. It would be good if we were to take this attitude. If we practice Vajrasattva, it is perfectly complete to simply practice that single yidam. One doesn't have to be constantly shifting to different deities afraid one will miss something, because there is absolutely nothing missing in the single yidam one practices.

A line from one tantra says, "I apologize for accepting and rejecting the yidam deity." Sometimes one feels tired with a particular practice, like "It's enough, practicing this one yidam!" Then you give up that one and try practicing another one, then after a while, another. Try not to do this.

As I said earlier, if you accomplish one buddha, then you accomplish all buddhas. If you attain the realization of one yidam, automatically you attain realization of all yidams at the same time. Of course, there is nothing wrong with practicing more than one. The point is to not skip around between them.

Practice whichever yidam you like best. You will naturally feel more inclined toward one yidam than another, and this feeling is a very good indication of which yidam you are connected to. The basic guideline is to choose whoever you feel most inspired by. Once you choose one, practice it continuously.

There are no essential differences between the yidams. You cannot say that there are good or bad yidams, in that all yidam forms are included within the five buddha families. It is not that one buddha family is better or worse than any of the other ones—not at all. People's individual feelings do make a difference, in that some people want to practice Padmasambhava as their yidam, while some want to practice Avalokiteshvara or Buddha Shakyamuni or Tara. The preference varies from person to person due to karmic inclination. It is not that there is any distinction in quality between yidams. If you take the one hundred peaceful and wrathful deities as your yidam, you have included everyone.

Once you reach accomplishment, you have simultaneously accomplished all enlightened qualities, regardless of which yidam you practice. It doesn't make any difference. For example, when the sun rises, its warmth and light are simultaneously present. If you accomplish one buddha form, you simultaneously accomplish all buddha forms. The reason is that all yidams are essentially the same; they differ only in form, not essence. The fundamental reason one attains accomplishment is because of recognizing mind essence while doing the yidam practice. The real practice is recognizing rigpa, and you use the yidam as the external form of the practice. Even though every yidam manifests various aspects of different qualities, in essence they are all the same.

You can describe the rising sun in all sorts of different ways: Some people will say that when the sun rises, it's no longer cold, or that there's no more darkness, or that it becomes light and you can see. It's the same with describing the different qualities of the enlightened state, in which all the qualities such as wisdom, compassion, and capability are spontaneously present.

Try to see yidam practice as a gift that the buddhas have given us because we have requested it. When we take refuge, we are asking for protection, to be safeguarded, and the real protection lies in the teachings on how to remove the obscurations and how to attain realization. The real protection is the yidam practice. Through it we can remove what needs to be removed and realize what needs to be realized, and thereby attain accomplishment.

Although we have this enlightened essence, it is like a butter lamp that is not yet lit, not enlightened yet. We need to connect with, to touch it with a lit butter lamp in order to light our own. Imagine two butter lamps together: One is not lit, the other is already enlightened. The one that is as yet unlit has to bow to the other in order to get the light.

In the same way, we already have the buddha nature, but we haven't caught on to it yet. We haven't recognized it, trained in it, and attained stability. There is great benefit in connecting with those other "lamps" because they *have* already recognized their buddha nature, trained in it, and obtained stability. Our butter lamp is ready to be kindled, to catch the flame, but it hasn't recognized itself, it hasn't trained, and it hasn't yet attained stability.

There is benefit in yidam practice. Mipham Rinpoche had a vision of Manjushri, his supreme deity, and through that he became a great pandita, an extremely learned scholar. Many of the Indian *mahasiddhas* practiced Tara sadhana. They combined recognizing mind-essence with yidam practice and attained accomplishment. All the life stories of those who became great masters tell of yidam practice. You never hear of anyone saying, "I achieved accomplishment and didn't use any deity. I didn't need to say any mantra." The yidam deity practice is like adding oil to the fire of practice; it blazes up even higher and hotter.

# 28

## ALL-ENCOMPASSING
## PURITY

*Tulku Urgyen Rinpoche*

Although their aim is the same, Vajrayana is far superior to Mahayana in its profundity because it offers so many methods. These include the different procedures for visualizing the peaceful and wrathful deities, making offerings and praises, reciting mantras, emanating and absorbing rays of light, and so forth. Vajrayana has few hardships and is meant for people of higher faculties. That's why Vajrayana is especially exalted.

We should understand that Vajrayana is not some clever system of invented techniques. The nature of the peaceful and wrathful deities is present as our own physical and mental makeup, as the basic nature of the aggregates, elements, and sense bases. These deities are also called the *three seats of completeness*. These three seats are of male and female tathagatas as the aggregates and elements, of male and female bodhisattvas as the sense bases, and of the male and female gatekeepers as the times and beliefs. They are what is mentioned when saying, "the hosts of the empowerment deities of the three seats of completeness, VAJRA SAMAYA!" That is referred to in the practices of Mahayoga when making the invocation, but the actual meaning is the pure aspects of our current state.

From Tulku Urgyen Rinpoche, *As It Is*, Volume I (Boudhanath: Rangjung Yeshe Publications, 1999), "All-Encompassing Purity."

The first seat is that the aggregates and elements are the five male and female buddhas. The natural purity of the aggregate of consciousnesses is Akshobhya. For the aggregate of forms it is Vairochana, for the aggregate of sensations it is Ratnasambhava, for the aggregate of perceptions it is Amitabha, and for the aggregate of formations it is Amoghasiddhi. Earth is Buddha Lochana, water is Mamaki, fire is Pandara Vasini, wind is Samaya Tara, and space is Dhatvishvari. The second seat is that the sense bases are the eight male bodhisattvas and their corresponding objects, the female bodhisattvas.

The third seat involves the actions and senses, sometimes described as the completeness of the male and female wrathful gatekeepers, sometimes as the natural purity of the four beliefs and four times. The four male gatekeepers are Amrita Kundali, Hayagriva, Achala, and Vijaya. The four beliefs are the notions of permanence, nothingness, self, and conceptions. The notion of nothingness means "there is nothing at all." The notion of self means thinking "I." The notion of conceptions means "earth is earth; water is water," and so on. The four female gatekeepers are the past, present, future, and the unfixed time. These are the power of action and the four times the power of karma.

There are other interpretations of this third seat of completeness. These deities can be combined in different ways, as the intent of the tantras is vast. You can find all the details of this in the *Guhyagarbha Tantra* and its commentaries, which are very extensive. However, in general it is as I have mentioned.

Here is how this applies to us: At some point our body dies and the thatness wisdom, our true nature, manifests outwardly. There is a definite benefit in realizing the deities of our body through practice because when we die, these forms of the deities will manifest at the time of the bardo. Moreover, when we practice Tögal and progress through the four visions, it is these very same deities that manifest.

Some people think that deities are someone's invention and don't really exist anywhere. On the contrary, we cannot claim that deities like the peaceful and wrathful deities do not exist, because to quote one tantra, "Rigpa lives in the mansion of light." Rigpa refers to primordial purity, which is indivisible from its own "mansion of light" of spontaneous presence. This is the dharmakaya that manifests as rupakayas—the form kayas composed of sambhogakaya and nirmanakaya. Dharmakaya is primordial purity beyond constructs, and rupakaya refers to the spontaneous presence—the forms of deities, which are indivisible from primordial purity. It is not that there aren't any deities. The deities are the unity of primordial purity and spontaneous presence.

So, the awakened state of rigpa lives in the mansion of light, and from here the deities manifest. Although they manifest from within our own nature, we still visualize them as being outside. This is one of the skillful methods of Vajrayana, the swift path for those of the higher capacity. Our basic state is not like physical space, a complete nothingness from which there is nothing to accomplish. The deities can be realized because they are our own light. The purpose of completion stage is to realize primordial purity, while for development stage it is to realize spontaneous presence. Development stage and completion stage in Vajrayana make the difference between an ordinary person and a Vajrayana practitioner. An ordinary person has no development or completion stage practice. In this regard, such a person is not much different from an ox. Someone who familiarizes himself or herself with the two profound stages of Vajrayana will have a great advantage when meeting death.

Let me repeat this important point: Development stage is spontaneous presence, and completion stage is primordial purity. The crucial point here is that primordial purity and spontaneous presence are indivisible. Our body is the buddha mandala. That is why the person of sharpest faculty can develop and realize the deities. The way to combine these profound teachings is to practice a sadhana. Understand that the Mahayoga tantras are contained within the Anu Yoga scriptures. They again are contained within Ati Yoga, while Ati Yoga is contained within sadhana practice. The sadhana itself is contained within your application. This is why you can quickly perfect the accumulations and purify the obscurations through sadhana practice. Even a small sadhana text embodies all the key points of the incredibly profound Vajrayana system in a way we can connect with and practice. A sadhana of even a few pages contains something extremely important and profound.

The body, speech, and mind of the buddhas as well as the body, speech, and mind of sentient beings can all be experienced in actuality. The three kayas of buddhahood—the three vajras as the essence, nature, and capacity—are intrinsic aspects of our buddha nature itself. This is the basis for their undeniable connection with the body, speech, and mind of all sentient beings. Without these three, without the buddha mandala, without the body, speech, and mind, there would be nothing. However, they are complete within the aggregates, elements, and sense bases.

A practitioner could also focus on some nihilistic void and assert that nothing whatsoever exists, but that would be untrue and useless. It's very important to understand this. If our basic nature were a nihilistic void, nothing would take place: We would be like empty space, experiencing nothing—which is definitely not the case. Once again, this way of acknowledging reality *as it is,* is the skillful means of the profound and swift path of Vajrayana. We apply the methods to realize just this. It is extremely important.

Everything is all-encompassing purity; this is the Vajrayana perspective. This approach is not imagination, making up something or thinking that what isn't is. Vajrayana is totally unlike that. All that appears and exists actually *is* all-encompassing purity. We really should understand that everything, all world systems and all beings—whatever appears and exists, meaning the "perceived" and the "perceiver"—all takes place out of the sphere of the three kayas. Everything originates from the three kayas, takes place within the sphere of the three kayas, and dissolves back again into the sphere of the three kayas. That is what is meant by all-encompassing purity. It is not the act of believing something that isn't true. It is not like thinking that wood is gold. To regard gold as gold, that is knowing what is to be *as it is.*

Once we have entered the path of Vajrayana, training in all-encompassing purity is training in the path of *what is.* The Buddha from the beginning clearly knew the development and completion stages, the intent of Vajrayana. All-encompassing purity is not mentioned in the Sutra system only because it wouldn't fit into that type of individual's perspective. That is the only reason the Buddha did not teach it, not because some teachings are better than others.

If one doesn't know things as they are, as all-encompassing purity, one thinks that earth is just earth, fire is just fire, and water is just water. From the beginning the door is blocked by preconceptions. In accordance with the all-encompassing purity, everything originates, remains, and dissolves within the expanse of the three kayas.

If you have to imagine the development stage you now practice, it is a still a resemblance. The way of imitation thinks, "This is the samadhi of suchness, the nature of mind, and it corresponds to dharmakaya. Out of dharmakaya unfolds sambhogakaya, the all-illuminating samadhi, the naturally cognizant aspect. The indivisibility of these two is the seed samadhi, the compassionate nirmanakaya. Out of the unity of emptiness and compassion, nirmanakaya takes place."

Whether one is carrying out the actual or the resembling development stage, at the beginning of the practice, we need to unfold the structure of the three samadhis. Then we unfold the "support and the supported," the palace and the deity. Gradually we become more and more accustomed to this. At the end of a sadhana, there is a reversal of what was initially unfolded. The nirmanakaya aspect dissolves into the sambhogakaya, and that dissolves back into the unconstructed sphere of dharmakaya. Yet, even though everything has dissolved, there is a reemergence. These two phases, dissolution and reemergence, are to destroy the wrong views of nihilism and permanence. They eliminate the tendency toward eternalism, the belief in the permanence of all things, as well as the tendency toward nihilism, the idea that nothing exists.

The Vajrayana perspective is very important to have. Literally translated, the term *Vajrayana* means "vajra vehicle," with *vajra* meaning "unchanging," "indestructible." For ordinary practitioners, development stage is like a resemblance, a mask or portrait of the real thing. It is like the painting of Padmasambhava here on my wall. It's not really Padmasambhava in person, because he actually resides in his pure land, the Glorious Copper-Colored Mountain. But it is his likeness, isn't it? In the same way, the ordinary development stage is a likeness or imitation of the real thing. Although it's a resemblance and not the real thing, it's not exactly false, because development stage is a valid exercise in seeing things as they actually are, rather than as something other. Completion stage is the true thing, the view, the natural state.

To practice these two stages as indivisible has incredible depth of meaning. Sentient beings are constantly experiencing impure phenomena. To change that into the experience of pure phenomena, we train in development stage. The basis for development stage is completion stage, the realization of dharmakaya, the view. The fruition is when the rupakayas again dissolve into dharmakaya. The place where the rupakayas abide is dharmadhatu. That is the profound meaning in the unity of development and completion stage.

While reciting the lines of the sadhana, we come to the seed samadhi. From the seed samadhi the mandala of the deity unfolds; this is also the way everything really is. In the case of our practice, the seed samadhi is being created by mind, but the reason we mentally create it is that, from the very beginning, all that appears and exists is the buddha mandala. Vajrayana training is the means to realize it as it is, that all that appears and exists is the buddha mandala. That is why we train in sadhana practice.

The new schools have the same basic intent; there is no difference whatsoever. In the Nyingma school there are the three inner tantras of Maha, Anu, and Ati, while in the Sarma schools there are the mother tantras, father tantras, and nondual tantras, as well as their quintessential and innermost essence tantras. These levels include the tantras and deities of Kalachakra, Hevajra, Guhyasamaja, Chakrasamvara, and Mahamaya. The deities may have different names, but there is no difference in the basic principle.

All sadhanas have a main structure that resembles the way that everything evolves, remains, and vanishes. All of reality unfolds from the three kayas. Dharmakaya is free of constructs, sambhogakaya possesses the major and minor marks and is like a rainbow, and nirmanakaya appears in the form of the vajra body endowed with the six elements. Each of these unfolds from the previous one, while dissolution occurs in the reverse order.

Completion stage is the origin. The path of development stage is a training in knowing things to be as they are. From the very beginning, we need to be in harmony with this. First, there is the unfolding of the buddhafield within the sphere of emptiness. In the center of the buddhafield is the celestial palace. Within the celestial palace we visualize the deities, the main figure and its entourage of the peaceful and wrathful deities. They are like the sun and the rays of light emanating from it.

After visualizing the details of the deities, who are the samaya-sattvas, they are sealed with the three vajras of the body, speech, and mind of all enlightened beings, marked with OM AH HUNG. Then they are empowered by being crowned with the five buddha families, usually while saying OM HUNG TRAM HRIH AH. Next, one invites the jñana-sattvas, the wisdom beings, from the realm of Akanishtha, the buddhafield of dharmadhatu. It is said, "The deities are oneself and oneself is the deities." It is the same meaning; they dissolve indivisibly within oneself. There is a mantra for this, whereby we request them to arrive and be seated. The meaning is, "Please remain indivisibly, by means of the four immeasurables." It is accompanied by a mantra such as JAH HUNG BAM HO KAYA VAKA . . . .

We then mentally create offerings. Since there is no duality in this type of mandala, the ones who make the offerings are emanations of oneself who turn around and make offerings to oneself. It is exactly like this in some of the god realms. For example, in the god realm called Mastery over Others' Creations lives Garab Wangchuk, who is the chief of the *maras*. The gods there mentally conjure up their own sense pleasures and enjoy them. Then they dissolve these, and again manifest. In this fashion, one emanates countless offering goddesses carrying all different kinds of sense pleasures. After that are praises. This corresponds to purifying the mundane tendencies to invite an important person, to cater to him, to flatter him, and finally to ask him for what you want. All this was for the accomplishment of body.

Next is the accomplishment of speech by means of the recitation. Recitation traditionally has four aspects: approach, full approach, accomplishment, and great accomplishment. Through this fourfold intent of approach and accomplishment, everything is accomplished.

After the mantra, the feast offering section can be added to mend breaches of samaya, meaning to relink or make up with the deities. Tormas are also presented to the protectors, and evil forces are suppressed by means of special requests to the Dharma protectors. An elaborate sadhana also includes the "threefold neigh of Hayagriva," meaning the "horse dance" at the end of the feast offering. The threefold neighing proclaims that the ultimate state of awakened mind, described as the three doors of emancipation, is totally beyond the constructs of past, present, and future. This ultimately will suppress all evil forces that might otherwise backfire or create hindrances for this realization.

At the end of the sadhana come the phases of dissolution and reemergence. Just as everything evolved out of the sphere of three kayas, the entire mandala again dissolves back into the sphere of the three kayas. The mandala gradually dissolves into the palace, the palace into the deities, the retinue into the central figure, and the central figure into the seed syllable in the heart center. It also dissolves and you remain as unconstructed emptiness. Then, once again you manifest as the single form of the deity and carry out your daily activities. Before closing the session, recite the verses of dedication, aspirations, and auspiciousness.

Taken together, these main sections of sadhana practice are extremely profound. We engage in them in order to purify habitual tendencies and delusion. The real nature of things is all-encompassing purity. All things in samsara and nirvana and the path are pervaded by the body, speech, and mind of the victorious ones. It is only temporarily that sentient beings do not know this. They have conceptualized and labeled the pure as being impure. The true nature of things is primordial purity, pure from the beginning, primordially enlightened.

Primordially pure, with nothing impure at all; that is all-encompassing purity. What happened is that we made the mistake of not recognizing mind nature. It is only temporarily that sentient beings do not recognize. Once the sun begins to shine in a dark place, the darkness doesn't remain. All of samsara and nirvana—all of existence and peace—is the great purity. That is why Vajrayana is so profound.

There is no difference whatsoever in what a deity really is between the old and new schools. There is not a single deity that isn't included in the five buddha families of Vajra, Ratna, Padma, Karma, and Buddha. Only one's own individual tradition differs. The fundamental aim is to accomplish the deity. One is taught this by means of training in the development and completion stages.

If one doesn't know mind essence, development stage is essentially blocked. It is very important to understand the basic principles of Vajrayana. In order to accomplish a deity, one must know the nature of the deity one is trying to accomplish. This is called identifying the deity to be accomplished. The names, colors, and attributes may differ, but a deity is actually the unity of primordial purity and spontaneous presence. In this way, development and completion are contained within Trekchö and Tögal.

Without the recognition of mind-essence, development stage practice is like laying bricks. It becomes a lot of hard work! This is most important. An incredible amount of evil deeds and obscurations are purified by this practice, if you know what is to be *as it is*. It is the path of pure perception. Know the origin. All of the worlds and beings unfold from the expanse of the three kayas. The three kayas are not over there. They pervade everything. If one doesn't know this, it is like doing masonry, laying down one brick at a time. Or else it's a flight of fancy, merely an act of imagination. What we really need to do is to begin with unfolding the samadhi of suchness. The real suchness samadhi is mind essence.

Unless you understand all-encompassing purity, the development stage becomes very simplistic. You sit and imagine that there is nothing whatsoever; everything is emptiness. Then you try to imagine that now there is a place for the mandala, and you try to build the mandala up, step by step, through your imagination. Such a practice is conducted with a materialistic sense of constructing a mansion and inviting over a group of beautiful rich people. The deities all have arms and legs and faces and wear special silk garments. In order to please them, you dish out exotic offerings, flatter them, and make them happy; then they give you something in return. That is some people's understanding of development stage.

We need a deeper understanding than that. Honestly speaking, there is no way around understanding all-encompassing purity. The five great elements are the female buddhas. The aggregates are the male buddhas. That is why I have repeatedly stated that the all-encompassing purity is the main principle to understand. I go on and on about this point because the principle of primordial purity is so vital to understand. *Everything* is of the nature of primordial purity. This is not something that is achieved through practice. It is an uncovering of how things actually are to begin with; that the minds of all sentient beings are, at this every moment, the unity of experience and emptiness. This is nothing other than Buddha Samantabhadra in union with his consort, the female buddha Samantabhadri.

The name Vairochana means "manifest in form" and refers to all experience of perceivable form. Forms experienced among the five aggregates are indivisible from emptiness itself. That is the nature called Buddha Vairochana. Speech is Buddha Amitabha, meaning that the semimanifest, such as sound and communication, is indivisible from emptiness. Mind is Akshobhya, the unshakable. The nature of cognition, the consciousness aggregate, is indivisible from emptiness. Similarly, all qualities are Ratnasambhava, and all activities and interactions are of the nature of Amoghasiddhi.

Although *aggregate* means a group or a conglomeration composed of many parts, the five different aggregates all have the same nature, which is the five buddhas. It is the same with the five elements. Everything in the world is made out of elements; therefore, everything is of the nature of the five female buddhas. In this way, we cannot find anything that is not already the mandala of the five male and female buddhas. This is what is meant by the phrase "all-encompassing purity." We need to pay close attention to this and try to understand it, because there is not anything that isn't all-encompassing purity. That is the true meaning of development stage.

The simplistic view of the palace, the ornaments, the offerings of delicious food, and so on is totally interconnected with the normal habitual tendencies of mundane people. It is not that deities of rainbow light have any concepts of near and far or that they are pleased by being praised. It is only for one's own benefit that this is done, in order to gather the accumulations and to purify bad karma and habitual tendencies. We should clearly understand the profound intent of the Vajrayana.

Please gain full comprehension of the principle of this practice! The materialistic way of practicing the development stage is not that effective. It becomes like the guy who visualized himself as Yamantaka and couldn't get out the entrance of his cave because his horns were too big. His guru called for him to come, and he sent back a message, "Sorry! I can't come out! My horns get stuck in the doorway."

To reiterate, a sadhana may have several sections. In the main section, one erects the basic framework of the three samadhis. The samadhi of suchness is the intent of primordial purity. The samadhi of illumination is the intent of spontaneous presence. The samadhi of the seed syllable is the nirmanakaya aspect, the indivisibility of primordial purity and spontaneous presence. This is how to start out the sadhana practice. Next, visualize the support, which is the mandala of the celestial palace, and the supported, the mandala of the deities. Bring to mind the details of all the deities and seal them with the syllables of body, speech, and mind. Crown them with the five syllables of the five buddha families, empowering the deities with deities. After that, consecrate the samaya-sattva, which has been visualized until now, with the jñana-sattva invited from the buddhafield of dharmadhatu. They arrive and dissolve into yourself indivisibly, like water dissolving into water.

Next are the outer, inner, and secret offerings. The outer offering is the offering cloud exemplified by the bodhisattva Universal Excellence; the inner offerings are the sense pleasures represented by amrita, rakta, and torma; and the secret offering is the unity of bliss and emptiness. The ultimate thatness offering is the offering of dharmadhatu indivisible from nondual awareness. Then, one makes praises. Both offerings and praises are performed by the offering goddesses who are emanated from oneself. They carry the offerings in their hands. At the time of making praises, they dance and perform mudras and sing the lines of praise, praising the body, speech, Mind, qualities, and activities of both the peaceful and wrathful deities. At the conclusion, the offering goddesses again dissolve into oneself.

Up to this point, we have completed what is known as the body aspect of the development stage. Next comes the speech aspect, which is the recitation. The recitation intent is nothing other than deity, mantra, and samadhi. Through the mantra, we acknowledge that whatever is seen is the body of the peaceful and wrathful deities; whatever is heard is their voices, the sound of mantra; and the nature of mind of all sentient beings is the state of nonconceptual, thought-free awareness, which is by nature an unconfined empty cognizance. Although the deities appear in inconceivably different ways, they are in essence identical in being the unity of basic space and original wakefulness. While keeping this in mind, one recites the mantra. This completes the speech aspect.

As I have repeatedly said concerning development stage, all phenomena, all deities, whatever appears and exists within samsara and nirvana, arise out of the sphere of the three kayas, remain within the sphere of the three kayas, and finally dissolve into the sphere of the three kayas. Nothing takes place outside of the three kayas. In order to train in accordance with this principle, at the beginning of the sadhana let everything unfold out of the three kayas by means of three samadhis. Then let everything dissolve back.

Among the concluding sections of a sadhana, the first is dissolution. The empty forms, empty sounds, and empty awareness dissolve back into basic space. After that is the reemergence. Whatever appears is the body of the peaceful and wrathful ones, whatever is heard is their voices, whatever takes place as natural awareness is the mind of the peaceful and wrathful ones. Following that is the dedication of merit and the making of aspirations. Finally there are the four lines for auspiciousness of dharmakaya, sambhogakaya, and nirmanakaya. This conclusion again reminds us of the sphere of the three kayas.

PART FOUR

# THE CONCLUDING ACTIVITIES

# 29

# TORMA

## *Tulku Urgyen Rinpoche*

When beginning a retreat, you should gather offerings and tormas. All the texts say that you should give a torma to the "local deity" and the "permanent deity" and that you should also offer a feast to the Three Roots. The purpose of such offerings is to eliminate obstacles and to swiftly accomplish the supreme and common siddhis.

There are two kinds of local deities, one called a permanent resident and the other a local resident, who has arrived temporarily. Torma is presented to both of these. Actually, according to custom, the property owner should be asked for permission first, "Please let me use your place. I am using it to practice virtue." The owner agrees and permission is obtained. Even if no one owns the land, there is still the local deity and the lord of the area. The lord at Nagi Gompa is the lord of the Shivapuri region, and the local deity is Maheshvara, the deity for all of Nepal, who is very influential in this country. Both are *kshetrapala*, Dharma protectors. We present them with a torma saying, "Please don't be displeased, have ill will, or feel envious. I am doing this practice to attain enlightenment for the sake of all beings as vast as the sky. My only purpose is to benefit all these beings, nothing else. Permit me to use this place for spiritual practice."

From Tulku Urgyen Rinpoche, *Vajra Heart* (Boudhanath: Rangjung Yeshe Publications, 1988), "Torma."

Torma is also offered to expel obstructing forces, the so-called *gek*. In this case, you first give a torma peacefully, insisting, "Now, don't stay here. Go elsewhere. I have many herukas on my side." Say the corresponding mantras and send the torma outside. Finally, in a wrathful way you emanate wrathful figures, rakshas, countless as dust particles, and chase them far, far away to the other side of the world ocean, imagining that they have been expelled. That is the wrathful way of the *gektor*, the torma to the obstructing forces. In short, there are peaceful, insistent, and wrathful ways of dispelling the obstructing forces.

The local lord and deity, on the other hand, should not be expelled but presented peacefully with the white torma and requested that there be no obstacles for accomplishing enlightenment. One should say, "Please lend me your land; enjoy this torma however you like," and imagine that permission is received, that the deities are pleased and satisfied.

The torma represents the five pleasurable sense objects: beautiful form, melodious sound, sweet fragrance, delicious taste, and soft pleasant touch. The mental object is an abundance of bliss and happiness. We imagine that we have made this present, that the deities are satisfied and content, and reply, "Child of noble family, use this place as you wish." Imagining that we have received this permission, we present the torma and have finished.

By presenting the *gektor* in the peaceful, insistent, and wrathful ways, we have expelled the obstructing forces far, far away. Don't imagine that because one practices Ati Yoga, one should abandon the act of presenting these offerings. The tantras should be combined with the scriptures, the scriptures with the instructions, the instructions with the sadhana ritual, and the ritual with the personal application. Do not disregard the application.

# 30

# FEAST

## *Tsoknyi Rinpoche*

We make a feast offering, a *tsok*, in order to be in harmony with all the masters of the lineage, the dakinis, and the guardians of the teachings. The Vajrayana feast mends any rift, reconciles any disharmony that may have taken place. When people don't get along for small reasons, they get together and throw a party so that everything is cleared up, forgiven and forgotten. In the same way, we may have fallen into disharmony with the teachings, or there may be disharmony among Dharma friends. All this can be cleared up by throwing a *ganachakra* feast. We make a party where we drink a little wine, eat good food, and have a good time together. This is the outer meaning.

The inner meaning of feast has to do with the fact that the food and drink, which have the nature of means and knowledge, enter your mouth and the mandala of your physical body in the form of unconditioned nectar. The nature of great bliss permeates the 72,000 channels in your subtle body, and this feeling of ease and bliss suffuses your physical being so that all the channels that were bent, withered, or tangled are straightened out and fully opened up. The deities that dwell in this mandala of your body, all the dakas and dakinis, are given this offering of unconditioned great bliss that

---

From Tsoknyi Rinpoche, *Fearless Simplicity: The Dzogchen Way of Living Freely in a Complex World* (Boudhanath: Rangjung Yeshe Publications, 2003), "Retreat."

is indivisible from emptiness. Imagine that they all get intoxicated with the taste of great bliss and are fully satisfied. This complete internal harmony is the inner meaning.

For the innermost level of feast, you acknowledge the basic space of your being, called dharmadhatu, the immensity of your empty nature, as the offering tray for the feast offerings. The feast articles themselves are the cognizant, awake quality that is present within this emptiness. Your unconditioned nature, manifest in actuality, its increase in experience and vision, your awareness reaching culmination, and the exhaustion of concepts and conditioned phenomena, as well as the six lamps and the display of awareness—all these are the innermost feast articles. In short, when these articles don't leave their tray, everything that appears and exists is part of the innermost feast. In this way, when everything is spontaneously experienced as being pure—a purity that is free of dualistic clinging to subject and object—everything on the innermost level is in harmony as well.

*31*

# FEAST SONGS

## Feast Song by Kunkhyen Jigmey Lingpa

On the wish-fulfilling tree of karma linked with good wishes
The youthful peacock of East India has landed.
Turn your tail parasol to face the sacred teachings
So we youngsters can also step onto the path of freedom.

In the Queen of Spring's chariot of merit
The melodious voice of the cuckoo bird from the jungle of south
    Bhutan has arrived.
With a song sweeter than the flute of celestial maidens,
We receive the auspicious omen of a joyful summer season.

Vajra brothers and companions, assembled here with harmonious
    karma and wishes,
Our teacher is present and has arrived at the gathering of Dharma.
During this feast of drinking the nectar of ripening and liberation,
I have the special task of singing a joyful song.
Amid this gathering of unchanging great bliss,

From *Crystal Cave: A Compendium of Teachings by Masters of the Practice Lineage* (Boudhanath: Rangjung Yeshe Publications, 1990), pp. 39, 101 — 103.

249

We behold the countenance of the yidam and guru even without
   meditation.
So let us request the siddhi of attaining the rainbow body of
   dharmakaya,
Through the vehicle of luminous clarity, the heart essence of the mother
   dakinis.


## Spontaneous Feast Song by Dudjom Rinpoche

A Ho Ye
In the center of the Akanishtha palace on the Glorious Copper-Colored
   Mountain,
The gathering of vidyadharas, dakas, and dakinis assembles.
Thinking of their enticing playfulness, the one hundred expressions of
   great bliss,
I miss my only father, Padmavajra, in the core of my heart.

Glorious subjugator of appearance and existence,[45] vividly present in the
   form with the major and minor marks,
The tones of your voice, the sound of the Great Secret,[46] resound like the
   melody of a sitar.
Your eminent mind is unconditioned luminosity, the nature of wisdom.
What can compare with the feast of beholding the joyful face of the guru?

Smiling and smiling, with glances of delight,
How melodious are the secret words and symbolic songs of the dakinis.
Moving in flashes, the wondrous spectacle of dance,
One has an overwhelming desire to behold it again and again.

The material eyes of this wretched young lad
Are covered with a dense cataract—the defilement of dualistic thinking.
I have no fortune to offer you; deep is my despair!
Padmakara, do you hear my wailing cry?

If you hear me, extend the golden scalpel of your wisdom compassion
And remove the dense cover, the obscuration of ignorance.
Take hold of the fingers of my hand, only father,

And lead me to the beautiful gardens of your dwelling place.

If I lack the good fortune to be taken there right now,
Send the vidyadharas, dakas, and dakinis to console me.
I will then gladly partake of the splendid feast of unconditioned great bliss
And gradually follow in the footsteps of the father.

When the body, the virtuous plain, is in the full bloom of youth—the
    triple faith,
The wings of united view and conduct are possessed.
The power of pure samayas is perfected
And the citadel of Lotus Light[47] does not lie far away.

You, gathering of sacred brothers and sisters of harmonious karma and
    fortune,
Make an aspiration, in the manner of the vidyadharas,
With the clear, resounding, joyful laughter of experience.
Do not leave me, but let us go together to the terrestrial pure land.

Like the cry of the young cuckoo bird,
This yearning song was spontaneously sung with the playfulness of the
    wheel of enjoyment.[48]
May it be a messenger invoking the mind of Guru Rinpoche.
Bestow the gentle nectar rain of your blessings this very moment.

This was uttered spontaneously in the valley of Pemako[49] by Jigdrel Yeshe
Dorje,[50] a fortunate youngster of nineteen years of age, on the tenth day of
the waxing moon of the first month of summer.

# 32

# DEDICATION OF MERIT

*Padmasambhava*

*The Wish-fulfilling Gem of Dedication* ❧

NAMO GHURU DHEVA DAKKINI HUNG

> I shall now explain the *Wish-Fulfilling Treasury of Precious Gems*,
> The method for dedicating your roots of virtue, as many as they may be,
> Whatever merit you have accumulated, will accumulate, or the merit in
>     which you rejoice,
> Toward the great and unexcelled enlightenment.

Well, now, rejoice in the resolve to dedicate these good roots made for the benefit of a particular person toward the unexcelled state of enlightenment! For this to happen, it is important that three factors concur: the virtuous deed to be dedicated, the recipient, and the thought of dedication.

For a practitioner of Secret Mantra, the master is regarded as the pure field of merit, just as the *Shri Guhyasamaja* mentions:

> At the outset of any offering,
> Set aside all other offerings
> And commence with an offering to your master,
> Since by pleasing him you attain accomplishment,
> The sublime state of omniscience.

---

From Padmasambhava, *Advice from the Lotus-Born* (Boudhanath: Rangjung Yeshe Publications, 1994), "The Wish-fulfilling Gem of Dedication."

According to the sutras, it is taught that the Sangha is the pure field of merit. As the *Sutra on the Furtherance of Virtue* says:

Being the treasury of all the teachings
And the opener of all doors,
The ones known as Sangha members
Are the Sangha to be supported by everyone.

In the general sense, the Three Jewels are accepted as the pure fields of merit. It is said:

There is no teacher like the Buddha.
There is no protector like the Dharma.
There is no field like the Sangha.
Thus I make this offering to the Three Jewels!

A sutra says, "The followers of the lower vehicles consider the elevated field to be supreme. For instance, when you sow seeds—the cause—in an excellent field, and carefully nurture them by supplying fertilizer, breaking up clods of dirt, and so forth, the crop—the effect—will be abundant. Likewise, the effect is magnified many times if the field of merit is pure."

The followers of Mahayana regard inferior recipients as more important and support those who are disabled, rejected, and friendless. A scripture mentions:

Those who are disheartened and friendless,
The sick and disabled,
The old, the indisposed, and those deprived of senses,
The destitute, the famished, and beggars—
Bodhisattvas should support these unprotected people.

To these pure recipients, whether high or low, the objects we offer are, in the case of the higher recipients, actually present and mentally created.

With unsurpassable offering clouds of Samantabhadra
Actually present and mentally created,
Vastly and fully displayed within pure space,
We present you with an ocean of outer, inner, and secret offerings.[51]

It is taught one should give necessary articles that are uncontaminated by wrongdoing, such as wrong livelihood, to the lower recipients by means of fourfold giving, as a sutra says:

> No articles from theft, robbery, or monastic holdings,
> Nor harmful things,
> But that which is treasured and delightful,
> And, at best, which is also needed.

Moreover, it is said:

> Assist the poor and disabled
> With the fourfold types of giving
> Of provisions and a variety of pleasant sense objects,
> But not objects mixed with evil deeds or weaponry,
> Nor food poisoned by improper earnings.

Motivate yourself in this way, with a pure attitude toward the pure field of merit. Generate trust in the ones above, compassion for the ones below, and the awakened mind of enlightenment. It is said:

> Motivated by trust and compassion,
> Give for the sake of others with the enlightened attitude.
> Guide with dedication and good wishes,
> And seal by not conceptualizing the three spheres.[52]

It is also said:

> While possessing a pure attitude
> Toward all pure objects,
> Offer or give the best things.
> When you dedicate them to the state of the supreme vehicle
> And seal by not conceptualizing the three spheres,
> This dedication is the most eminent.

In this way, the accumulation of merit is created by connecting object, article, and attitude with the virtue to be dedicated. Now, to what should these virtuous deeds be dedicated? And to which cause or end should they be dedicated?

To quote the Great Mother Prajñaparamita, "The bodhisattva spiritual guide should dedicate all virtue or good roots toward the state of complete omniscience, and not toward the state of a shravaka or pratyekabuddha."

Thus, dedicate to the cause for attaining the fruition of complete omniscience, the state of all-knowing buddhahood. Regarding the different types of masters who make the dedication, Padmavajra has said:

The ones who realize the natural state of the view,
Who are adept in the samadhi of meditation,
Who possess the compassionate enlightened mind,
And all the marks of being qualified—
Such sublime spiritual friends
Are the most eminent masters to dedicate the merit.

Best is when such a master is within reach; if not, it is said:

For whomever has supreme faith and resolve
The buddha will be present as if in person.

And also:

At the right time, such as on the new moon, full moon, and the eighth
(of the lunar month),
Dedicate the good roots in the presence of the Three Jewels.

It is also permissible for the faithful to dedicate in the presence of a shrine for the Three Jewels.

Next, for whose sake is the dedication made? Do not dedicate just for the sake of a certain person, but for the sake of all sentient beings headed by so-and-so.[53] As is said:

Directly and also indirectly,
Only do what is for the benefit of beings.
For the sake of all sentient beings,
You should dedicate all merit to their enlightenment.

For a person who is alive, simply use his or her name; for someone who has passed away, use "the late so-and-so."

When dedicating for the sake of all sentient beings headed by a certain person, instruct him or her by saying:

"Keep your body and mind respectful, join the palms, and imagine that in the sky before you sits our main teacher, the transcendent perfect conqueror, the victorious one, Buddha Shakyamuni, adorned with the numerous major and minor marks, surrounded by all the buddhas and bodhisattvas of the ten directions, as well as by the gurus, yidams, dakinis, and the loyal guardians of the Dharma. Offer your body and wealth, power and glory, and all your good roots, thinking, 'So that all sentient beings headed by so-and-so may attain supreme, true, and complete enlightenment, I dedicate all the virtuous roots resulting from the merit and wisdom gathered by myself and all others since beginningless samsara!' With a respectful voice, repeat the words of the dedication."

If the dedication is made for someone else, then the word "you" should be substituted (for "I"). If a congregation of four (ordained Sangha members) are present, request them to add their good wishes. The master himself should personally, without wavering from the words and their meaning, focus on this resolve:

"Buddhas and bodhisattvas who dwell in the ten directions, please pay heed to so-and-so! Gurus and deities of the yidam mandala, please pay heed!

"The good roots created since beginningless samsara and resulting from giving, discipline, meditation, and so forth, which the person known as so-and-so has created, caused others to create, or rejoiced in their creating, and the good roots resulting from merit and wisdom created in thought, word, and deed in this very life or in the future—just as all noble beings accomplished in the power of truth have done, I fully dedicate them as a cause for the supreme, true, and complete enlightenment for the sake of so-and-so, as well as all other sentient beings!"

If the dedicator's realization is superior to your own or if he is a great master, then make the request to bear witness and change the end of the dedication and aspiration for the benefit of all sentient beings as follows:

"May all sentient beings headed by so-and-so swiftly attain the precious state of supreme, true, and complete enlightenment!"

Having repeated that three times, say:

"Until achieving the aim of the aspiration, throughout all lives and rebirths, may all sentient beings attain the level of a god or a human in the higher realms, without being interrupted by any other rebirth!

May they possess all the qualities of a high rebirth including the most noble character!

May they meet with a spiritual guide who upholds the lineage of sublime masters, and be accepted into his following!

Accomplished in the three pleasing ways,[54] may they enjoy the wealth of the unexcelled teachings of the supreme vehicle through learning, reflection, and meditation!

Through possessing perfect dwelling place, companions, and favorable conditions, may they extensively turn the profound and serene Dharma wheel of the unexcelled and supreme vehicle!

Through immeasurable compassionate activity endowed with the boundless love and empathy of the awakened mind, may they accomplish, effortlessly and spontaneously, the welfare of all sentient beings, taming each in whatever way is appropriate!

Journeying to the all-encompassing ocean of boundless buddha realms, including the mandalas of the gurus, yidams, and dakinis, may they be protected by the realization of their marvelous deeds! May they enter into the following of all these gatherings! May they follow in their footsteps! May they be equal to the buddhas in realization, compassion, deeds, and activity!

On the path of accomplishing this, may all unwholesome and adverse elements such as difficulties, obstacles, distractions, laziness, wrongdoing, and error subside! May they possess perfect circumstances and an abundance of these qualities of well-being and happiness: long life span, good health, attractive form, deep faith, sharp intelligence, great compassion, strong vigor, plentiful wealth, joy in giving, pure samaya commitments, perfect discipline, and so forth!"

If the dedication and aspiration is made for the sake of a deceased person, at this point perform the ritual for purifying obscurations. If it is for a living person, then say any other suitable aspiration, as well as the following:

"In this very life may they possess longevity, good health, and abundant wealth and excellence!

May all their sickness and evil influences, misdeeds and obscurations, transgressions, mistakes and misfortunes, outer and inner obstacles, and all evil and discordant forces be pacified!

May they abide by the Dharma in thought, word, and deed, and, while enjoying the flawless words of the victorious ones, may they have all their wishes fulfilled, just as if they possessed the wish fulfilling powerful king of precious stones!

When the time of death arrives, may they not suffer the misery of the life force being interrupted, but may all conceptual states of disturbing emotions subside, and may they joyfully and delightfully remember their guru and the Three Jewels!

May they be completely protected by the wisdom mind of all noble beings endowed with great compassion who are the unsurpassable objects of refuge! May they not undergo the fear and terror of the bardo, and may all the doors to the lower realms of existence be closed! As the ultimate, may they soon attain the precious state of unexcelled, true, and complete enlightenment!

By the blessings of the Buddha's attainment of the three kayas,
By the blessings of the unchanging truth of dharmata,
By the blessings of the unshakable resolve of the Sangha,
And by the blessings of the guru, yidam, and dakini,
May whatever I dedicate be accomplished!
May all my wishes be powerful!"

Having uttered this, conclude by sealing with the threefold purity of non-conception.

There are boundless virtues in sealing with the precious dedication in this way and making flawless aspirations. The *Sutra Requested by Unending Intelligence* mentions:

Just as a drop of water falling into the great ocean
Does not dry up until the ocean itself does,
In the same way, the virtue fully dedicated toward enlightenment
Does not vanish before enlightenment is attained.

It is also said:

In the presence of the Three Jewels,
The deity, your master, or the like,
With an attitude of faith, gather the accumulations
And thus make vast aspirations.
The virtue of this lies beyond expression!

Having gathered the accumulations of merit and wisdom, the shortcomings of failing to seal with the precious dedication are described as these four causes of depletion:

After creating a virtuous root,
To neglect dedicating, to make a perverted dedication,

To boast about it to others, or to feel regret—
These are the four causes of depletion.

Therefore, it is essential to dedicate in the following way. Imagine that an effulgence of light rays streams forth from the heart center of the Buddha and touches the body, speech, and mind of the beings for whom the dedication is being made, completely purifying their misdeeds, obscurations, faults, and failings. They become spheres of light that dissolve into the heart center of the Buddha. The Buddha and his retinue depart into the expanse of invisible basic space, like a rainbow vanishing into the sky. Sealing thus, by not conceptualizing the three spheres, becomes the true and supreme dedication. As Lord Maitreya said:

The extraordinary, complete dedication
That is most eminent to perform
Is the attitude free of conceptualized focus,
With the attribute of nondelusion.

He furthermore said:

Moreover, the unexcelled supreme dedication
Is to fully know that there is no real nature
In the merit created, in its fruition,
In the dedicated, or in the act of dedicating.

Therefore, bury all virtue created for a particular purpose as an inexhaustible treasure mine, and complete it by sealing it with the Mahayana dedication. Then pay respect while rejoicing with heartfelt joy and gratitude.

This was the way to instruct. Samaya.

Basically speaking, when wishing to make a dedication, there are three general points: the dedication that fully protects the meritorious gift of a benefactor; the dedication after an extraordinary practice of Secret Mantra or after turning the wheel of the profound Dharma; and the dedication that perfects the accumulation of merit within the basic space of original wakefulness.

The first occurs immediately after the benefactor presents the offering, or right after enjoying it. Repeat the following, or any other suitable aspiration, three times:

All buddhas and bodhisattvas dwelling in the ten directions, pay heed to this benefactor! Masters and Sangha of pure monks, please pay heed!

As demonstrated by this virtuous root,
May whatever virtue the benefactor creates throughout the three times
Be dedicated to vastly increasing an inexhaustible fruition!
May unexcelled enlightenment be swiftly attained!

The second occurs at the conclusion of any outer or inner spiritual study, teaching, and meditation, or any of the (ten) spiritual activities. Dedicate in the following way:

Buddhas and bodhisattvas of the ten directions, gurus, yidams, dakinis, and all mandala deities, together with your guardians and protectors, please pay heed to me!

Within the immense great mandala of Samantabhadra,
May all the virtuous roots created throughout the three times
By the guru vajra holder and others,
And by all vajra brothers and sisters,
As exemplified by this turning of the wheel of Dharma,
Be dedicated to the attainment of perfect buddhahood!
May everyone everywhere attain the state of Samantabhadra!

Dedicate in this way and rest in the supreme true state of the ultimate.

The third occurs at the conclusion of whatever you wish to dedicate and whenever you dedicate, or at the end of any type of activity. Make this dedication from within the state of the "great sealing":

Victorious ones and your sons of the ten directions, pay heed!
May whatever virtue created by thought, word, and deed
By myself or any other of all the sentient beings
In the three times of past, present, and future
Be dedicated toward the great sphere of enlightenment!
May the supreme fruition of the unexcelled nature be attained!

At the beginning of any kind of dedication, visualize the Three Jewels before you as the witness. Imagine that they accept you with words of dedication and good wishes. Next, utter the words of dedication while sealing without conceptualizing what you dedicate and the objects of the dedication, the deed, and doer of the dedicating. At the end, remain in the state beyond word, thought, and description, within which all the phenomena composed of samsara and nirvana at first have not arisen, in between do not remain, and in the end do not cease.

*Samaya.*

*These skillful means of bringing virtuous causes to full maturity, the oral instructions on dedication entitled The Wish-Fulfilling Gem of Dedication, were given by the vidyadhara Padmasambhava. I, Tsogyal, wrote them down in the form of notes and concealed them as a secret terma treasure. May they meet with worthy people possessing the karmic destiny!*

*Concealment seal.*
*Entrustment seal.*
*Treasure seal.*
*Samaya.*
*Dathim.*

*This was revealed from the Great Cave of Puri by me, Sangye Dorje (Sangye Lingpa), a mendicant follower of Shakyamuni.*

# FACILITATOR GUIDELINES

We now embark on the continuing practice and study program in the style of the kusulu, the simple meditator. Since there are so many significant points to understand, it is always helpful to review the basics before exploring new material; revisit *The Dzogchen Primer* to find out how much has been correctly understood and assimilated. The facilitator should try to encourage discussions about people's doubts, misinterpretations, and limited understanding, to help dispel these.

We should always keep in mind that the purpose of our study is to enhance our understanding and support our practice. We should never separate practice from study. As it is the simple meditator's style of study, naturally practice is integral to each meeting. Please keep that focus.

We often think that we should see some results from our efforts in study and practice. As Thrangu Rinpoche notes:

> An obstacle that might arise is looking back and thinking, 'I have spent a lot of time practicing but I haven't achieved anything.' One can then become discouraged and lose faith in the Dharma. The main guideline for measuring our progress is how much our negative emotions and selfishness have diminished and how much our compassion, devotion and renunciation have increased. There is a saying, 'The sign of learning is to be calm and gentle.' The more we learn and the more insight we have, the less conceited and proud we should be; that is the sign of actually understanding the teachings. It is also said, 'The sign of train-

ing is to have fewer negative emotions.' Take meditation training as the direct remedy against any shortcomings. In short, the true signs of success are to be kinder, more considerate, more loving and more compassionate.[55]

Your initial group meetings are the time to check your motivation, which should be no less than practicing in order to benefit countless beings and reach true and complete enlightenment. On the subject of motivation, Tsoknyi Rinpoche states:

> Someone may relate to Dharma merely as a remedy to be used when he or she is confused or upset or unsettled. This is not the real purpose of spiritual practice. In this situation, you do some practice till you have settled down and then you set it aside and forget all about it. The next time you get upset, you do some more practice to feel good again. Of course, reestablishing one's equilibrium in this way is one of the minor purposes of practice, but it's not the real goal. Doing this is a way of using the Dharma as if it was a type of therapy. You may of course choose to do so, but I do not think it will get you enlightened. Feel a little bit unhappy, do some Dharma, get happy. Feel a little bit upset, then fine, then again unhappy. If you continue holding the very short-term view in mind, there is no progress in the true spiritual sense.

Do not practice in this way. Dharma practice is not only meant to make oneself feel better: the whole point of spiritual practice is to liberate oneself through realization, and also to liberate others through compassionate capacity. To practice to feel better only brings you back up to that same level—you never make any genuine progress. With this attitude of *merely feeling good* becoming the type of Buddhism that spreads in the West, we may see a huge scarcity of enlightened masters in the future. They will become an endangered species.

Please understand that the pursuit of "feeling better" is a samsaric goal. It is a totally mundane pursuit that borrows from the Dharma and uses all its special methods to fine-tune ego into a fit and workable entity. The definition of a worldly aim is to try to achieve something "for me" with a goal-oriented frame of mind "so that I feel good". We may use spiritual practice to achieve this, one good reason being that it works much better than other methods. But if this is how you practice, you don't get anywhere in the end. How can one ever become liberated through selfishness?

There comes a point when we start to lose faith in the illusions of this world: our level of trust in illusions begins to weaken, and we start to get disappointed. Using spiritual practice to nurture our ego back into good health while still retaining trust in these illusory aims does not set us free. True freedom does not mean having a healthy faith in illusions; rather, it is to go completely *beyond* delusion. This may not sound particularly comforting, but it is true. It may be an unpleasant piece of news, especially if we have to admit to ourselves, "I have really been fooling myself all along. Why did I do all this practice? Am I completely wrong?" What can you do to pretend this isn't true? Facing the truth is not pleasant.

The real help lies in continually correcting and improving our motivation: understanding why we are practicing and where we are ultimately heading. Work on this and bring forth the noble motivation of bodhichitta: then all methods and practices can be used to help you progress in that direction.[56]

## INTRODUCTION

In his unique and direct style, Tsoknyi Rinpoche explains the key points of the next phase of this program. Read this introduction together with Padmasambhava's "Quintessence of Wisdom Openness" as you continue to assess what needs to be cleared up and clarified. "The Quintessence of Wisdom Openness" contains the words of Padmasambhava and is a treasure revelation by Chokgyur Lingpa and Jamyang Khyentse Wangpo. While highlighting the preliminaries and development stage practice, it also outlines the scope of the material in *Dzogchen Essentials*. Use as supports *The Light of Wisdom*, Volume I; *The Jewel Ornament of Liberation;* and *The Words of My Perfect Teacher.*

Once most of the difficult points have been investigated to the best of the facilitator's ability, move on to part 1 on empowerment.

Whenever a student presents a question that cannot be resolved in the study group, write it down and ask it publicly in a retreat with an experienced teacher. If there is a way to e-mail the question to such a teacher, that also is helpful. Please have each member of the study and practice group commit to attending every year at least one of the many wonderful programs that teachers in this and similar traditions conduct. The curriculum in this book encourages students to be in contact with qualified teachers as much as possible.

## CHAPTERS 1 THROUGH 5

To reconnect with our enlightened body, speech, and mind, we receive empowerment. Empowerment is the way to be authorized to practice the instructions. As Tsele Natsok Rangdröl says, "The basic seeds for the empowerments are already spontaneously present within one's own nature. The master's blessings and the symbolic indications provide the circumstances for their growth." Engage in discussions on the ideas of ripening. Ask the students to define, from their own understanding, what it means to be ripened and empowered.

The easiest way to understand the theory of transmission and empowerment is through Chögyam Trungpa Rinpoche's brilliant analogy of the guru as an electrician: "to electrify the student's vessel and then to pour essence into it." Work with analogies such as basic seeds and transmitters to generate comprehension in the students.

As a support for these chapters, read *The Small Golden Key* by Thinley Norbu, pp. 57–63 (Shambhala Publications). Another good source is the chapter entitled "Transmission" in *Meditation in Action* by Chögyam Trungpa, pp. 52–61 (Shambhala Publications).

## CHAPTERS 6 THROUGH 10

It is good to review the teachings on the ground from *The Dzogchen Primer*, expanding to consider the basis, the buddha nature, before delving into the development stage in detail. Look over the first two Dharmas of Gampopa and Longchenpa. After that, continue with studying the path phase, which is the state of confusion. Here you can return to the final chapters of *The Primer* to reclarify how the nature of mind is insubstantial and also how the misapprehension of what we experience takes place. Do we accept that we are perhaps deluded? Again through in-depth discussion, examine our way of defining the world and ourselves.

Encourage as much debate as possible on these topics. Primarily focus on what the state of confusion means and how the path is the way to remedy it. Study the selections in this section carefully in an effort to expose any resistance to the development stage practice as a means of purifying the "temporary stains" of incorrect, habitual tendencies.

Tulku Urgyen Rinpoche points out a key aspect of development stage practice, "By training in the development stage consisting of deity, mantra, and samadhi, we actualize what we already are ... . We may think that this is a product of our imagination, but in fact it is an exact replica of the original state of all things ... . Do not consider development stage to involve imagining. Even though visualization is at this point an artificial construct, a mentally fabricated act, still it is an imitation that resembles what is already present in us. Until we are able to practice the ultimate development stage, we need to visualize or mentally create pure images in order to approach that absolute state."[57]

Yidam practice should never be seen as separate from nonduality. As Dzongsar Khyentse Rinpoche expresses it, "The nonduality aspect, the great vastness, is unchanging. It has never been fabricated, nor is it something that we re-create. What does this mean in practical terms? Devotion is integral to being a practitioner. Wanting to be free of delusion implies accepting that we are deluded. Within our deluded state, we have to learn and believe that we need to create a pure reality."

And Mingyur Rinpoche states, "Another reason for yidam practice is that all the qualities, kayas, and wisdoms of buddhahood are present in all beings and are pure from the very beginning. The nature of confusion is emptiness and therefore is the dharmakaya of all buddhas. We too possess these spontaneously present kayas and wisdoms. Deity practice is a way to acknowledge and remind ourselves that, since the very beginning, "I am a deity." When meditating, everything we see and hear and all mental events in our consciousness are all naturally the original state of wakefulness, the buddha nature. By doing yidam practice, we are recognizing what is for what it is." If we fail to prepare ourselves, just as we would prepare the soil for a garden, we will not become a suitable, receptive medium in which the seeds of the ensuing practices can be planted. The hardness of doubt and hesitation prevents the experience of our basic nature. The ngöndro loosens this soil and allows the development of a fertile, receptive frame of mind. Moreover, the preliminaries are a swift method to purify negative actions, obscurations, and habitual tendencies as well as to gather the accumulations to act as a conduit for recognizing and sustaining the true view. Finally, the preliminaries are the foundation, the basis for the whole path.

## CHAPTER 11

Here, Kyabje Dilgo Khyentse Rinpoche outlines the entire path in general and the preliminaries in particular. This section is extracted from the *Mind*

*Ornament of Samantabhadra*, a commentary on the practice of *Kunzang Tuktig*. The student does not have to engage in this particular practice. It merely provides a model for understanding the comprehensive framework of Dzogchen practice.

## CHAPTERS 12 THROUGH 14

These selections on the preliminaries can be read in conjunction with the chapters on Vajrasattva and mandala offering in *The Words of My Perfect Teacher* by Paltrül Rinpoche, pp. 263–95 (Shambhala Publications), and *The Light of Wisdom*, Volume II, pp. 68–80 (Rangjung Yeshe Publications). Another helpful source book is *The Torch of Certainty* by Jamgön Kongtrül, pp. 79–117 (Shambhala Publications).

In particular, chapter 13 on Vajrasattva can be practiced on an individual basis or with the group. It conveniently offers places to meditate. During these times, the students are encouraged to gain as much familiarity as possible with a state that is nonconceptual and awake.

## CHAPTERS 15 THROUGH 19

Many practitioners nurture a deep-seated resistance to the preliminaries and development stage practices. Partially this could be caused by laziness—we cannot deny that the preliminaries require effort. Another reason is, of course, incorrect motivation, not really wanting to destroy ego from its root but just engaging in the "feel-good Dharma." Or the problem could be incorrect understanding, arising from a belief that the practice of Dzogchen is to suspend the attention in a vacuous state and that practices with form should therefore be avoided entirely. One other possible source of reluctance is not having connected in a genuine way with a teacher. Without relying on the guidance of a qualified lineage holder, it is difficult for the student to relate to these practices. Devotion is a necessary component that spurs us to utilize the methods that in the beginning seem complicated and inessential. It opens us up to be able to commit to these practices. Out of trust, we accept direction. To be able to actually follow through with the preliminaries and development stage practices, we additionally need the right karmic mindset and positive aspirations.

Dzogchen is not merely a self-help technique. It requires more than buying the book, logging on to the Web site, and getting a certificate after

X number of years in the program. The receptive student needs to connect with a qualified teacher. Genuine transmission needs to take place. And this transmission needs to be received in a personal, experiential way. Our Western attitude of self-reliance—"I can do it myself, I'm strong and clever"—is not appropriate here. To be genuine Dzogchen practitioners, we need a teacher who holds that tradition, and we need to follow the path laid out by our teacher.

For these reasons and because of the profound link between devotion and the Dzogchen view, a large section of this book is dedicated to the practice of guru yoga. This essential connection is "to surrender to groundlessness," as Chögyam Trungpa Rinpoche explains in his chapter on transmission. The vital point is our relationship with a guru. Without it, accomplishment, in the Dzogchen tradition, is unobtainable.

All the tantric scriptures dedicate several chapters to the need to examine and receive the support of the qualified master. The different reasons, aspects of practice, and methods are all included in this book. It is essential to note that it is the responsibility of the student to examine the teacher before committing to following him or her. Certainly there are false gurus out there to be avoided. Likewise the teacher needs to examine the student before accepting him or her. As Dzongsar Khyentse Rinpoche says:

> Karmic links exist and they have an effect. It amazes me that Western people have connections with Guru Rinpoche. You have only just heard of Guru Rinpoche for the first time, yet you still have this karmic link. This is why, for many of us, visualizing the guru in the form of Guru Rinpoche is much better than visualizing the guru in the form of Madame Blavatsky.
>
> But this feeling of having a link is only one level, the emotional level, and there is a danger here. Should you simply trust in your so-called devotion? What if you end up having devotion to someone like that Japanese guru Asahara, who tried to poison people, or to Jim Jones, who formed a suicide cult? Their students had devotion, probably much more than most Buddhists have for us lamas. Lamas have trouble getting students to do something as important as the four foundations, which involves 100,000 prostrations. Sometimes we don't even dare suggest it. Yet devoted students of these other gurus will gladly and obediently put plastic bags over their heads and kill themselves. There

are many fake gurus like these. That's why I call this "feeling of connectedness" only one level of devotion.

So what do we do? We need the theory, the tantras, and the whole system. Without them we have no insurance, and we do need reference points. We need to examine what the guru says. Does it contradict what the Buddha said or not? The Four Pillars of the Buddha are so important.[58] That is why Jigmey Lingpa said, "First one has to learn how to examine the guru, how to examine the path, how to examine the method." We do so by having a strong background or knowledge of the whole system, and this understanding forms the second level of devotion.

For someone like me who is so full of doubt, hope, and skepticism and who has a complete lack of pure vision, the theoretical framework is very necessary. "Is my guru teaching anything that contradicts the Four Pillars of the Buddha? Is he teaching that some things are permanent? Is he teaching that some emotions are actually bliss? Or that everything is emptiness, except one particular thing? Is my guru teaching me that enlightenment is an actually existing state of being?" It is necessary to become clear about this much. Even if your guru teaches in a very, very unconventional way, using all kinds of outrageous methods, is he still in line with the Four Pillars? If so, and if you can handle this unconventional guru with your devotion, you are on the right path. Nothing much can go wrong. Understanding devotion on the theoretical level is quite important.

Devotion needs to be more than emotion. Most of our devotion is only on the level of emotion, feeling some kind of connection or inspiration. When a manifestation of the buddha nature, such as devotion, is met with merit, then, as a beginner, you feel inspired. The guru will give you proper instructions. As you practice and gain merit, your devotion will grow, and you will actually see everything as the guru.[59]

Students who, after examining themselves, do not feel suited for this path of the Great Perfection, Dzogchen, should take the time to meet other teachers and to study other traditions. It is best, however, to first try to keep an open mind about the guru principle and the various Vajrayana practices, such as the preliminaries and development stage practice. If this doesn't work, then change your approach or course of practice. The teachings of the Buddha are offered in nine different vehicles. Each one is perfect within itself and may provide a more appropriate method for your inclinations.

Our materialistic tendencies combine with the skillful marketing techniques of various Dharma promoters—the emphasis on Dzogchen as the ultimate practice—to heighten our interest. But following the Dzogchen path requires much more than an elitist attitude. Moreover, one may not yet have awakened the karmic propensity for Dzogchen. In the Tibetan tradition, Milarepa is generally considered the greatest yogi, the one who possessed the utmost diligence and faith. When he met a Dzogchen master and received Dzogchen teachings, he neither followed the teacher nor persisted in the practice. That did not mean that there was anything wrong with the teacher, the teachings, or the student. Practicing Dzogchen simply was not Milarepa's karmic destiny at that point in his life. We need to carefully examine and be honest with ourselves before embarking on this path.

Thrangu Rinpoche offers additional reasons a teacher is so important: "Some people may argue it's possible for us to figure the ultimate truth out for ourselves. We can read books and ponder the meaning; we can gain an intellectual understanding of how to practice. That may very well be true. But the profound nature of emptiness, the true natural state, is seldom the object of our thoughts. Indeed, it's not within the reach of ordinary thinking. For this reason it's extremely important to receive proper guidance and pith instructions in Mahamudra and Dzogchen from a living lineage master."[60]

Combine this section with careful study of the guru yoga chapters in *The Words of My Perfect Teacher,* pp. 309–47. For a complete and comprehensive way to practice the preliminaries, it is extremely beneficial to read and emulate the ngöndro meditation practice explained in *The Small Golden Key* by Thinley Norbu, pp. 102–109.

The group can henceforth engage in the guided meditation beautifully explained by Tulku Thondup in chapter 18. If the discussion has gotten too intellectual, end with this simple and profound sitting.

## CHAPTERS 20 THROUGH 28

These nine chapters explain all aspects of the development and completion stages in both the ordinary and extraordinary manners. Moreover, the method of yidam practice and sadhana is examined step by step from beginning to end. Whereas the section on the liberating instruction (chapters 6 through 10) describes the main theory for development and completion stage practice, here we have a hands-on guide to the actual application of these practices.

Once more let's examine the theory, beginning with the quotation by Jamgön Kongtrül: "The basis of purification, that which is to be purified, that which purifies, and the result of purification." So, the basis of purification is "the unformed realm of reality, the buddha nature." What needs to be purified are "the temporary stains of confusion," and the way to do this is through "the Vajrayana methods of deity, mantra, and samadhi," in this context. Lama Putse expands upon some of the more complex points touched on by Jamgön Kongtrül. Next, Padmasambhava clearly elucidates the traditional way to actually engage in visualization practice.

The subsequent pieces by Tulku Urgyen Rinpoche and Tsoknyi Rinpoche explain the context of sadhana practice with practical advice about combining the recognition of rigpa with the development stage, the essential intent being to integrate these trainings with the view of the Great Perfection. This is Tulku Urgyen Rinpoche's approach:

> The way to train in the unity of development and completion is without leaving behind the continuity of the completion stage. Without ever parting from the samadhi of suchness, allow all of the visualization to take place ... .
>
> If we have not been introduced to the natural state of nondual awareness, we must create the visualization through thought ... . This is not the authentic development stage; rather, it's an imitation of the real development stage ... . The authentic way of practicing development stage is to allow the visualization to unfold as the natural expression of rigpa.
>
> There is another way to unify development and completion: Include the completion stage within the development stage. While trying to imagine oneself as the deity, palace, and so forth, at some point remember to recognize mind-essence: "What is it that imagines this? What is it that thinks this?'" In the moment of recognizing mind-essence, development and completion stage are a unity, because the empty quality of that which visualizes is and always was dharmakaya.

Tsoknyi Rinpoche teaches in a similar way: "There are two ways of practicing visualization or development stage as the means, and completion stage or knowing rigpa as the knowledge aspect. The first way is that you don't combine or unify the two. You practice the development stage, and then at some point you give it the stamp of the completion stage. In other words, you try to adorn or embellish development stage with completion stage during the session. The other way is when you allow the visualization or development stage to unfold out of the completion stage, indivisibly, without separating means and knowledge. Whether one practices the first way or the second depends entirely on the individual."

These are vital points of application. Discuss the meaning of the words in the group and integrate them in your own practice as much as possible. It is important to note that at this stage of the practice and study group, the facilitator should be someone who has completed the preliminary practices as well as yidam recitation. Most sadhanas in the Tibetan tradition are similar. The facilitator should be familiar with this structure and be able to explain the reasons for it and how to engage in sadhana practice.

Look through *As It Is*, Volume I, by Tulku Urgyen Rinpoche (Rangjung Yeshe Publications) for additional pieces on these topics. Especially try to study the "Various Applications" chapter. Another way to understand visualization is by reading the chapter titled "Visualization" from *Journey Without Goal: The Tantric Wisdom of the Buddha* by Chögyam Trungpa (Shambhala Publications). It adds an additional perspective to engaging in this extremely profound practice.

## CHAPTERS 29 THROUGH 32

The feast offering is an enjoyable and special way to employ skillful means in our practice. It is an extremely beneficial method to clear up any broken or damaged samayas and create positive circumstances. If members of the practice and study group share the same practice and have received empowerment, this is a good opportunity to do a feast offering together. It can be in the manner of rejoicing and celebrating having journeyed together through the third of the Four Dharmas of Gampopa and Longchenpa and perhaps having clarified a bit of confusion!

Feast is an outlet for appreciation as well. The offering of song is one such skillful means. When engaged in feast, try your best to relax into the natural state and sing songs with an open and devoted heart. Thrangu Rinpoche says, "At times, it is good to sing the vajra songs of the siddha lineage. Sing them out loud, as it creates a very favorable imprint in our minds. It is through reading biographies and singing songs that trust and devotion saturates our hearts and renunciation for samsara wells up. Rather than attachment, we feel more detached; rather than being lazy, we want to persevere; rather than being disinterested in the sublime Dharma, we gain more sincere interest. This is why I encourage people to read and sing the spiritual songs of the past masters of India and Tibet. As Machik Labdrön, the great female master and founder of the *Chö* system of teachings, said, 'Sing in your own voice, linking words and tune. That is the key point of chanting.'"[61]

Additionally, reflect on how fortunate we are to have met such precious teachings as these and to have met our own teacher in particular. Offer up this wonderful feeling to unlimited beings. And of course dedicate the merit of this and all other virtuous actions to infinite numbers of beings so that they may one day play in the unceasing happiness of the enlightened state.

Once again I would like to quote Thrangu Rinpoche: "We can rejoice in the fact that our Dharma practice is personally beneficial and even though we have not yet attained full realization, we should still appreciate our opportunity to practice and dedicate any benefits to the welfare of all beings. Others often do not have the same opportunities we do, they have little or no chance to receive teachings, let alone understand or put them into practice. Therefore, thinking of all those sentient beings who helplessly suffer in samsara, we should repeatedly generate compassion and dedicate the results of our practice to their welfare."[62]

# NOTES

1. Padmasambhava, *Dakini Teachings* (Boudhanath: Rangjung Yeshe Publications, 1999). pp. 69-70.

2. Chökyi Nyima Rinpoche, *Present Fresh Wakefulness: A Meditation Manual on Non-conceptual Wisdom* (Boudhanath: Rangjung Yeshe Publications, 2002), p. 133.

3. Tsoknyi Rinpoche, *Fearless Simplicity*, (Boudhanath: Rangjung Yeshe Publications, 2003) p 15.

4. Thinley Norbu, *The Small Golden Key*, (Boston: Shambhala Publications, 1993) (pp 57-63).

5. Tulku Urgyen Rinpoche, *Vajra Speech*, (Boudhanath: Rangjung Yeshe Publications 2001) p 19.

6. Tulku Urgyen Rinpoche, *Vajra Speech*, (Boudhanath: Rangjung Yeshe Publications, 2001) p 134.

7. Tulku Urgyen Rinpoche, *Vajra Speech*, (Boudhanath: Rangjung Yeshe Publications, 2001) p 134.

8. Though of identical purpose with the general vehicles of the Buddhadharma.

9. The stake of concentration [samadhi], the stake of the essence mantra, the stake of the activity of emanation and absorption, and the stake of unchanging realization. For more details, see *Light of Wisdom*, Volume II, page 108 onwards.

10. To reiterate, these seven empowerments are for the vase and crown, tiara-streamer, vajra and bell, yogic discipline, name, and permission blessing.

11. For more details about the *Eight Sadhana Teachings of the Assemblage of Sugatas*, see *The Lotus-Born*, Rangjung Yeshe Publications, 2004.

12. The term "upwardly embodies" means that the intent and meaning of the vehicle below are essentially contained in the one above.

13. The teaching cycle of *Lama Gongpa Düpa*, the *Embodiment of the Guru's Realization*, was revealed by Sangye Lingpa (1340–1396) and is still renowned as *Lama Gongdü (bla ma dgongs 'dus)* in eighteen volumes of approximately 700 pages each.

14. The nine vehicles (theg pa dgu) are: Shravaka, Pratyekabuddha, Bodhisattva, Kriya, Upa, Yoga, Maha, Anu, and Ati.

15. Ubhaya, meaning "both," combines the conduct of Kriya with the view of Yoga Tantra. The vehicle is otherwise called Upa or Charya.

16. This refers to the initiation into the mandalas of the nine gradual vehicles according to the system of Anu Yoga.

17. A fully enlightened buddha teaches beings in accordance with their individual capabilities and inclinations. All of these levels of vehicles are, nevertheless, ways to full awakening through the ultimate vehicle. In the tradition of *Düpado*, the disciple is initiated into nine mandalas representing the nine gradual vehicles.

18. The three yogas refer to Maha, Anu, and Ati.

19. The word 'incalculable' is the number ten followed by fifty zeros.

20. In the case of development stage as inference and completion stage as direct perception, the latter refers to completion stage with attributes. [Jokyab Rinpoche]

21. For an explanation of the defilement of the habitual tendencies of transition, see *The Light of Wisdom*, Volume I (Boudhanath: Rangjung Yeshe Publications, 1999), pp. 281–82.

22. *Light of Wisdom,* Volume II covers the practice connected with the vase empowerment. The practices connected with the three higher empowerments will be the subject of subsequent volumes.

23. Since it is of exceeding importance to identify the object to be accomplished, the sugata-essence, which by nature is the utterly pure dharmadhatu, is the samaya being that is present as the ground continuum of all sentient beings. The deity that is of the identity of wisdom is the wisdom being of dharmakaya, the wisdom that is the mind continuum of all victorious ones. These two, the samaya being and the wisdom being, as the ground continuum and (enlightened)

mind continuum, are neither different nor separate, so samsara and nirvana are primordially the indivisible unity of the samaya and wisdom (beings). The deities with attributes that manifest from their blessings or expression are the Three Jewels and the Three Roots. It is by all means vital to understand these characteristics. (Jamyang Drakpa) repeatedly said this. [Jokyab Rinpoche]

24. In the word vidyadhara, vidya refers to awareness-wisdom (rigpa'i yeshe), and the one who has realized it is a vidyadhara. [Tulku Urgyen Rinpoche]

25. The deity to be accomplished is luminous awakened mind, the natural state of unconfined empty cognizance–the identity of essence, nature, and capacity that is primordially present without distinction in all beings. This is the state in which all phenomena included within the aggregates, elements, and sense sources are primordially pure as being the mandala deities of the three seats of completeness. In particular, the extremely subtle three doors are from the beginning the identity of the deity of the three indestructible vajras. The lack of understanding due to the mistaken conceptualizing of the perceiver and perceived as separate, which happens because of not recognizing your natural face, is the object of purification, the temporary defilement.

26. To explain the deities to be accomplished: The ground is the luminosity of awakened mind endowed with the three aspects of essence, nature, and capacity. This is the samaya being that is primordially present in all beings without difference, remaining right now as your natural possession even though you are an ordinary person. Nevertheless, just as a jewel that is covered in mud and not free from defilement cannot perform its function, at the present time we are in the delusion of not recognizing our nature as the real, basic state.

27. The *Detailed Explanation* describes both the means for accomplishing the root mandala and the means for accomplishing the all-encompassing activities based on the root mandala. Please read the rest in *Light of Wisdom*, Volume II.

28. The phonetics pronounced by the Tibetan tradition differs slightly from the Sanskrit spelling of the mantra: OM VAJRA SATTVA SAMAYA. MANU PALAYA. VAJRA SATTVA TVENOPA. TISHTHA DRIDHO MEBHAVA. SUTOSHYO MEBHAVA. SUPOSHYO MEBHAVA. ANU RAKTO MEBHAVA. SARVA SIDDHIM ME PRAYACCHA. SARVA KARMA SUCHAME. CHITTAM SHRIYAH KURU HUNG. HA HA HA HA HOH. BHAGAVAN SARVA TATHAGATA VAJRA MAME MUNCHA VAJRI BHAVA MAHA SAMAYA SATTVA AH. ༔

29. OM VAJRA SATTVA AH ༔

30. The *Seven Notions* or *Seven Enquiries*, the root tantra of Bhairava.

31. *Lamrim Yeshe Nyingpo* and *Lekso Sumgyi Döntri*. Both are available from Rangjung Yeshe Publications.

32. The phrase "to offer one's realization" refers to the tradition of presenting one's experience of the natural state (rigpa) to the meditation master so he can validate it. Once it has gotten the stamp of approval, then comes the main practice of training in rigpa to attain stability.

33. The *Tigle Gyachen* is the guru sadhana of Longchen Rabjam.

34. From *The Last Public Teaching of Lama Kalu Rinpoche,* Sonada, March 28, 1989, courtesy of The International Translation Committee, Drajur Dzamling Kunchab.

35. Although separated in time by some four centuries, Jigmé Lingpa was tremendously inspired by the teachings of Longchenpa, and during a three-year retreat in the caves of Chimphu between 1759–62, he invoked him fervently with a guru yoga he had composed. Longchenpa appeared to him in three visions, through which he received the blessing and transmission of the wisdom body, speech and mind of Longchenpa, empowering him with the responsibility of preserving the meaning of the teachings of Longchenpa, and of spreading them. Longchenpa appeared to him three times: first he appeared as quite old, the second time he appeared he was younger and smiled at him, and the third time he was very youthful; he came alive, took the whole teaching in the form of a book and placed it on his head, granting him the *Rigpé Tsal Wang.* At that instant his mind became one with the wisdom mind of Longchenpa.

36. Dilgo Khyentse Rinpoche, *The Wish-Fulfilling Jewel,* p. 83.

37. The dharmapalas are considered the wisdom protectors that are manifestations of enlightenment. These are not worldly spirits or deities that have a protective function.

38. A synonym for all-accomplishing wisdom.

39. For details, see *Light of Wisdom,* Volume II, p. 100.

40. The second of the four vidyadhara levels.

41. The third of the four vidyadhara levels.

42. The question is constructed since it was missing in the original manuscript.

43. In general this word (bsnyen pa) simply means "recitation," but in particular it refers to the first of the four aspects of approach and accomplishment.

44. In this context, *mahamudra* means the "sublime bodily form" of a deity.

45. Another name for Guru Rinpoche.

46. The Great Secret is a synonym for Vajrayana.

47. The name of the palace of Guru Rinpoche.

48. Poetical expression for the throat center.

49. A province in the southern part of Tibet. The name means "Lotus Arrayed."

50. The name of H.H. Dudjom Rinpoche.

51. These four lines are taken from *The Ineffable Confession of the Ultimate*, the fourth chapter on Confessing Disharmony with the Wisdom Deities, extracted from the *Tantra of the Immaculate King of Confession*.

52. The three spheres are subject, object, and action, or, in the instance of giving, the giver, the act of giving, and the recipient.

53. For "so-and-so," substitute the name of the person for whose benefit the dedication is made.

54. The three pleasing ways are personal practice; service in thought, word, and deed; and providing material things.

55. Khenchen Thrangu Rinpoche, *Crystal Clear: Practical Advice for Mahamudra Meditators* (Boudhanath: Rangjung Yeshe Publications, 2003), p. 132.

56. Tsoknyi Rinpoche, *Fearless Simplicity*, p. 25.

57. Tulku Urgyen Rinpoche, *As It Is,* Volume I (Boudhanath: Rangjung Yeshe Publications, 1999), p. 70.

58. The Four Pillars of the Buddha are also known as the Four Seals or Four Summaries of the Dharma: (1) Everything conditioned is impermanent. (2) Everything defiling is painful. (3) All phenomena are empty and devoid of self. (4) Nirvana is peace. See Chökyi Nyima Rinpoche, *Indisputable Truth: The Four Seals That Mark the Teachings of the Awakened Ones* (Boudhanath: Rangjung Yeshe Publications, 1996), and Jamgon Mipham Rinpoche, *Gateway to Knowledge,* Volume 3 (Boudhanath: Rangjung Yeshe Publications. 2002).

59. Dzongsar Khyentse Rinpoche, unpublished teachings.

60. Thrangu Rinpoche, *Songs of Naropa: Commentaries on Songs of Realization* (Boudhanath: Rangjung Yeshe Publications, 1997), p. 23.

61. Thrangu Rinpoche, *Crystal Clear,* (Boudhanath: Rangjung Yeshe Publications, 2003), p. 176.

62. Thrangu Rinpoche, *Crystal Clear,* (Boudhanath: Rangjung Yeshe Publications, 2003), p. 120.

# RECOMMENDED READING

Chokyi Nyima Rinpoche. *Present Fresh Wakefulness: A Meditation Manual on Non-conceptual Wisdom.* Translated by Erik Pema Kunsang. Boudhanath: Rangjung Yeshe Publications, 2002.

Dudjom Rinpoche. *Counsels from My Heart.* Translated by the Padmakara Translation Group. Boston: Shambhala Publications, 2001.

_____. *The Nyingma School of Tibetan Buddhism: Its Fundamentals and History.* Translated and edited by Gyurme Dorje and Mathew Kapstein. Boston: Wisdom Publications, 1991.

Goleman Daniel, ed. *Healing Emotions: Conversations with the Dalai Lama on Mindfulness, Emotions, and Health.* Boston: Shambhala Publications, 1997.

H. H. the Dalai Lama. *Dzogchen: The Heart Essence of the Great Perfection.* Translated by Geshe Thupten and Richard Barron. Ithaca, N.Y.: Snow Lion Publications, 2002.

Jamgön Kongtrul, *The Autobiography of Jamgön Kongtrul: A Gem of Many Colors.* Translated by Richard Barrons. Ithaca, N.Y.: Snow Lion Publications, 2003.

Khandro Rinpoche. *This Precious Life: Tibetan Buddhist Teachings on the Path to Enlightenment.* Boston: Shambhala Publications, 2003.

Khenchen Trangyu Rinpoche, *Crystal Clear.* Translated by Erik Pema Kunsang. Boudhanath: Rangjung Yeshe Publications, 2003.

Khenpo Ngawang Pelzang. *A Guide to the Words of My Perfect Teacher.* Translated by Padmakara Translation Group. Boston: Shambhala Publications, 2004.

Rangdröl, Tsele Natsok. *Empowerment.* Translated by Erik Pema Kunsang. Boudhanath: Rangjung Yeshe Publications, 1993.

_____. *Mirror of Mindfulness.* Translated by Erik Pema Kunsang. Boudhanath: Rangjung Yeshe Publications, 1993.

Thondup, Tulku. *Boundless Healing: Meditation Exercises to Enlighten the Mind and Heal the Body.* Boston: Shambhala Publications, 2001.

_____. *The Healing Power of Mind: Simple Meditation Exercises for Health, Well-Being and Enlightenment.* Boston: Shambhala Publications, 1998.

Tsoknyi Rinpoche. *Fearless Simplicity: The Dzogchen Way of Living Freely in a Complex World.* Translated by Erik Pema Kunsang and Marcia Binder Schmidt. Boudhanath: Rangjung Yeshe Publications, 2003.

# CONTRIBUTORS

ADEU RINPOCHE, TRULSHIK. A major living master of the Drukpa Kagyü and Nyingma lineages. Resides currently at Nangchen Tsechu Gompa in Kham.

CHÖGYAM TRUNGPA RINPOCHE was a Buddhist meditation master, scholar, artist and visionary. He was the founder of Naropa Institute, Boulder, Colorado, and of Shambhala Training and the former abbot of the Surmang monasteries in Eastern Tibet. His seventeen years of teaching in the United States and Canada has left an indelible mark of authenticity on the practical application of American Buddhism. For his biography, read *Born in Tibet*, Shambhala Publications. (www.shambhala.org)

CHÖKYI NYIMA RINPOCHE is the oldest son and a spiritual heir of the widely renowned late Dzogchen master Tulku Urgyen Rinpoche. He is the author of *Indisputable Truth* and *Union of Mahamudra and Dzogchen,* Rangjung Yeshe Publications. His Holiness the 16th Karmapa recognized Chökyi Nyima as a reincarnate bodhisattva and advised him to turn his efforts toward instructing Western practitioners, transmitting Tibetan Buddhism to the rest of the world. He is the abbot of one of the largest Buddhist monasteries in Nepal, located at the sacred Boudhanath Stupa in Kathmandu. (www.shedrub.org)

DILGO KHYENTSE RINPOCHE (skyabs rje ldil mgo mkhyen brtse rin po che). (1910-1991). Regarded by followers of all four schools as one of the foremost masters of Tibetan Buddhism. Among his other names are Rabsel Dawa and Tashi Paljor, and his tertön names Osel Trulpey Dorje and Pema Dongak Lingpa. His two root gurus were Shechen Gyaltsab Pema Namgyal and Dzongsar Khyentse Chökyi Lodrö. His collected works fill numerous volumes.

DUDJOM RINPOCHE (1904-1987) The incarnation of the great treasure revealer Dudjom Lingpa. His Holiness was the supreme head of the Nyingma lineage after exile from Tibet. He is regarded as one of the most prominent scholars of our time.

DZONGSAR JAMYANG KHYENTSE RINPOCHE was born in Bhutan in 1961, and was recognized as the main incarnation of the Dzongsar Khyentse lineage of Tibetan Buddhism. He has studied with some of the greatest contemporary masters, particularly H.H. Dilgo Khyentse Rinpoche. From a young age he has been active for the preservation of the Buddhist teaching, establishing centers of learning, supporting practitioners, publishing books and teaching all over the world. Dzongsar Khyentse Rinpoche supervises his traditional seat of Dzongsar Monastery and its retreat centers in Eastern Tibet, as well as his new colleges in India and Bhutan. He has also has established centers in Australia, North America and the Far East. These are gathered under Siddhartha's Intent (www.siddharthasintent.org).

JAMGÖN KONGTRÜL ('jam mgon kong sprul). (1813-1899). Also known as Lodrö Thaye, Yönten Gyamtso, Padma Garwang and by his tertön name Padma Tennyi Yungdrung Lingpa. He was one of the most prominent Buddhist masters in the 19th century and placed special focus upon a non-sectarian attitude. Renowned as an accomplished master, scholar and writer, he authored more than 100 volumes of scriptures. The most well known are his *Five Treasuries*, among which are the 63 volumes of the *Rinchen Terdzö*, the terma literature of the one hundred great tertöns.

KUNKHYEN JIGMEY LINGPA ('jigs med gling pa) (1729-1798). The great master of the *Nyingtig* tradition who had three visions of Longchenpa and received his direct lineage renowned as the *Longchen Nyingtig*. He collected and organized the tantras known as *Nyingma Gyübum* and made a catalogue with a full explanation of the lineal history. Among his immediate reincarnations are counted Jamyang Khyentse Wangpo, Paltrül Rinpoche and Do Khyentse Yeshe Dorje.

LAMA PUTSE, PEMA TASHI was the head-chanter, *umdzey*, at Neten Monastery in the tradition of Chokgyur Lingpa. A learned, low-key meditator, he also edited the publication of the *New Treasures, Chokling Tersar*.

MINGYUR RINPOCHE (b 1976). The seventh in the incarnation line of Yongey Mingyur Dorje, the youngest son of Tulku Urgyen Rinpoche, was brought up in the Karma Kagyü and Nyingma lineages. His main teachers are Salchey Rinpoche, Tai Situ Rinpoche, Nyoshul Khen Rinpoche and his father. He currently teaches at Dharma centers world-wide. (www.mingyur.org / www.yongey.org)

PADMASAMBHAVA is the miraculous great master who brought Vajrayana to Tibet in the eight century. He is also referred to as Guru Rinpoche, the precious teacher. For his biography, please read *The Lotus-Born*, Rangjung Yeshe Publications.

SOGYAL RINPOCHE. One of the most renowned Buddhist teachers of our time and author of *The Tibetan Book of Living and Dying*. He lectures world-wide and at his main centers in France and United States. (www.rigpa.org)

TSELE NATSOK RANGDRÖL. (b. 1608) Important master of the Kagyü and Nyingma schools. His published works in English include *Mirror of Mindfulness*, *Lamp of Mahamudra*, *Circle of the Sun*, *Heart of the Matter*, and *Empowerment*. About this master and his writings, Chökyi Nyima Rinpoche said: "People who harbor no ambition to become a great scholar, but who want to focus on truly realizing the ultimate point of Vajrayana training should study just a few of the writings of Tsele Natsok Rangdröl. In these, they will find the pith instructions that are the very heart of the Dharma."

TSOKNYI RINPOCHE, Drubwang was recognized by His Holiness the 16th Gyalwang Karmapa as a reincarnation of Drubwang Tsoknyi, a renowned master of the Drukpa Kagyü and Nyingma traditions. Later he was brought up by the great master Khamtrül Rinpoche. Among his other teachers are Dilgo Khyentse Rinpoche, his late father Tulku Urgyen Rinpoche, Adeu Rinpoche of Nangchen, and Nyoshul Khen Rinpoche. Rinpoche is the head of the Drukpa Heritage Project to preserve the literature of the Drukpa Kagyü lineage. He is also the abbot of Ngedön Ösel Ling in the Kathmandu valley of Nepal and author of *Carefree Dignity* and *Fearless Simplicity*, Rangjung Yeshe Publications. (www.pundarika.org)

TULKU THONDUP, is an exceptional teacher and translator of the Nyingma Lineage. He is the author of *Masters of Meditation and Miracles, Enlightend Living, Enlightened Journey, Hidden Treasures, The Practice of Dzogchen, The Healing Power of Mind* and *Boundless Healing*, to mention a few. (www.tulkuthondup.com)

TULKU URGYEN RINPOCHE was born in eastern Tibet on the tenth day of the fourth Tibetan month in 1920 and passed away in Nepal on February 13, 1996. H. H. Khakyab Dorje, the 15th Gyalwang Karmapa recognized him, as an incarnate lama. He studied and practiced the teachings of both the Kagyü and Nyingma orders of Tibetan Buddhism.

In the Nyingma tradition, Tulku Urgyen held the complete teachings of the last century's three great masters: Terchen Chokgyur Lingpa, Jamyang Khyentse Wangpo and Kongtrül Lodrö Thaye. He had an especially close transmission for the Chokling Tersar, a compilation of all the empowerments, textual authorizations and oral instructions of Padmasambhava's teachings, which were rediscovered by Terchen Chokgyur Lingpa, his great-grandfather.

Tulku Urgyen established several monasteries and retreat centers in Nepal. The most important ones in the Kathmandu region are at Boudhanath, the site of the Great Stupa, at the Asura Cave, where Padmasambhava manifested the Mahamudra Vidyadhara level and at the Swayambhunath stupa. He primarily lived at the Nagi Gompa Hermitage above the Kathmandu Valley. He is the father of tulku sons, Chökyi Nyima Rinpoche, Tsikey Chokling Rinpoche, Drubwang Tsoknyi Rinpoche and Yongey Mingyur Rinpoche.

Rinpoche instructed a growing number of Dharma students in essential meditation practice. He was famed for his profound meditative realization and for the concise, lucid and humorous style with which he imparted the essence of the Buddhist teachings. His method of teaching was 'instruction through one's own experience.' Using few words, this way of teaching pointed out the nature of mind, revealing a natural simplicity of wakefulness that enabled the student to actually touch the heart of awakened mind.

# CREDITS

"The Quintessence of Wisdom Openness" is from the fourth chapter in Sheldam Nyingjang, *The Essence Manual of Oral Instructions, Lamey Tukdrub Barchey Künsel*, The Guru's Heart Practice, Dispeller of All Obstacles, by Padmasambhava, © 1995 by Erik Pema Kunsang. Reprinted by arrangement with Rangjung Yeshe Publications, Boudhanath, www.rangjung.com.

"The Ripening Empowerments" is from *Empowerment* by Tsele Natsok Rangdröl, © 1993 by Erik Hein Schmidt. Reprinted by arrangement with Rangjung Yeshe Publications, Boudhanath, www.rangjung.com.

"Sowing the Seeds" is from *The Light of Wisdom*, Volume II by Padmasambhava and Jamgön Kongtrül, © 1998 by Erik Hein Schmidt. Reprinted by arrangement with Rangjung Yeshe Publications, Boudhanath, www.rangjung.com.

"Awareness-Display Empowerment" is from *kun bzang dgongs pa zang thal gyi rig pa rtsal gyi dbang gi 'grel ba* by Padmasambhava, © 2002 by Erik Pema Kunsang. Reprinted by arrangement with Rangjung Yeshe Publications, Boudhanath, www.rangjung.com.

"Transmission" is from *Journey without Goal: The Tantric Wisdom of the Buddha* by Chögyam Trungpa, © 1981 by Diana Mukpo. Reprinted by arrangement with Shambhala Publications, Inc., Boston, www.shambhala.com.

"Empowerment and Samaya" is from *Present Fresh Wakefulness* by Chökyi Nyima Rinpoche, © 2001 by Chökyi Nyima Rinpoche. Reprinted by arrangement with Rangjung Yeshe Publications, Boudhanath, www.rangjung.com.

# CONTACT ADDRESSES FOR TEACHINGS AND RETREATS

For information regarding programs,
recorded and published teachings in the lineage
of Tulku Urgyen Rinpoche,
please access one of the following websites:

Rangjung Yeshe Gomdé, USA
WWW.GOMDEUSA.ORG

Rangjung Yeshe Gomdé, Denmark
WWW.GOMDE.DK

Ka-Nying Shedrub Ling Monastery, Nepal
WWW.SHEDRUB.NET

Rangjung Yeshe Publications
WWW.RANGJUNG.COM

Pundarika
WWW.PUNDARIKA.ORG